Evangelicals and the Arts in Fiction

Evangelicals and the Arts in Fiction

Portrayals of Tension in Non-Evangelical Works Since 1895

JOHN WEAVER

McFarland & Company, Inc., Publishers
Jefferson, North Carolina, and London

LIBRARY OF CONGRESS CATALOGUING-IN-PUBLICATION DATA

Weaver, John A.
 Evangelicals and the arts in fiction : portrayals of tension in non-evangelical works since 1895 / John Weaver.
    p.   cm.
 Includes bibliographical references and index.

 ISBN 978-0-7864-7206-2
 softcover : acid free paper ∞

 1. American fiction — History and criticism.
 2. Evangelicalism in literature.   3. Christianity in literature.
 I. Title.
 PS374.E87W43 2013
 813'.509382—dc23   2013008634

BRITISH LIBRARY CATALOGUING DATA ARE AVAILABLE

© 2013 John Weaver. All rights reserved

No part of this book may be reproduced or transmitted in any form or by any means, electronic or mechanical, including photocopying or recording, or by any information storage and retrieval system, without permission in writing from the publisher.

Cover images © 2013 Thinkstock

Manufactured in the United States of America

McFarland & Company, Inc., Publishers
 Box 611, Jefferson, North Carolina 28640
  www.mcfarlandpub.com

To my parents, for their love.

And to Gayle Whittier,
for a mentorship and friendship
that is more precious to me
than any scholastic success.

Acknowledgments

I would like to thank a few people in particular. Joshua Lewis looked at early drafts of this work and provided valuable feedback on many of the ideas contained herein. I have used him as a constant sounding board for some of the best ideas I have had, and he always has proved to be a good listener.

Mikhail Gofman, similarly, helped me with finding some of the scientific research that eventually found its way into chapter 1.

My father, Daniel Weaver, has saved numerous backup files for me and generally served as an all-around troubleshooter for this work. It was thanks to my father and mother's kind offer that I was able to stay at their home the year this work was completed.

My colleague Dr. Nick Nace provided numerous book recommendations that turned out to be useful.

I would like to especially thank the staff of *Image* journal, the staff of *Christians in the Visual Arts* (CIVA), and Dr. Daniel Turner of Bob Jones University for answering questions about publications of their organizations, often providing copies of these publications to me when I could not afford them (which in Dr. Turner's case was his own publication). Though I imagine there may be some ideological disagreement between, say, CIVA's position and my own, I do support all these organizations' desires for a healthy, spiritually enriching evangelical movement.

Finally, I would like to thank my dissertation committee, Bob Micklus, Elizabeth Tucker, Thomas Dublin, and especially Gayle Whittier, for looking at this work during the dissertation stage. Gayle's advice has continued afterwards, and it is largely thanks to her influence that this work greets you, my reader, today.

Table of Contents

Acknowledgments	vi
Preface: Becoming an Iconoclast	1
Introduction: Evangelicalism and Artistry in Conflict	3
1. The Current Crisis of the Evangelical Art World	15
2. Romantic Realism: The Damnation of Evangelicalism	37
3. Lonely-Hearted Fascists: The Evangelical Community in Disarray	65
4. The Fifties: Creativity and Creationists	84
5. The Age of Fantasy	111
6. Feminisms, Fanaticism and Evangelicalism	142
7. More Problems, Added Possibilities	165
8. You Picks Your Worldview, You Takes Your Chances	188
Glossary	193
Chapter Notes	197
Bibliography	201
Index	211

Preface: Becoming an Iconoclast

> CARLA: Look, we can fight Him and be crushed or we can submit...
> DANNY BALINT: And be crushed.
> CARLA: What if ... submitting, being crushed, being nothing, not mattering, what if that's the best feeling we can have?—*The Believer*

This book is very unusual in its formation, presenting a nearly six-year process of development. It started out, in almost totally different form, as a dissertation on evangelicalism for Binghamton University, colorfully entitled "Jesus Freaks, Freaking Jesus: Evangelicalism and American Literature." That work, though it satisfied me in many ways, by its conclusion could not address one of the central questions I had come to ponder upon while writing the dissertation: What should be the relationship between the evangelical community and the arts?

I had first started formulating this question during the third year of my doctoral studies, ironically more initially for pleasure than for profit. During that year I became fascinated with the relationship between fascism and aesthetics, and how that relationship was (unintentionally) mirrored in evangelical aesthetic theorizing. Three works that were absolutely central to my then-embryonic understanding of the connection between aesthetics and politics were Menno Meyjes's courageous fictional biopic depiction of Hitler, *Max*, with its tag line "Art + Politics = Power"; Peter Cohen's *The Architecture of Doom* (1989), which showed me the link between biological and aesthetic racism; and Frederic Spotts's *Hitler and the Power of Aesthetics* (2002), which was a powerful indictment of Hitler's condemnation of Modernist art and artists, as well as a telling narrative of Hitler's own megalomaniacal artistic ambitions.

I fairly immediately began seeing connections between Hitler's theorizing and that of evangelical aesthetician Francis Schaeffer, though I by no means thought that Schaeffer was in any way an ideological equivalent of Hitler. Rather I felt that Schaeffer's artistic philosophy (described in chapter 1), outlined particularly in *Art and the Bible* (1973) and *How Should We Then Live?* (1976), and fully delineated by other artistic theorists such as Gene Veith,

Tim Keller, and Karen Mulder, had politicized evangelical aesthetic theory in a way I found contrary to the long-term survival interests of the evangelical community. By seeking to engage "culture," evangelical art critics ended up becoming one with the "world" they so often condemned, thereby lessening evangelicalism's potential to both survive the next century and make meaningful cultural change. As a descendant of pietistic fundamentalists (though no longer even evangelical myself), I felt the evangelical movement was better served by a policy of cultural separatism than by its rather selective history of political engagement over the last fifty years. Evangelical belief was about saving souls for pietists, not about conquering culture.

What allowed me to develop this criticism into a generalized critique of the secular art world's depiction of evangelicals was the influence of two scholars: Larry Shiner and John Carey. Carey's *What Good Are the Arts?* (2006) was the single most influential text in shaping this work. From Carey, I developed a largely proletarian critique of both evangelical and secular high culture, not unlike Carey's critique of the operation of high culture within British society. Shiner's *Invention of Art* (2001) allowed me to understand how closely tied our view of the arts is to prevailing socioeconomic conditions.

The text that has resulted is unique in a number of respects. It is the first primarily secular text to examine the evangelical art world, though Daniel Siedell's *God in the Gallery* (2008) has made a noble, somewhat similar attempt, albeit from an entirely different interpretative angle. This is also the first work to explore secular narratives of evangelicalism in the 20th century in anything like a comprehensive form, let alone narrative typological depictions of artists and artist stand-ins. For those interested in evangelical narratives of evangelicalism during that same period, Jan Blodgett's *Protestant Evangelical Literary Culture and Contemporary Society* (1997) is an excellent, albeit introductory, source.

This book seeks to explain why a secular stereotype of anti-art evangelicalism emerged during the late 1920s and why it continues till this day. In so doing, this work also attempts to address why evangelicals should embrace that stereotype rather than run from it. Stereotypes only have power over their victims so long as those victims accept those stereotypes as accurately reflecting what the stereotyped individual should ideally be like. And in the case of art, evangelical iconoclasm may have more value than the community ever anticipated.

Introduction: Evangelicalism and Artistry in Conflict

> Every latrine is a drawing room, every drawing room a latrine. The distinction between sublime and vulgar no longer makes sense—Vergine 909
>
> BECKY FISCHER: And while I'm on the subject, let me say something about Harry Potter. Warlocks are enemies of God and I don't care what kind of hero they are, they are an enemy of God and if it had been in the Old Testament, Harry Potter would have been put to death. You don't make heroes out of warlocks—*Jesus Camp*

Artists and evangelicals seem to be two groups diametrically opposed to each other, at least if one reads the prevailing fictional narrative tradition of non-evangelicals during the last hundred years. Starting with *The Damnation of Theron Ware* (1896), continuing through texts such as *Elmer Gantry* (1927), *Miss Lonelyhearts* (1933), *Inherit the Wind* (1955), *The Handmaid's Tale* (1985) and many others, there is a dominant assumption that the study or practice of aesthetics and evangelical belief are at best alienated from one another; in more extreme texts, there is the suggestion that evangelicals will try to suppress the work of artists and artistic theorists. Evangelicalism represents the fundamentalist Other, which seeks to burn books, ban books, inhibit children's mental growth, and serve as an overall artistic killjoy. This work seeks to complicate that characterization of evangelicalism by exploring the aesthetic/anti-aesthetic typological classification of characters in novels about evangelicalism.

Basically, such typologies of characters deal with evangelicals or non-evangelicals in whose lives the aesthetic or artistic realm plays a large part. In many of these works, the artist or anti-artist type is directly present, through depictions of graphic novelists (*Blankets*), advice columnists (*Miss Lonelyhearts*), musicians or music lovers (*Damnation of Theron Ware*), poetic reporters (*Inherit the Wind*, the film version of *Elmer Gantry*), or fictional memoirists (*Handmaid's Tale*). In all but a handful of these narratives, the evangelical or evangelical-like characters are either against the arts or must overcome their evangelical heritage in order to become true artists. Please note that by typological classification, I do not mean biblical typology, but its more broad definition as provided in the *Oxford English Dictionary*: "The study of classes with common characteristics; classification, esp. of human products, behavior, characteristics, etc., according to type; the comparative analysis of structural or other characteristics; a classification or analysis of this kind" ("Typology"). Or to put it more bluntly, this is an analysis of a certain set of character types, all revolving around the arts, that secular or non-evangelical texts set up when dealing with evangelicalism. It is emphatically not an attempt to draw biblical parallels to characters in modern fiction.

In addition, in some of these works, as well as others not listed, scientists or fictional messiahs stand in for the artist-hero: *Inherit the Wind*, *The Planet of the Apes* movies, and the *Dune* series are excellent examples of this. Characters that react strongly against aestheticism — almost inevitably, evangelicals — are also covered here (for instance, Elmer Gantry in the original novel of the same name). This work argues that the concern with the artist's relationship to evangelicalism remains one of the central artistic concerns of twentieth century non-evangelical novelists who explore evangelical belief. The fear of evangelicalism's iconoclastic nature, the secret concern that maybe evangelicals are better modernists than contemporary novelists, lies at the heart of the twentieth century secular narrative of evangelical culture.

The mission of this book is not to condemn Becky Fischer or her allies. Instead, this book seeks *to defend their viewpoint* as one of the most principled reactions to (though not necessarily against) the relativization of aesthetic standards in the twentieth century, including the relationship of aesthetic standards to religious moral codes. This book will therefore seek to contrast contemporary evangelical artistic thinking (primarily in the visual arts, but also in literature) with novelistic depictions of evangelicals. A central argument will be that evangelicals, rather than embracing the contemporary art scene (whether it be high literature, the visual arts, or the various products of the culture industry), should instead seek to embrace their iconoclastic past.

That iconoclasm, far from being a threat to the visual arts, instead offers an alternative way of looking at the arts that points to the drawbacks of glorifying aesthetic productions while ignoring the plights of the populations that do not get to enjoy the arts — indeed, populations that are often exploited so that the contemporary West may enjoy both its high and its pop art.

Model: Dispensational Marxism, a Description of "Commie Fundies"

The interpretive mechanism being used here is one unique to this study: dialectical dispensational Marxism (DDM). Historian George Marsden has pointed out the similarities between dispensational and Marxist beliefs:

> Marxism ... has some formal similarities to the nearly contemporary development of dispensationalism. History is divided into distinct periods, each dominated by a prevailing principle or characteristic. Each age ends in failure, conflict ... and the violent introduction of a wholly new era. History thus proceeds in dramatic steps toward a final age of peace. The crucial difference is that in the Marxist scheme the scientific approach to history assumes that the laws of change are governed by wholly natural factors of human behavior [Marsden 64–65].

Marsden throws this comment out almost as an aside, yet the similarities between evangelical and Marxist ideas have been noted in many other authors' works, including Glen Shuck's *Marks of the Beast* (Shuck 2005, 40) and this author's dissertation, "Jesus Freaks, Freaking Jesus: Evangelicalism and American Literature" (Weaver 2010, 48). Marsden's unique contribution to this dialogue is to point out the specific elements within dispensationalism, rather than evangelicalism in general, that have Marxist or Hegelian overtones.

The basic format of DDM is simple. Each dispensation of the church reflects a dispensation of art, in which particular artistic modes of expression (not necessarily artistic schools) dominate. Each age has a central conflict, which evangelicals almost always eventually lose. But there's always the promise of "The Rapture of the Arts," when traditional anti-art evangelical views will be accepted. Hopefully, this will lead to the dictatorship of the "spiritual proletariat," ruled by those populist evangelicals who do not subscribe to Christian worldview, Emergent, or other more elitist evangelical artistic ideologies.

The reason evangelical churches fail to reach this iconoclast, egalitarian ideal are, of course, complex. This work will focus on what I've termed the "spiritual capitalist impulse" as the central culprit against the Rapture of the Arts. Spiritual capitalists seek to aggrandize money and/or power to dominant theological bodies of the time (which often change from era to era). For the Dispensational Marxist, religious struggle between the spiritual bourgeoisie, who control the spiritual (and often material) economy, and the spiritual proletariat, who make up the oppressed masses, is fundamental. The secular novel, in almost all instances, is the enemy of evangelicals, because it seldom tries to elucidate what evangelical concerns are, and instead either directly works for the spiritual bourgeoisie[1] or indirectly supports either the spiritual or materialist bourgeoisie narrative of evangelicalism, usually through simplistic depictions of the evangelical anti-artistic impulse (works in this vein include *The Devil and Daniel Silverman*, and the overstated, but much more fair, *Elmer Gantry*).

The study groups the history of the last century's evangelical narratives (starting just before the opening of the twentieth century, in 1895) into six periods, each period being covered by one chapter. Chapter 1 sets the parameters of this study by exploring the reasons an iconoclastic evangelical artistic vision is needed, and why that vision is currently endangered by some contemporary evangelical aestheticians. After that, each chapter progresses in chronological order. The first period covered is Romantic Realism, or simply Realism, depending on how one defines *The Damnation of Theron Ware*. The two major works in this period are Sinclair Lewis's *Elmer Gantry* and Harold Frederic's *The Damnation of Theron Ware*. Both works' central artistic concern is with whether evangelicalism has any meaning in a secularized age. During this period, the balance of power slowly shifts from conservative evangelicals to liberal Protestantism (see Marsden 2006, 85–93, but elsewhere in that work as well). Mainliners and their secularist allies, such as Sinclair Lewis, represent the dominant spiritual capitalist force in this period, which does not mean these groups were totally reactionary. In many ways, they were more principled, or at least as principled, as the evangelical movement that opposed them.

The Modernist era covers 1930 to 1950, and I have chosen two works from that period, *Miss Lonelyhearts* and *It Can't Happen Here* (1935). Here, the big issue is the evangelical as quintessential existential man, facing existential anguish and literal voicelessness, which are the essential oppressing forces of the era. The evangelical in West's *Miss Lonelyhearts* becomes the emblematic failed artist, unable to achieve artistic transcendence (Lorch 17). Yet without meaning to, the artistic modernism West supported laid the foundation for the Christian Right's later critique of the "modernist" movement as supporting "fragmentation" and "abstractions" (Schaeffer, 1973, 58–60, 90; 1976, 190). Therefore, the ghost that haunts West's works is a future ghost — that of major evangelical thinker Francis Schaeffer's unintentionally fascistic analysis of modern art. In both Lewis's and West's works, it is the fear of the essential ties of evangelicalism to fascism that serve to oppress evangelicals. These fears are partly justified, but only if directed against the old Christian right; Schaeffer's later quasi-fascism was stopped from developing into full-blown fascism by that thinker's own internal sense of justice (though the same cannot be said of all his followers). Resistance to this sense of spiritual anemia could at the time be found among philosemitic evangelicals and fundamentalists, but these resistance forces are covered very little in this section because they did not much operate either within the novels covered or within the artistic culture at large.

Late Realism is a period from 1950 to 1960 exemplified by three central texts: *Inherit the Wind*, *Go Tell It on the Mountain* (1953), and the film version of *Elmer Gantry* (1960). The main cultural problem non-evangelicals saw with evangelical belief during this period was its anti–Communist and anti-black aspects, which fit into a dominant mainline Protestant narrative of evangelical backwardness. This analysis of evangelical belief was not totally wrong, but it failed to note the diversity of evangelical viewpoints on race, as well as the checkered anti–Communist record of many mainline Protestants and some secularists (for instance, Ayn Rand).[2] The resisting force, which again does not play much of a role in my description of the texts themselves, is separatist fundamentalism. In an irony mentioned in chapter 4, neo-evangelicalism ended up also operating as a spiritually capitalist force in the fifties, despite the fact that in the short term, it was a more spiritually progressive force (particularly in regards to racism) than fundamentalism. This period also began Hollywood's roughly thirty-year interest in art's relationship to evangelicalism, which is why analyzing the film *Elmer Gantry* as a central mythos of the Late Realist era is vitally important.

The Age of the Fantastic dates from about 1960 to roughly 1985. During this era, the most important narratives of evangelicalism are in the science fiction and horror genres. Many of these narratives are on film, and many are actually British, not American. The preference in the Age of Fantasy for generic, rather than so-called literary, depictions of the artist's relationship to evangelicalism explains why so many excellent depictions of evangelicalism during this period came from the cinema. The novel *Stranger in a Strange Land* (1961) juxtaposes an eroticized evangelical-like religion against a combination libertarian and countercultural vision of religious paradise. The *Dune* series, though not directly about evangelicalism, can be seen as a text with wide implications for both Christian and Islamic fundamentalism. I have included the British film *Privilege* (1967), despite its national origins, because it so eerily and presciently predicted the rise of the seeker-sensitive and church-growth movement and the consequent wedding of evangelical musical artists to capitalism. The first two *Apes* films, using scientists as artistic and intellectual stand-ins, decry fundamentalist positions on race and the atom bomb. The artists of this era saw two central dilemmas with evangelical belief during this period. Almost every tale in this era warned of government manipulation of the masses, while a significant number also studied how the destruction of messiah figures changed fundamentalist or evangelical belief. However, an implicit assumption of many of these tales—particularly *Dune* and *Planet of the Apes*—was that fundamentalist and evangelical beliefs could only work in a "primitive" cultural environment. *Stranger in a Strange Land*, meanwhile, thought only "chumps" could really buy into the magic of evangelical belief (see Heinlein 1961, 274). As admittedly good as all these critiques of evangelicalism were, only *Privilege* truly contended with evangelicalism in its contemporary, increasingly sophisticated ideological form; other works essentially consigned the evangelical movement to the past. *The Wicker Man* (1973), for instance, powerfully evokes the death of Christianity in its portrayal of a triumphant paganism (Grant 1997, 1012–1013).

The Age of the Fantastic represents the first era when American evangelicalism produced significant aesthetic theorists, ranging from Francis Schaeffer to Nicholas Wolterstorff (both helped by Dutch aesthetic theorist Hans Rookmaaker and the writings of C.S. Lewis and J.R.R. Tolkien). The dominant evangelical aesthetic theorists of this period were all Reformed evangelicals.[3] While their influence was in, immediate terms, salutary for evangelical intellectual development, their long-term influence was disastrous, because theorist Francis Schaeffer helped to unite postmillennial and amillennial Reformed evangelicals, particularly Presbyterians, with dispensational premillennialist evangelicals, both Arminian and Calvinist (see W. Martin 2005, 354 and Detwiler 1999, 110–111, in particular). Schaeffer, a premillennialist Reformed individual, but not a dispensationalist (Hankins 2008, 13–14), thereby convinced evangelicals to unite the worst elements of short-term dispensationalist apocalypticism with the long-term goal of cultural conquest shared by many of the more extreme members of the Reformed movement. The Reformed movement was also aided by the seeker-sensitive churches that started popping up during this period. Though the two groups vehemently disagreed on theology, both were motivated by a spiritually capitalist desire to gain cultural power and influence. Similarities between these developments in the evangelical community and simultaneous developments in the arts can be seen in *Dune*, and particularly *Privilege*, the latter work foresightedly predicting the corroding influence of materialist values on evangelical spiritual life. The dominant secular narrators of evangelical belief during this period generally followed a mainline, even New Left, vision of evangelical belief, but did so in a more ironic, idiosyncratic way than authors in the Late Realist or Early Postmodern era. Resistance to this New Left narrative was scant until 1976, the Year of the Evangelical. Once resistance was offered, it was co-opted by a coterie of Reformed elites, supported by non-separatist fundamentalists and parachurch leaders (e.g., James Dobson and Tim LaHaye). While separatist fundamentalists and pietists continued to resist the allure of artistic, spiritual, and material capitalism, the rest of evangelicalism seemed to give in to all three of these cultural phenomena.

The Early Postmodern phase of evangelicalism, covering such works as *The Handmaid's Tale* (a Canadian work dealing with American evangelicalism), *Portofino* (1992), and the *Parable* series, is full of hyperbolic feminist characterizations of evangelical belief, in which, in the name of protecting feminist voices (particularly writers' voices), feminist writers ignore how fundamentalist and evangelical voices have themselves been silenced over the last century. However, these overreactions are somewhat more understandable when taken in the larger context of the anti-feminist backlash of the eighties and nineties. The dominant religious forces of this era were Reformed and seeker-sensitive, even though this was not always immediately apparent. Pentecostals were both dominant and subversive, depending on where they fell on the prosperity gospel. Forces more firmly opposed to spiritual capitalism did still exist among pietist groups, Holiness individuals, and separatist fundamentalists, but such groups found it increasingly hard to maintain their numbers, with Christian right activist James Dobson, himself a child of the pietist traditions, characterizing the pietist factions as largely "shattered" (W. Martin 2008, 202, 204).

In terms of evangelical portrayals, the current era is the Late Postmodern. This period is characterized by evangelicals now entering mainstream fiction and visual art as a major force. Novels such as Leif Enger's *Peace Like a River* and visual artworks such as the paintings of Makoto Fujimura now compete with secular or ex-evangelical depictions of evangelicalism, such as the graphic novel *Blankets* (2005) or Theodore Roszak's *The Devil and Daniel Silverman* (2003), for control of the public's perception of evangelicals. Within the evangelical community, significant non–Reformed voices are being raised for the first time to challenge the dominance of Christian worldview theory. Rival artistic methodologies, such as Tolkien's mythopoeics and Brian McLaren's crude version of Derridaen deconstruction, are being offered up as possible substitutes for worldview art criticism. In this closing chapter, I will briefly touch on why I believe the anti-art iconoclasm offered by the DDM model is a preferable alternative to the artistic theories being offered by the worldview movement and the Emergent Church.

The DDM model works better as an explanatory model for some eras than others. In general, its prediction of an overarching spiritual capitalist force works extremely well in describing the Late Realist, Age of the Fantastic, and Early Postmodern periods, as these are eras when the narratives of evangelicalism belonging to the two prominent non-evangelical spiritual capitalist groups (mainline Protestantism and feminism) are in fullest operation. Our current period, the Late Postmodern, does not fit as well into the DDM model, nor is it intended to, because the current period is still quite contested, and it is unclear if it has any common vision of evangelicalism's relationship to the arts. The Romantic Realist period does show a combat between spiritual capitalists and the spiritual proletariat, but the fact that writers during this period still had contact with a religious culture means that their work was relatively uncolored by the prejudice that would seep into later narratives. The Modernist era is the hardest to define thematically or in terms of oppressive theological impulses, primarily because the only two major novels dealing with evangelicalism and the arts during this period—*It Can't Happen Here* and *Miss Lonelyhearts*—are thematically very different, united only by a shared dislike of fascistic anti-art impulses, which both novels apparently find in evangelicalism. Since, however, one cannot skip over twenty years of evangelical history, this section seeks to explain how literature transitioned from the complex and nuanced depictions of evangelicalism seen from 1895 to 1927 to the modern, largely caricatured vision of evangelicalism and its relationship to the arts seen in the vast majority of texts from the fifties onward.

I have chosen Dispensationalism, despite its Reformed origins, as an interpretative mechanism, because so many Arminians now follow dispensationalist ideals. However, despite my personal preference for Arminian, or even non–Reformed mainline theology, over Reformed viewpoints, this work is meant to be as inclusive as possible. My own theological viewpoints would be considered heterodox by all these groups, so I do not wish to anathemize the Reformed movement simply because its theology does not fit into my own. Despite the fact that I am not an evangelical, and barely Christian, this work attempts to construct a cohesive evangelical artistic theory that can explain developments in depictions of evangelicals over time, while still retaining enough theological conservatism to please most evangelical readers. My motivation for such a seemingly obscure undertaking is complex, and need not be related here; however, one element propelling me to such an effort is my feeling that while evangelicalism is a religion, it is also a culture. I may no longer be religiously evangelical, but I remain very much culturally invested in the survival of evangelicalism.

Definition of Evangelicalism

The most commonly used definition for evangelicalism focuses on four characteristics that have been "special marks" of evangelical belief: "conversionism, the belief that lives need to be changed; activism, the expression of the gospel in effort; biblicism, a particular regard for the Bible and what may be called crucicentrism, a stress on the sacrifice of Christ on the cross" (Bebbington 1989, 2–3). Bebbington's definition is one of the most comprehensive yet offered and covers groups ranging from seeker sensitive to fundamentalists. The Biblicism element, however, is starting to shift somewhat within the Emergent church, which drifts more in the direction of contemporary liberal Protestant interpretative practices (including using a generous amount of deconstructive theory as well as just enough higher criticism to impress young adult "seekers") (Bielo 2011, 8–11). The "activism" element, though common to all evangelicals (and a trait shared by mainline Protestants), is practiced in radically different ways by different groups of evangelicals: while most evangelicals for the last century have believed that such activism should be spiritual and not be motivated by the "social gospel," this viewpoint has come under increasing attack from a wide variety of Christian leaders, including Francis Schaeffer and Brian McLaren (Bielo 2011, 8–9; Hankins 2008, 109– 122, 180–208). The division between more socially oriented traditions — pietists of various stripes, many of the Reformed, many Pentecostals, and the Emergent Church — and the more spiritually oriented groups (usually fundamentalists and seeker-sensitives), which do not believe in the social gospel, is a strikingly wide contemporary division within evangelicalism. Therefore while Bebbington's definition serves as a starting point, it cannot be an end-all and be-all.

Denominational definitions are equally problematic. For instance, some Lutherans and Anabaptists are classified as evangelicals (indeed many of them would label themselves as such) (Sweeney 2005, 19); however, other members of these groups would feel insulted at this comparison. Similarly, despite the Orthodox Presbyterian Church's (OPC) crucial role in the foundation of fundamentalism and its subsequent development, few members of the OPC would wish to be classified as fundamentalist or even neo-evangelical, instead preferring the more traditional "Reformed" label. What does one do with Episcopalians or Methodists? Chronology is important as well, because a denomination that has been evangelical in the past may not be so today. Practically every Protestant denomination in America could be claimed for the evangelical tradition if people went far enough back in time. Therefore, fixed denominational definitions are simply too unyielding to provide much support for this kind of labeling.

Clustering evangelical groups might be a slightly better option. Fritz Detwiler's *Standing on the Premises of God* (1999), a perceptive study of the Christian Right, divides it into six constituent parts (one of which is Catholicism). The five evangelical groups are fundamentalists, Holiness, Pentecostal /charismatic, born-again evangelicals (roughly equivalent to what are called neo-evangelicals in this text), and Reformed Christians (Detwiler 1999, 150– 155). These distinctions are important, though somewhat incomplete. Fundamentalism was a movement that, during its period of national prominence during the 1920s, opposed theological modernism and evolutionary theory (Marsden 2006, 3–4). As Marsden points out, fundamentalism is a "loose, diverse, and changing federation of co-belligerents" (4). Over time, fundamentalism has gradually modified itself due to changing circumstances; for instance, old-earth creationism is now much less accepted than it was at the time of fundamentalism's greatest national prominence (Numbers 1992, x). Similarly, fundamentalism, which was initially associated with the north and urban areas (Marsden 2006, 188), is now typically seen as primarily, though hardly exclusively, a Southern rural phenomena. Holiness Christians emphasize "religious behavior and the moral life as the marks of a true Christian" (Detweiler 1999, 152). Nazarenes, Wesleyan Churches, and the Pilgrim Holiness movement exemplify this relatively small subsection of evangelicals. The most significant Holiness leader in evangelicalism, by far, is James Dobson (152). Pentecostals and Charismatics are distinguished by the "gifts of the spirit," such as speaking in tongues (152) or, more rarely, miraculous healing. While there are differences between true Charismatic churches and Pentecostal churches, those differences are not germane to this particular work, so the terms are used somewhat interchangeably.

On the other hand, one should carefully distinguish between the term evangelicals (referring to the movement as a whole, as defined by Bebbington) and neo-evangelicals. Neo-evangelicals, what George Marsden has called "new evangelicals," arose after World War II, mainly thanks to evangelical leader Billy Graham (identification with Graham often was a convenient shorthand for determining whether an individual was fundamentalist or evangelical). Neo-evangelicals, though retaining many fundamentalist distinctives, abandoned some of the more militant aspects of fundamentalism in the hopes of gaining more cultural influence (Marsden 2006, 233–234). They tend to be slightly softer on biblical inerrancy and evolution than fundamentalists. The Reformed tradition, according to Detwiler, "draws its defining characteristics from the theological teachings of John Calvin" (154). The problem is that definition is not particularly helpful. Most Protestant traditions in America evolved from the Calvinist tradition, including some that many ardent Calvinists would now consider heretics (including a large chunk of mainline Protestantism). In addition, some groups that have a much more Arminian history, such as Pentecostals, have in recent years been occasionally adopting Calvinist theological positions (for instance, Sovereign Grace Ministries) (Hansen 2008, 99–103). The most ardent Calvinists believe one must be a 5-point Calvinist to truly be considered a proper Calvinist believer; other Calvinists are much less doctrinaire. The differences between Dutch, Presbyterian, and the few remaining truly Reformed Congregationalist Protestants is also quite considerable. For the purpose of this work, Reformed Protestantism, unless otherwise specified, refers to conservative Calvinism, though not necessarily "5 Point" Calvinism. In other words, for the most part this study lets Calvinists define themselves.

Indeed, in the final analysis that will be this work's guiding principle for interpreting evangelical belief. There is no truly all-encompassing definition of evangelicalism, whatever the claims to the contrary. It does not matter which way I define evangelicalism. What matters is how the term was or is interpreted by both evangelicals and non-evangelicals in such successive historical period. For too long, evangelicalism has been narrowly defined by both hostile critics seeking to marginalize the community and by members of the community who want to exclude unpopular theological groups (such as the Emergent Church). But to write the story of evangelicalism is to write the story of all those in the community who sincerely wish to bear that name.

1
The Current Crisis of the Evangelical Art World

Why should evangelicalism's seemingly extreme viewpoints on aesthetics be respected? At root, the answer to this question lies in the increasingly troubled relationship between art and so-called non-art at the close of the twentieth century. In 1913, Marcel Duchamp asked, with his typical subversive wit: "Can one make works which are not works of 'art'?" (Tomkins 1996, 131). In 1917, his entry of *The Fountain* into the 1917 Independents exhibition forever changed the nature of art (180–186). *The Fountain*, a "readymade" (found-object), which was simply a signed urinal, called into question existing definitions of art. Was an object a piece of art simply because someone designated the object a piece of art or did the object have to agree to some Platonic or religious concept of an aesthetic ideal?

No one has yet provided an adequate answer to these questions. Perhaps the best answer comes from Arthur Danto's school of artistic criticism, which holds that an artwork is an artwork not because of any inherent values in itself, but because it gains such value through a group of people known as the "art-world" (Carey 2006, 19). It is the art-world, not compliance to essentialist ideals, that makes a work of art a piece of art. John Carey, however, points out the essential problem with the Dantoian school of criticism, which allows an aesthete elite to determine what is high and low art: "I have suggested that those who proclaim the superiority of high art are saying.... 'What I feel is more valuable than what you [the low art supporter] feel'" (25). Aside from the obvious ethical objections to such a potentially classist and elitist position, this viewpoint simply makes no sense psychologically:

> Because other people's feelings cannot be accessed.... He [the champion of high art] would have to mean that the experiences he derived from high art were in some absolute and intrinsic sense more valuable than anything the other person could get from low art. How could such a claim make sense?... It could have meaning only in a world of divinely decreed absolutes [Carey 2006, 25].

The elitism that says one person's artistic viewpoints are more valuable than another's, while a great way of promoting tenure for art critics and English professors, makes little sense in a post–Duchampian world, where practically anything, from bicycle wheels to urinals, can be art. Carey's definition of art, by contrast, makes much more sense logically, even if it is distasteful to artistic purists like Danto: "What makes it [the potential artwork] a work of art is that someone thinks of it as a work of art.... A work of art is anything that anyone has ever considered a work of art, though it may be a work of art only for that one person" (Carey 2006, 29).

The man on the street might respond that some things are simply "obviously not art," for instance, human waste products, like urine. Yet, as John Carey points out, Piero Manzoni published an edition of tin cans reputed to contain 30 grams of his own excrement. The Tate Gallery put it in its collection. Absolute emptiness? Yves Klein conducted an "exhibition in Paris consisting of an entirely empty gallery" (4). If art cannot involve the body, what about the recorded plastic surgeries of French artist Orlan (5)? What about tattooing, or bio-art, or landscape art, or musical compositions contained only in one's head? By Carey's definition, the most rational definition currently being offered, all of these phenomena would be considered art.

But such phenomena are relatively mild and do not bring up the larger ethical and moral problems that aesthetic relativism — that is, the lack of any absolute standard of artistic excellence or barometer by which to distinguish between art and non-art — forces current aesthetic theorists to confront. What about snuff films? Certainly one could imagine an aesthetically well-made movie in which a person is killed in "real life." What about 9/11? German composer Karlheinz Stockhausen, an important figure in European music, called the attack on the World Trade Center "the greatest work of art that is possible in the whole cosmos" (Tommasini 2001). And if 9/11 can be art, at least to one person, then why not that most terrible of human events: the Holocaust? Indeed, the aesthetic dimensions of the Holocaust have been noted for many years, by a variety of intellectuals. Documentarian Peter Cohen's film *Architecture of Doom* (1989) has chillingly commented, "Mass murder was the ultimate consequence of Hitler's ambition to create the new man. The cosmetic of the Nazi beauty cult finally found its way into the gas chambers. The killing was a biological mission, a holy tribute to pure blood. The death factories were anthropological sanitation facilities, instruments to beautify the world." If Hitler's Final Solution was conducted with an aesthetic intent, does that makes its results, whether they be mass graves, shrunken Polish heads, or SS tattoos, authentic works of art?

There are no easy answers to these questions. One of the greatest ironies of twentieth century art is that it was the relativist definition of art promoted by largely anti-fascistic Modernists, which sought to embrace as many objects and ideas as possible, that now allows those who will to define atrocities like Bosnia, 9/11, or the Holocaust as art. Reacting in moral indignation to critics such as Cohen or Stockhausen is not only counterproductive but disingenuous. Both men raise serious points about art that cannot be easily addressed. And though it was aesthetic relativism that leads moderns to view these events today as potential art, it was a code of aesthetic absolutism, in which only one view of art was correct, that led Hitler to many of his anti–Semitic views on artistic modernism. Hitler commented on Jews, whom he equated with the broader Modernist movement, that they "contaminate art, literature, the theatre, make a mockery of natural feeling, overthrow all concepts of beauty and sublimity, of the noble and the good, and instead drag men down into the sphere of his own base nature" (Spotts 2002, 19). The Soviets, despite their ostensible support for moral relativism, also eventually attacked modernism for its "bourgeois individualism" (the equivalent of sin in the Soviet system), while extreme anti–Communists such as Senator George Dondero accused Modernists of Communist tendencies (Dondero 2003, 665). In the evangelical movement it was the most theocratic elements—specifically, the Reformed movement—that promoted something approaching aesthetic absolutism, though fortunately the leading aestheticians of the movement, such as Francis Schaeffer and Gene Veith, were too smart to totally buy into an aesthetically absolutist view of art.

Therefore, even assuming aesthetic relativism is morally bankrupt, the imposing of arbitrary and absolute aesthetic codes on a population, as practiced by the Soviets, Nazis, and McCarthyites is not a viable option. Supporters of worldview theory, the dominant evangelical aesthetic paradigm operative at the moment, would argue that without an absolute aesthetic code (not as Francis Schaeffer points out, of style, but of message within the style [1973, 76–77]), one risks the possibility of an anything-goes attitude, where everything from child pornography to Skittles can be art. This may be regrettable, but it does not invalidate the logical soundness of Carey's argumentation, nor Duchamp's radical break with traditional aesthetic standards. Other evangelicals would argue, more plausibly, that if God exists, he presumably has some code of aesthetic standards that would prevent us from viewing such "works" as art. This may very well be true, but one cannot know God's views of aesthetic "truth" with the certainty of, say, empiricist science. Given the historical precedents of Nazi, Soviet, and McCarthyite artistic absolutism, decreeing an absolute aesthetic preference for one style or message type within art seems both questionable to implement in theory and doomed to both artistic and ethical failure in practice.

This work argues that evangelicals, therefore, have two other options open to them. First, they can accept the aesthetic relativism of Duchamp wholeheartedly and seek to produce modern art that fits into the contemporary art scene, rather than the classicism that seems to be preferred by (most) Christian worldview theory supporters. For those evangelicals that love modern art — or pretend to love modern art — this certainly sounds like a viable option. With the success of Japanese-American evangelical painter Makoto Fujimura's blend of abstract expressionism and Nihonga (a specific form of Japanese watercolor painting), the embrace of contemporary aesthetic standards, including modernist art forms, may sound like a viable option for contemporary evangelicals, a way of entering the cultural elite (see Lindsay 2007, 137 for a brief overview of Fujimura's stylistic preferences). Indeed, many contemporary evangelical elites look down their noses at more populist evangelical artistic depictions. Sandra Bowden, head of the influential Christians in the Visual Arts (CIVA) organization, has condemned such populism in the works of Thomas Kinkade: "It's [Kinkade's works] not good art. Technically, it's been done a million times" (Lindsay 2007, 126). Fujimura comments on Kinkade that his art is "very superficial" (126). Such comments, of course, echo the secular world's similar condemnation of Kinkade, indeed mimic that condemnation like parrots.

The problem is that such condemnation, besides representing an increasingly all-too-typical elitism on the part of the evangelical artistic community, makes no rational sense, whether it comes out of the mouths of secular authors such as Sinclair Lewis and Margaret Atwood or the contemporary Christian art scene. By what standards does an aesthetically relativist world label Kinkade worse than Fujimura, or Rembrandt, or Duchamp? Such distinctions are at best, purely arbitrary. At their worst, they represent simple snobbery. Can anyone seriously argue that Thomas Kinkade's paintings of light are any worse, than say, this description of an elite Goldsmiths art student by Goldsmiths tutor David Mabb?[1]: "A student two years ago came in [for her final project] ... and then she got up on the table, lowered her shorts and did a big shit into ... a big glass bottle, with a lot of grunting and groaning and stuff and then put a lid on the bottle and sprayed it gold and left the room" (Goldsmiths: *But Is It Art?*)? One could perhaps pardon the *canaille* if they preferred Kinkade to such peerless exhibitions of artistic greatness.

The truth is that art, among most novelists, academics, painters, sculptors, and musicians, is a religion, a religion whose believers are far more pathologically fundamentalist, in their own way, than Becky Fischer ever could be. Robert Hughes, writing in the *Guardian*, proclaimed, "When you have the super-rich paying $104m for an immature Rose Period Picasso— close to the GNP of some Caribbean or African states— something is very rotten. Such gestures do no honor to art: they debase it by making the desire for it pathological" (R. Hughes 2004; Carey 2006, 26). When an unmade bed

1. The Current Crisis of the Evangelical Art World 19

is valued at £150,000 and yet an African child's life is not valued at a dollar, something is seriously wrong with the values art promotes (Carey 26). The assumption that art is of value is usually based on the corollary idea that the aesthetic products people imbibe enrich human life and (among the more naïve) ennoble both the individual and civilization. Critic John Berger, by contrast, according to John Carey, denounced art "as a monument to privilege, inequality, and social injustice" (106). And indeed, when the study of "high" art was formalized in the eighteenth century, the working class, minorities, and women were held to be largely incapable of showing good artistic "taste" (Shiner 2001, 137–139). The history of Western art, as Larry Shiner points out, only gradually divided artists from working class artisans (13), mainly as the result of the industrial revolution. Many of the values typically associated with great art, at least till *The Fountain*'s arrival on the artistic scene, represented a deeply classist bias. For instance, the demand that great art not be mass produced, or if it was, only by a great artist (say Andy Warhol), represents a typically anti-proletarian bias, since most of the work the proletariat would produce (clothes, cars, etc.) would occur at factories. For an evangelical community, which should ideally be concerned about the poor and disenfranchised, the adoption of such an overtly wasteful system would be reprehensible. In so far as evangelicals ape "the world" in dividing art into "high" and "low" (already a vanishing distinction) and setting prices accordingly, they minimize the evangelical community's culturally subversive potential. Nor is an adoption of refined artistic tastes likely to bring the evangelical community new allies. To many secular artists who promote the anti-aesthetic vision of evangelicalism — Theodore Roszak or Barbara Kingsolver, for instance — evangelicals will always remain those "dumb hicks," no matter how many great paintings or novels the evangelical community produces.

Instead, this work argues that evangelicals should adapt a radical form of iconoclasm that seeks to fulfill the anti-art promise of Dada and Duchamp, but with a Christian spin. Tristan Tzara, one of the chief formulators of Dada, expressed this desire: "There is a great negative work of destruction to be accomplished. We must sweep and clean. Affirm the cleanliness of the individual after the state of madness" (Tzara, 2003, 256). The problem is Tzara never went far enough. Reformed Protestantism (from which the evangelical wing of the Protestant church evolved), from its very beginnings, has been drawn towards iconoclasm, seeking to reduce art either to nothing or to its most basic level (MacCulloch 2003, 249–250, 558). Therefore the project of Protestantism is not so dissimilar from the project of Dada. Dada was anti-art but was unable to fulfill the logical implications of that position because of the Dadaists' love of art. Evangelicals, particularly the pietist, fundamentalist, and Pentecostal evangelicals that this work is meant to defend, can much more logically work out the long-term implications of such an iconoclastic position.

There are limits to such iconoclasm today, of course, limits that the Dada movement did not see. For instance, if anything can be art, including concepts, there really is no way one can conceive of totally destroying the aesthetic. The point here is not to destroy art, but to reject the capitalistic philosophy behind the modern art world. In so far as artists like Duchamp or the Dadaists tried to attempt to destroy the aesthetic, they were chasing at windmills that could never be brought down. But the evangelical movement is uniquely positioned, from long practice, to strip the beautiful of all its essentialized, reified, "eternal" values. Nor is this an unprincipled or "anti-human" move to make. The evangelical community's love of people and organisms that other individuals have often considered ugly — such as the malformed, the disabled, the mentally disabled, fetal life — represents one of the most honorable and long-lasting spiritual traditions within evangelical belief. In so far as people try to essentialize beauty into certain forms and aesthetic standards, one can see that the desire for definite definitions of beauty is a root cause of much racial and eugenic prejudice. Again, a true evangelical theory of aesthetics would seek to move beyond such essentializations. It could never move totally beyond them — even when one chooses a mate one is usually making an aesthetic choice — but the evangelical community can help minimize how much such essentializations influence humanity's perception of racial, disabled, and non-human Others, by a continuous, never-ending destruction of the grounds on which purveyors of aesthetic essentialized elitist standards make their stand. In so doing, pietists of all stripes, fundamentalists, and Pentecostals will be at once both iconoclastic and modernist in their actions, avoiding the played-out elitist classicism of the older supporters of Francis Schaeffer's worldview movement, with its allegiance to a rather narrow reading of both the contemporary literary and artistic canons, as well as the muddled postmodernism of Derrida–loving members of the Emergent Church (the Emergent Church is a group of evangelicals who combine postmodern, ancient, and evangelical forms of theological expression). In such a system, the iconoclasm of Becky Fischer and the iconoclasm of Duchamp are brought together, but always with the significant caveat that, while evangelicals have the right to enforce their artistic ideals upon their individual selves, it is not in the evangelical community's long-term interests to try to enforce such prohibitions on other people via coercion.

The Contemporary Evangelical Art Scene

Evangelicals are, of course, a diverse group, and a chapter in one book could hardly detail the movement's entire history of aesthetic theorizing.

1. The Current Crisis of the Evangelical Art World 21

Roughly speaking, "official" modern evangelical aesthetic theory can be grouped into a couple of camps. The first, worldview theory, is the product of the mind of Francis Schaeffer. Partly influenced by the thinking of Dutch Reformed thinker H.R. Rookmaaker (Hankins 2008, 124), Schaeffer's theory split world history into a series of ages in which there was always a battle between a humanist and a biblical worldview (Detwiler 1999, 112–114). Though each worldview had its strengths, humanism ultimately led to disaster (114).

Schaeffer explored his artistic ideology in two works, *How Should We Then Live?* (1976) and *Art and the Bible* (1973). Schaeffer's worldview theory emphasized driving opponents to a "point of pressure" where, as Fritz Detwiler puts it, "their presuppositions collapsed, leaving them without any protection against the world." Schaeffer called this process "taking the roof off" (Detwiler 1999, 159). Schaeffer hoped to replace these opponents "humanist" worldviews with God–centered ones (159). When extended to the realm of art, therefore, worldview theory tended to emphasize the thought content of artpieces. For Schaeffer, "as far as a Christian is concerned, the world view that is shown through a body of art must be seen ultimately in terms of the Scripture" (Francis Schaeffer 1973, 64). This did not mean that an artwork had to be explicitly Christian in content, but that it would in some way reflect Christian values. Worldview proponents tended to take a dim view of artists who argued that their work was ideologically "contentless," pointing out (probably correctly) that even such a claim of contentlessness is itself a claim about content. Worldview theory therefore seeks to promote an evangelical aestheticism based largely on careful attention to the intellectual and moral form of artworks, though these are not its only criteria for judgment.

Worldview theory was a valuable first step in creating a workable evangelical artistic theory. It helped encourage many young evangelicals in the sixties and seventies to embrace the arts (Dennis 1976, 9–10). As a theory of art, however, it had certain inherent limitations. First of all, both Schaeffer and his theological descendants (particularly Gene Veith and David Hegeman) tended to preach a kind of Christian cultural triumphalism that, at times, seemed to have distinctly theocratic overtones. Theocracy itself, of course, need not produce poor art; one need look no further than the Catholic Church during the Renaissance for proof of that assertion. But this theocratic focus on producing great Christian artists and great Christian art tended to, in worldview theory, degenerate into producing a mirror Christian high art world that was not sensitive to either the secular high arts or to the more "humble" Christian and secular culture industries, with their pop music, rock, and paperback sci-fi, inspirational, romance, and western novels. In more elitist evangelical thinkers such as Franky Schaeffer, son of Francis and a prominent leader till he left the movement for the Eastern Orthodox

Church, this led to condescending slams against the "evangelization propaganda" of pietist Christians (Franky Schaeffer 1981, 69), even as these thinkers were often themselves merely recopying the thoughts and artistic ideas of a few Anglican and Catholic writers, such as C.S. Lewis and J.R.R. Tolkien. This triumphalism also led many Reformed evangelicals to see themselves as a kind of cultural elite within the evangelical church. David Hegeman, for instance, argued that "differentiation and specialization in culturative tasks are inescapable as societies mature and will normally lead to a governing order and a cultural elite" (1999, 49); his work leaves little doubt that that cultural elite will be principally Reformed evangelicals.

Worldview theory also had at least two other flaws: It did not adequately address either modernism or the relationship between capitalism and art. These two problems are interconnected. Worldview theorists tend to emphasize the "fragmentation" and "disjointedness" of modern art. For instance, abstract art "alienated" viewers (Francis Schaeffer 1973, 60), while Schaeffer expressed skepticism about the disassociation of language of modern novels from "the normal use of language" (58). Schaeffer's single-minded focus on the faulty communicatory problems of modern art led him to underhistoricize the significance of modern art. For Schaeffer modern art was simply symptomatic of modern man's leap from reason into the area of "non-reason" (1976, 202), a leap he found impossible to accept with his rationalist presuppositions. Modernism, for Schaeffer, was simply another of man's excuses for not embracing Christ, though it must be said in Schaeffer's defense that he (unlike his spiritual descendants) was never happy at this prospect. Schaeffer felt that for modern people, modernism provided a form of art in which there were "no human or moral categories" and "no certainty, no categories upon which to distinguish between reality and illusion" (202). For Schaeffer the illusory aspects of modern art prevented people from realizing the ultimate truth — Christ — that should lie behind truly good art. With no moral categories to define art, art soon became lost in abstraction or, in worse cases, moral degeneracy. And as art went, so went the culture.

What Schaeffer neglected to see was a much deeper cancer in modern art, one that would also infect the more classicist and Reformational art that he preferred: the triumph of capitalism over the production of the arts. As of 2011, "creative expressions from the arts and entertainment industries" were estimated to consume $1.7 trillion in world output (Singh 2011, xxi). As far back as Adorno, artistic theorists have pointed to the dangerous use of popular culture — TV, video games, comic books, etc.— as a kind of artistic narcotic. Schaeffer and his Reformed allies did not fall into that particular trap, though many other evangelicals did enjoy the products of the culture industry. Instead, they tended to too easily believe in the myth of Kantian

1. The Current Crisis of the Evangelical Art World   23

disinterestedness, in which the viewer's relationship to an art object should be purely based on an emotional and intellectual detachment from what is being viewed. The Kantian critique of art stressed that there should be no mundane concern with cash or popular taste where art is concerned ("Pierre Bourdieu"). For instance, Gene Veith, a Reformed critic in the worldview tradition, complains that "concepts such as beauty, order and meaning are being challenged by the new aesthetic theories in favor of ugliness, randomness, and irrationalism" (1991, 21). Veith complains of artistic elitism (15), yet the glorification of beauty, order, and meaning are the very foundations of artistic elitism, and other forms of elitism as well. Would racist whites, for instance, continue to justify racism, were it not for their view that other races are aesthetically unpleasing?

Nor are racists the only group that seeks to justify their social position based on aesthetic judgments. Pierre Bourdieu pointed out that "aesthetic judgment ... is a sorting process through which modern societies both produce and legitimate economic and status inequalities" ("Pierre Bourdieu"). Bourdieu argued that social status was not simply economic, but cultural. In other words, status was partly economic, partly a matter of social taste, so that no matter how far one rises, one can never truly enter the social elite. One could use for an example here the business mogul who no matter how much money he makes, is still considered vulgar ("Pierre Bourdieu"); one could think of Jack London's fictional novelist Martin Eden as well, a brilliant working-class writer who is denied any station in the middle class, despite his immense learning, until it is too late for that social station to matter.

When it comes to depictions of evangelicalism and the evangelical elite's reaction to those depictions, Bourdieu's notion of aesthetic judgment as a central standard by which social classes police their boundaries is crucial. Bourdieu felt that "modern aestheticism is central to the cultural elite's self-understanding and to the general willingness of society to grant it authority and prestige" (1806). The rapid rise of what evangelical scholar D. Michael Lindsay has called "cosmopolitan evangelicalism," that is the urban, intellectual evangelicalism of the evangelical elite, has led these evangelicals to contest secular narratives of their culture as backward, anti-intellectual, and artistically impoverished (2007, 220). One of the most important elements of this backlash against secular perceptions of evangelicalism's anti-artistic identity has been an attempt to reassert for the evangelical church the image of a pro-art, culturally enriched Christianity; as a consequence, any evangelicals who attempt to question the wisdom of endorsing the Christian worldview movement or other evangelical artistic methodologies or who seek to return to a supposedly more primitive "anti-art" stance are automatically labeled as anti-intellectual, both by the evangelical church and by its opponents.

Complaints about evangelicalism's anti-art stance are frequent and vociferous from worldview supporters. Francis Schaeffer was at the forefront of condemning populist evangelicalism's rejection of the arts, complaining, "As evangelical Christians, we have tended to relegate art to the very fringe of life. The rest of human life we feel is more important" (1973, 14). Franky Schaeffer, while still an evangelical, condemned the folk art of evangelicalism as "Christian graffiti" (Franky Schaeffer 1981, 21) and Sandra Bowden, the former president of Christians in the Visual Arts, has complained, "The local church is supposed to be a place for personal and spiritual development, but most Christian artists find themselves lonely with few to help them work through theological or practical issues of concern to them" (2006, 1). These complaints are of course understandable coming from supporters of the arts, but Schaeffer and his followers are so ashamed of the secular narrative of evangelicalism (with its condemnation of evangelicalism's anti-artistic viewpoints), so eager to condemn the populism of Harry Potter burners, Christian "graffiti" makers, and other supporters of evangelical anti-art or pop art that they neglect to consider the possibility that perhaps the iconoclasts are on to something. Instead, iconoclasm and evangelical folk art become the whipping boys by which worldview supporters announce their entry into America's social elite. Far from being a socially neutral or culturally enriching action, this kind of lock-step betrayal of evangelicalism's iconoclastic heritage is an action motivated intensely by a class-conscious decision to avoid any association with evangelicalism's "hick," lower-class heritage.

D. Michael Lindsay has called this social distancing from evangelical cultural heritage among cosmopolitan elites—many, or probably most, whom are supporters of the Christian worldview movement—a reflection of "status concerns" (2007, 219). In an unintentionally hilarious section of his study, he reflects, "People went out of their way to say they had never read *Left Behind* or purchased a painting by Thomas Kinkade.... One business leader told me he prefers to read Leo Tolstoy or Dorothy Sayers rather than the 'evangelical kitsch' at his local Christian bookstore" (219). With movies such as *Saved!* (2004), documentaries such as *Jesus Camp* (2006), television shows such as *Law and Order* and major novels such as *The Abstinence Teacher* (2007) and *The Handmaid's Tale* routinely portraying evangelicals as ignorant, tongues-speaking, book-burning extremists somewhat akin to the Third Reich or the firemen of *Fahrenheit 451* (1953), worldview supporters seem to be intent on proving to themselves their own elite credentials, not by agreeing with the secular art world (whose non-classicist art standards they reject), but by creating a false dichotomy between elite, cosmopolitan Christians (usually hailing from Reformed or deeply liturgical Protestant churches, such as the Anglicans and Lutherans) and the supposedly more culturally wild and impoverished Christianity that purportedly characterizes Pentecostal and fundamentalist churches (such as the Independent Baptists).

The most crucial consequence of the worldview movement's distancing of the evangelical art world from populist art or populist concerns about art is that evangelicals have divorced the arts from their relationship to the development of our modern economic and social class system. Franky Schaeffer, when asked if the arts are elitist, responded, "Wealth is a byproduct of creativity and freedom anyway. Therefore art, which is one part of creativity is part of the process that creates abundance for all people. To say one is 'for the poor,' but be against freedom, creativity and art is a contradiction of terms" (1981, 85). For the younger Schaeffer (at the time, anyway), the arts were unconnected to economic issues. Schaeffer naively felt that since enjoyment of high art is free and "many museums" and "retrospectives" were also of little cost, aesthetic appreciation was only somewhat influenced by hierarchical, class-based concerns (84–85). As a whole, *Addicted to Mediocrity* (1981), Schaeffer's artistic opus, distinctly aligned itself with the kind of naïve renderings of art and literary history one would have seen in nineteenth century or pre–Marxist art history texts. There also seems to be a concern among evangelical aestheticians and literary theorists that art not be associated with either a profit or utilitarian motive, as if the arts are somehow "higher" and more "noble" when they are disconnected from everyday material concerns. Thus H.R. Rookmaaker condemns "Christian utilitarianism," which sees art only as "an aid to evangelism" (1981, 154). Similarly, one of the crucial determinants of artistic excellence for Francis Schaeffer is "validity," by which he meant "whether an artist is honest to himself and to his world view or whether he makes his art only for money or for the sake of being accepted. If an artist makes an art work solely for a patron ... his work does not have validity" (1973, 63). For the senior Schaeffer, artistic excellence must be divorced from economic necessity. Art that fulfills a function on the market, providing the artist a livelihood, is false art. Though some Christian worldview aestheticians have made an effort to give a more economically nuanced reading of art history (Gene Veith in particular), overall the movement has an impoverished view of how economic and cultural history has influenced the history of the arts.

Why is this important? One of the crucial contentions of many (though not all) contemporary artistic theorists is that the contemporary category "art," including literature, though it in some sense always existed, did not take on its modern form of "fine art, the artist, and the aesthetic" until the eighteenth century (Shiner 2001, 14). One crucial by-product of this rise of the artist figure, particularly the artist-hero, was that the artisan, or craftsperson, was devalued. In ancient times, the division between artisans and artists did not exist, nor was there the "modern emphasis on imagination, originality, and autonomy" (23) that has come to characterize the artist figure. In other words, many trades were viewed as fundamentally similar to what we would term the "fine arts" (21). Shoemaking, for instance, could plausibly be seen as an art (20–21). Thus the artisan was not necessarily a disrespected figure until the eighteenth century. Then, "facility and inspiration ... innovation and imitation ... freedom and service were pulled apart.... Whereas the artist was said to act with the spontaneity of nature, the artisan was said to act 'mechanically,' following rules, using imagination only to combine, serving only by filling orders" (115). Though this process did not happen all at once (115), the end by-product of it was that Chinese sweatshop workers or American working class laborers could slave away for 12 hours a day, 52 weeks a year, making medical cabinets that would bring them at best the minimum wage of their respective country, while Damien Hirst could do the same thing, put a few pills in the box, call it *Lullaby Winter*, and have it sell for $7.4 million (D. Thompson 2008, 25). Anti-art evangelicalism has always been deeply suspicious of such ridiculous over-valuations of artistic objects and of art in general. Indeed, the Orthodox Presbyterian Church from which Francis Schaeffer split is famous for its conservatism in this regard; it is not unknown to find such churches debating about the propriety of stained glass windows. Among non–Reformed fundamentalists, the break with the arts is even more extreme. Any work of bestselling Christian fiction is questioned, particularly if it comes from artists favored by the evangelical elite; one need not look far on the Internet (or even in the publishing industry) to find sites, books, and YouTube videos devoted to the evils of C.S. Lewis, J.R.R. Tolkien, and Charles Williams, let alone non-evangelical authors such as Dan Brown and J.K. Rowling. Yet, now, the evangelical art world seeks to assimilate the values of the "artistic genius," the creative *übermensch*, at the very time that secular critics such as Larry Shiner, John Carey and Roger Taylor are calling into question the sentimentalized glorifications of these figures.

One should be careful not to overstate the case here. Some worldview supporters, in particularly Gene Veith, take a rather dim view of the artistic genius, correctly pointing that the "cult of the artist is profoundly anti-art" (1991, 95). Veith, unlike the Schaeffers, also seems to be aware of how profoundly Romanticism altered our concept of the artist, creating the cult of artistic genius that exists today (see 71–73). But other worldview supporters continue to persist in the creation of a new artistic elite whose exact mission is unclear, but whose artistic superpowers seem to know few limits. Tim Keller, a prominent Reformed pastor whose church is famous for its art outreach, has written, "Artists have a special capacity to recognize the 'other country' and communicate with the rest of us regarding the greater reality"

(2006, Keller 120). Later, Keller gushes, we need "the greater reality" because we "can't understand truth without art" (120–121). Still further, Keller asserts, "We cannot praise God without art" (122). Assuming that Keller considers art a distinct entity, as apart from everything else in the world, one immediately runs into problems. According to Keller's model, a Christian hospice worker cleaning up someone's excrement cannot properly be considered praise, because it is not art. On the other hand, the church organist at the local Reformed Church is by definition praising God a hundred times more fully than the hospice worker, even if the hospice worker's motives and actions are more self-sacrificing and loving than the organist. Keller's claims seem to take on a sort of magical quality. People do not need the fine arts to tell them how to understand what 2+2 means, and yet it's doubtful that Keller would admire such numerical formulae as works equal to the masterpieces of the Reformation. Yet mathematical formulae may tell us more about truth than any artistic work.

But of course the real motive for the worldview movement's interest in the arts is no more aesthetically-based than the secular bourgeoisie or elite upper-middle class academics who write works such as *The Handmaid's Tale* and *The Poisonwood Bible* (1998), condemning the evangelical "rubes." In both cases, what is at stake is cultural capital. The mystification of taste by which modern art supporters declare C.S. Lewis a second-rate novelist and Phillip Pullman a great artist is mirrored in evangelicalism, where Lewis is declared a first-rate novelist, but more populist writers, such as Hal Lindsay, Tim LaHaye, and Frank Peretti, are labeled second-rate. Dave Hegeman, for instance, assures the worldview movement that the "ravages of popular culture" can be defeated if Christians accept "the inevitability of an elite class of God–gifted individuals whose job is to *serve* the rest of society by crafting texts, objects, and structures of real (not pretended) depth and substance" (1999, 52). Hegeman's facile use of the term *serve* is as about as convincing as George Bush's oxymoronic "compassionate conservatism"; Hegeman, like other worldview supporters and cosmopolitan evangelicals, expects to be in charge of the new evangelical movement. And he expects the populist evangelical class to accept their marching orders.

The only major alternative to worldview criticism and aesthetics among evangelicals today is the mythopoeic system of reading and criticism favored by many of the Inklings (a Christian writers' group that included C.S. Lewis and J.R.R. Tolkien). Mythopoeics is not exactly a defined school of criticism; rather, it is a means of reading that focuses on the qualities of scripture as "true myth" and the power of authors as "sub-creators" who, as servants of God, imitate God's creative process when they are working in harmony with Him. Crucially, for Lewis's and Tolkien's fellow Inkling, Owen Barfield, mythology was the "very origin of speech and literature" (H. Carpenter 1979, 41). Barfield argued that at the dawn of language there was no distinction between "the 'literal' and 'metaphorical'" (41). For instance, the Latin *spiritus* could roughly be translated as "spirit-breath-wind." Therefore, "when the wind blew it was not merely like someone breathing: it was the breathe of God" (41). Thus language took on a mythological quality. Language itself was a form of myth, or at least a myth-making system. For the Inklings, at least for Tolkien and Lewis, this meant that pagan myths were not lies, or falsehoods, but reflections of eternal truth, to be valued for their reflection of the "real Dying God" myth seen in all the pagan stories (44).

The Inklings thought here bears perhaps an unacknowledged debt to Frazier's *Golden Bough* (1890) and to Wittgenstein's careful dissection of philosophical language, but its implications went even further than the Inklings realized. Today, we can see that not only language, but also perception itself, can in some sense be considered mythological. It is a truism of philosophical and scientific thought that human beings never see the world as it actually is. Our brain interprets the sensory data inputted by the external world and then creates an image of the world as it appears to that particular brain (*EB*, s.v. "Primate"). But different brains will perceive the world in different ways — the senses of color, taste, hearing, and sight will vary from individual to individual and species to species. Perception, therefore, is not simply perception, but also interpretation. Each being perceives the world in idiosyncratic ways, so that even simple questions like "Is the sky blue?" are really not that simple. A dog's answer to that question would be different from ours, yet whose perceptual bias is "correct"? Color is a phenomenon created by how our eyes and brains perceive light, as well as by how our mind remembers colors and processes visual data (*EB*, s.v. "Color"). This means that on a fundamental level, if perception is mythological, then interpretation must also be mythological as well. The *Weltanschauung* individuals create of the world is a result of their own unique sensory experiences, which no other individual shares. Those experiences (perceptions) create the reactions (interpretations) with which individuals greet the universe. To be a believer then, in anything, including non-belief, is to be inherently mythological in one's thinking. One can no more escape myth than one can escape breath.

The inherently religious quality of language — that it depends on "faith" or "belief" in communication, or language games as Wittgenstein would have it — for two people to successfully use it, is certainly good news for religion as a whole, and renders mythopoeic criticism (which never explicitly stated the religious nature of language, but did acknowledge its mythic character) a much more advanced and well thought out artistic ideology than worldview criticism, though Tolkien and Lewis never really worked out its implications for the visual arts. Indeed, the fact that mythopoeics was centrally concerned with aural and written communication means that its understanding of the visual arts was, by definition, less profound, thus exposing one of the few limitations of the mythopoeic school.

The other main drawback to widespread adoption of mythopoeic criticism is more fundamental, however, and that is that the kind of implications mentioned above are deeply unsettling to believers as well as non-believers. For instance, if perception is mythological, how does one trust in communication at all? And if people cannot trust in communication, how can they trust in the guarantee of John 1:1 that "In the beginning was the Word and the Word was with God and the Word was God" (*NIV*)? For everyday believers, even in the cosmopolitan evangelical camp, these are questions that people would rather not deal with. While difficult to prove, it is also probable that the growth of the Emergent Church and other elements of postmodern evangelical biblical interpretation have hindered the acceptance of mythopoeic criticism. When taken to its logical conclusion (as above), mythopoeic criticism sounds to many evangelicals like a thinly veiled Christian version of Jacques Derrida or the souped-up deconstructionist rhetoric of Emergent Church leader Brian McLaren, who despite his vaguely evangelical allegiances is deeply unpopular for his questioning of core evangelical beliefs.

The idea of the artist as sub-creator has, overall, been less controversial than the Inklings' theories on language, though some prominent evangelical aestheticians have rejected the emphasis the Inklings placed on that aspect of artistic creation (see Seerveld 1980, 26). The artist's role as a sub-creator is seen by many evangelical artists (and Christian artists in general) as a corrective to the denigration of the arts found in contemporary evangelicalism. For instance, James Romaine's essay "Creator, Creation, and Creativity" in the Christian–worldview–influenced *It Was Good: Making Art to the Glory of God* (2006) shows clear signs of mythopoeic influence, emphasizing the value of the true artist as a creator of something "deeply mysterious and supernatural" that echoes the divine (Romaine 2006, 109). Romaine attempts to split the difference between the viewpoint of Dorothy Sayers (a sort of honorary Inkling who shared many of Tolkien's and Lewis's views on the art) and Calvin Seerveld's reservations about the uses to which the mythos of the sub-creator was being put (109).

The danger of viewing humanity as sub-creator is that instead of creating a respectable middle ground between what Martin Eden calls the "clod and God" schools of writing, in which writers either glorify man utterly or debase him utterly, is that the role of sub-creator is increasingly taking on a Christianized version of the "cult of genius" that secular artists promote, thus dividing the artist from the populace and enshrining him as something special and elite (London 1909, 209). Nor can it be said that this is totally an unexpected development coming from Tolkien and Lewis, considering their well-known social and political conservatism. One need not, of course, support egalitarianism in politics or art any more than in any other field. But neither is it required of the working class critic or the populist evangelicals that such critics would hopefully support, to endorse an artistic viewpoint that neglects to account for their aesthetic and cultural tastes.

If mythopoeic criticism is limited by its lack of appeal to both cosmopolitan and populist evangelicals, the deconstructionist methodologies of the Emergent Church are even more problematic, because they offer nothing distinctively evangelical in their approach to the arts, instead doing very bad impressions of Derrida and Lyotard.[2] The problem here is not that deconstructionism is inherently a destructive ideology (though it certainly tends to be), but that evangelicalism is not really an ideological system ideally equipped to handle deconstructionist thinking. Denominational groupings more equipped to deal with the delicate balance between mythic-ness and facticity in Scriptures, such as the Episcopalian Church, can find much of value in deconstructionism and even in Emergent thinking, without having to rethink the entire epistemological system on which their theology is based. For evangelicals, however, Emergent thinking suggests a break that is too radical and too quick.

A more fundamental problem of Emergent thinking, however, is that it simply accepts the secular narrative of evangelicalism too easily, without stopping to wonder how much of that narrative is constructed by the media, and in particular, the arts. For instance, Brian McLaren in *A Generous Orthodoxy* (2004) appeals to secular readers:

> You may not be a Christian and wondering why anyone would want to be. The religion that inspired the Crusades, launched witch trials, perpetuates religious broadcasting, presents too-often boring and irrelevant church services with schmaltzy music — or else presents manic and overly aggressive church services with a different kind of schmaltzy music — baptizes wars and other questionable political programs, promotes judgmentalism, and ordains preachers with puffy haircuts (and others who are so superficial as to complain about puffy haircuts...) ... it doesn't make sense to you why anyone would want "in" on that [McLaren 2004, 19].

McLaren here appeals to the media image of evangelicals that non-evangelicals will typically encounter. At no point does he point out that this is, in fact, a stereotyped image of Christianity with little nuance. Instead, he seeks to promote an "I'm cool, you're cool" sort of evangelical identity, that negates real cultural distinctives on the part of evangelicals. Yet, even assuming the image of evangelicalism here is true, it is definitely an image abetted and maintained by the secular media and entertainment industry. How else, for instance, can one explain why Jerry Falwell was continuously called on to provide his "representative" voice for evangelicalism, even though his actual popularity rating among evangelicals was under 50 percent (Simon 2005)? How does one explain *Jesus Camp*'s implication that the children at the camp in the film represent "normal" evangelicals, when they are actually a by-product of a subset of Pentecostals known as Joel's Army, with admittedly real, but also currently limited, power (Sanchez 2008)?

Meanwhile, with some exceptions (such as *The Rapture* [1991] and *The Apostle* [1997]), evangelical characters in film typically are some sort of psychotic killer or serial killer (*Night of the Hunter* [1955]), hypocritical preacher (*Elmer Gantry*, *Inherit the Wind* [1960]), gay-hating homophobe (*The Laramie Project* [film, 2002], various episodes of *Law and Order* [1990–2010]), or oppressed woman yearning to breathe free (*Handmaid's Tale*, *Saved!*). It is not so much that all these narratives are false as that their almost-monolithic presentation of evangelicalism does not allow for alternative views of evangelical belief. The Emergent movement, a simulacrum of real deconstructionism, thus sees itself primarily through this shaming narrative, and like the worldview movement, never bothers to ask why that narrative is constructed or whom it benefits. That crucial question represents the primary subject of this book.[3]

The Secular Master Narrative: Tying Evangelical Views of the Arts to Secular Literature

But what does all this concern over evangelical views of aesthetics have to do with the typological classifications of evangelicals in mainstream fiction? To understand that dilemma, we have to return to Bourdieu. Bourdieu noted that a "class is defined as much by its *being perceived*, as by its *being*" (1984, 483). What is at stake in mainstream fiction's rather continuous assault on evangelicalism over the course of the twentieth and twenty-first century is a desire, sometimes conscious, sometimes unconscious or even against a writer's consciousness, to marginalize evangelicals as an inferior social class while simultaneously also labeling evangelicals as a socially dominant class, thereby creating the odd whiplash effect of an evangelicalism that is at once both a hillbilly concoction and a dangerous theocratic force. Therefore one sees in works such as *Elmer Gantry*, *Inherit the Wind*, the *Planet of the Apes* series (where the evangelical-like characters are literally sub-humans or mutants), Sinclair Lewis's *It Can't Happen Here*, the film version of *Elmer Gantry*, *The Poisonwood Bible*, and the works of Flannery O'Connor (notably *The Violent Bear It Away* [1960]), a marginalized, economically impoverished, usually dumb, and almost always hypocritical evangelical populace (further examples could be provided almost ad nauseum). On the other hand, in an image that is not only perplexing, but indeed totally contradictory and incompatible, evangelicals are also powerful conniving theocrats, particularly in the feminist dystopias of the eighties and nineties (*The Handmaid's Tale*, The *Parable* series).

At first such depictions happened almost out of necessity. At the beginning of the twentieth century and into the 1920s, there was still a good deal of debate about "which Protestantism (mainline liberal "Modernist" Protestantism or fundamentalism) would speak for the whole" (Marty 1991, 157). A narrative of right-wing evangelical Protestantism was needed that would cast it in the darkest possible terms; secularists and their liberal Protestant allies feared, with some justification, that certain fundamentalist preachers had grown inordinately powerful. The "colorful" exploits of evangelical leaders such as J. Frank Norris and John Roach Straton provided an ideal context for marginalizing fundamentalists and other members of the Protestant right. Since fundamentalists and their allies had made few friends during this period—antagonizing Catholics, secularists and even sometimes Jews—it was relatively easy for left-wing writers to cast fundamentalists as both marginal and dangerously elite.

How much this conflicted identity reflected reality is difficult to determine. As George Marsden points out, at the time of the culture wars of the 1920s, the split between modernists and fundamentalists was "widely perceived as a conflict between urban and rural culture" (Marsden 2006, 201), one exacerbated by a new mass media system that tended to simplify the roots of existing cultural division (202). While Marsden acknowledges that there may have been some particular appeal of evangelicalism to the working class, he associates that appeal mainly with the "respectable" Protestant and northern European working class and warns his readers against an essentially sociological reading of evangelical history, in which class concerns are paramount (203). On the other hand, Nathan Hatch's study of nineteenth century Christianity, *The Democratization of American Christianity* (1989), seems deeply skeptical of divorcing evangelical history from sociological analysis, pointing out that fundamentalism is a mixture of modern ideas of democracy mixed with a rejection of "modernity as it is expressed in high culture" (1989, 219).

What is clear is that the narrative of evangelicalism from the fifties on at best found evangelicalism to be a problematic movement, and at worst saw evangelicals as representing an inferior social caste, to be marginalized by non-evangelicals (primarily secularists, but also mainline Protestants and occasionally other religious groups), while at the same time denying such marginalization was taking place. For Bourdieu, operating in a society where religion was a less determinate factor in fixing social class, such repression was typically represented through "the eternal sociodicy, such as apocalyptic denunciations of all forms of 'leveling,' 'trivialization' or 'massification'" (1984, 469). These apocalyptic predictions usually take the form of "an obsessive fear of number, of undifferentiated hordes indifferent to difference and constantly threatening to submerge the private spaces of bourgeois exclusiveness" (469). Such images of evangelicals (and of fundamentalist Muslims, for that matter, who also get typed in this regard) are easy to find. One thinks of the foreboding military imagery in *Jesus Camp*, child soldiers threatening a jihad against Margaret Atwood in her palatial, middle-class estate. The mindless Cylons of the new *Battlestar Galactica* and the Fremen of *Dune*, with their fanatic monotheisms and terroristic intentions, are good examples of this trend (here probably directed at Christians and Muslims mutually), as are the gorilla and mutant armies of the original *Planet of the Apes* (serving under telepathic mind-reading, bomb worshiping mutants or fundamentalist orangutans), and even (perhaps) the association of armed militant Tea Party hordes with right-wing evangelicalism, ready to take over the country.

Evangelicals threaten to bring back a form of religion that mainline Protestants, atheists, and (some) secular Jews had hoped was lost in America—a faith that is kinetic, frenetic, fanatical, and most of all, *public*. The intrusion of evangelical faith practices into public life—witnessing, public prayers, Tebowing, religious valedictory speeches—threatens to unseat the secular bourgeoisie's sense of a safe, progressive, secular America. It also highlights the undercurrents of racism and classism that underlie much of secularism's critique of the Christian Right. It is more than a little suspicious, for instance, that secular narratives of evangelicalism, such as the documentaries *Jesus Camp* and *Hell House* (2001), as well as the movie *Saved!*, focus most negatively on Pentecostal and charismatic practices, particularly speaking in tongues and the physical movements associated with that phenomena, spiritual healing, and the seemingly (to non-believers) bizarre forms of prayer and call-and-response found in many charismatic churches. It is precisely these practices that have allowed Pentecostalism's phenomenal growth among non-white minority groups, particularly blacks and Latinos, many of whom came from churches that had similar worship styles (if not beliefs). The association of emotionalism with social inferiority walks hand in hand with the secular bourgeoisie aesthete's (documentarian or filmmaker's) concern for "mind over body" and "muted over gaudy" (Bourdieu 2001, 1807). Because Pentecostal and minority churches exhibit a more emotional worship style, they are typified as the dangerous hordes of child jihadists and theocratic foot soldiers that the right wing so desperately needs.[4] The working class and the minority hordes are thus conveniently marginalized as right-wing fanatics who do not want what is "right for America," while secular bourgeoisie writers such as Margaret Atwood and Barbara Kingsolver represent themselves, or at least their works, as championing the oppressed against these right-wing fanatics, many of whom do not make one-tenth the amount of money that either author earns in a year.

Thus it is literature and film — art, in other words — that make the marginalization of evangelicals, particularly fundamentalists and Pentecostals, both possible and desirable for the secular left. Whether or not Bourdieu was correct in pointing to aesthetics, and to Kantian disinterestedness in particular, as one of the crucial elements by which the social elite justify their cultural position, it is clear that when it comes to evangelicalism, Bourdieu was essentially correct. What is interesting about the evangelical experience of marginalization is that evangelicals compose the horde that is also supposedly the master class. One can understand why evangelicals remained perplexed at the secular contestation that they controlled the Bush–era government, for instance, when there was not a single evangelical on the Supreme Court and when evangelicals were (according to David Kuo, an evangelical member of the Bush White House) routinely referred to as "crazies" and "nuts" by the supposed evangelical-loving Bush administration staffers (Lindsay 2007, 262).

One can understand, therefore, even sympathize somewhat, with cosmopolitan evangelicals' attempts to distance themselves from their populist, "lower class" brethren, particularly when it comes to the arts. Here, they feel, they can find a common meeting ground with secular elites, an area of grace and thought where what matters is the cultural seriousness and merit of one's work; here evangelicals will be judged not by their faith but by the quality of their work. And if that work proves to be of high quality, then the cultural prestige of evangelicalism is raised, and its consequent social influence is extended. Yet the evangelical cosmopolitan elite, as bourgeoisie as the secular bourgeoisie that they contend with, believe in an illusory idol: the ideal that the meritorious in the arts rise to the top, that there are really no undiscovered great talents, that anyone with the inborn talent and drive will rise to the top of the artistic heap. As Bourdieu points out, this is merely the myth of meritocracy. In reality, the two greatest predictors of success are "the socioeconomic status of one's parents and one's success in school" (Bourdieu 2001, 1807). The secular left, seeing itself as "higher" if not "richer" than evangelicals, is not simply going to grant evangelicals cultural merit because they desire it. If the secular left were to do so, it would complicate the left's self-understanding, as well as its analysis of itself as the protector of the poor and the downtrodden. This is assuredly a position the left does not want to put itself in.

It is the very denial of that merit in evangelicalism, the denial of the correctness of evangelical "taste" even in debatably decent evangelical writing such as the works of novelists Stephen Lawhead and Kathy Tyers, that serves as the means by which the secular left legitimates the "social and economic inequalities" that working-class evangelicals face. The marginalization of populist evangelicals in fiction and the popular arts is made possible primarily — one is tempted to say exclusively — through the automatic denial to evangelicals of any artistic or cultural authenticity or originality. It does not really matter how good Christian rock ever gets (one could argue, for instance, that in the late nineties it was quite good); it will never gain legitimacy, even if it develops its own authentic aesthetic forms. Similarly, genres such as the spiritual warfare novel, even though they represent authentic folk art, will find it impossible to gain support among a wide body of secular and non-evangelical readers or art connoisseurs. The folk cannot have an art form and still remain an Other to the secular left; therefore anything that appears to be art within evangelicalism must be denied. From this wellspring, the need for spiritually persecuted bourgeoisie heroes and heroines — Offred, Frank Shallard, Cates, and Colonel Taylor — appears.

The worldview movement's answer to this dilemma is to merely replace a secular aesthetic with a Christian aesthetic, or at least an aestheticized Christian viewpoint about the world and the arts. That's fine if one is not struggling economically and socially against the accumulated cultural baggage the secular left has placed on evangelicals. But for a working class evangelical, art's influence is essentially pernicious; as Roger Taylor so graphically puts it, "As a form of life, art is like cancer. It takes over and colonizes other forms of life so that it becomes difficult to distinguish one from the other" (Home [2012]). Art mutates and takes shape, forming small colonies that either deny the reality of populist evangelical art (Frank Peretti, Thomas Kinkade, Jack Chick, etc.) or incorporate that art into a secular *Weltanschauung*, where the art produced by the great Christian artist is denied any status as Christian art (as one could argue happened with Johnny Cash).

The aim of this work is to in some small way contribute a third option to evangelicalism, which is to return to its iconoclastic roots. There is nothing ignoble or wrong in rejecting the arts, or in preferring Cyril Cusack's book-burning Captain to the repentant Guy Montag, rotely memorizing books whose words he may not even fully understand. If evangelical art is not to be accepted on its own terms, if the evangelical is always to be seen as an enemy of the arts, regardless of his actual ideological position, why not simply turn the secular stereotype on its head by saying, "Yes, we hate the arts. Shouldn't you?" The secular stigma of anti-art evangelicalism is only a stigma if one accepts that being against the arts is a bad thing. If evangelicals refuse to accept this illogical conclusion (that being against art is bad, immoral, evil, or ignorant), then they have a new means open to relating to art that avoids embracing the view of either the secular bourgeoisie or elitist Christian worldview supporters. And this means of viewing the figure of the artist and the arts, far from being anti-modern, allies anti-art evangelicals with the quintessentially subversive thinkers of modernism and contemporary art: Duchamp, the Dadaists, and all others who protested against the stink of secularized religion — or as the more anti-religious thinker Stewart Home puts it, the "rotten egg smell of the idea of God" present in art today — that art now exudes (Home [2012]). This is company populist evangelicals should be proud to be in, as they struggle to find their own cultural identity against hostile secular and cosmopolitan evangelical forces.

2

Romantic Realism:
The Damnation of Evangelicalism

Introduction: Damning with Good Intentions

The Damnation of Theron Ware and *Elmer Gantry* represent the two foundational texts in discussing the artist's relationship to evangelicalism. The reason for these texts' foundational nature is in both cases somewhat obvious. *The Damnation of Theron Ware* was the first significant work to note the essentially anti-aesthetic nature of contemporary evangelical belief; many of its comments on evangelicalism were prescient in predicting how later formulations of nineteenth century evangelical belief, such as fundamentalism, would come to view the arts. Yet *The Damnation of Theron Ware* is also in many ways anomalous, in that it, like this study itself, did not assume that anti-art or anti-aesthetic viewpoints were necessarily socially maladaptive. Indeed, despite Frederic's obvious linguistic and artistic skill, the novel gives the distinct impression that Frederic sympathizes at least as much with Theron's fundamentalist-like congregation as he does with either the aspiring aesthete Theron or his Catholic, art-loving friend, Celia.

Elmer Gantry, written three decades later, reflects very different concerns. Secularism and mainline Protestantism are on the ascendance; more conservative theological beliefs are considered at best misguided, at worst dangerous. For Lewis, art and evangelical belief are in dialectical opposition. Lewis, like Frederic, does not seem entirely happy with this situation. One can find traces of sympathy for evangelical belief in Lewis that would often be lacking in later works such as *Inherit the Wind* or *The Devil and Daniel Silverman*. For Lewis, as for Frederic, the passing away of religious belief at the beginning of the twentieth century represents the major dilemma facing those artists who seek to portray evangelical belief. But while Frederic had a healthy skepticism about the arts' cultural "value" and a contempt for what he saw as the dandyism and elitism of many of evangelicalism's critics, Lewis wholeheartedly threw his support behind the Menckenite derision of evangelical and fundamentalist belief, and its often far-fetched equation of fundamentalism with sinister cultural forces such as fascism. Through Lewis, many of the modern artistic clichés surrounding evangelicalism were formulated: the hypocritical minister, the hysterical female revivalist or evangelist, the anti-intellectual, anti-art evangelical rube, the Billy Sunday Christian masculinist, etc. Lewis's depiction is not necessarily problematic, when considered from a factual standpoint. He guys evangelicalism quite accurately, and his depictions of Elmer's rise through Methodist ranks is particularly well done. But in setting the initial formula by which artists read evangelical belief through the twentieth century, Lewis has been a largely negative force. Lewis depicts Elmer's anti-art, anti-intellectual views with great sympathy, but in the end Elmer is basically a dangerous, censorious rube. What Lewis, unlike Frederic, does not consider, is that evangelicals like Elmer may be as perceptive, perhaps more so, in their iconoclastic views of art as Lewis is with his own artistic self-validation.

In so far as spiritually capitalistic forces operated in this period, they were often innocent. Modernist or liberal Protestants, conservative non-fundamentalist evangelicals, and fundamentalists were all trying to accrue power during this period, and though by the end of the period modernists were largely dominant, the battle had been hard fought, with unnecessary wounds inflicted by both sides. While modernists and liberals did end up suppressing the cultural coherence of the evangelical church, their motivation for doing so was often quite noble. There had been a regrettable tendency in modern evangelicalism, present as far back as D.L. Moody, to deemphasize social concerns as opposed to saving souls (Marsden 2006, 85). From 1900 till 1920, the rise of the Social Gospel went almost hand-in hand with the collapse of revivalist social concerns (91). Lewis, and many of his religious contemporaries, expressed concern at what they saw as the growing union of capitalism and evangelical religion, which they felt marginalized minority groups and the working class.

The problem for liberals is that in many ways their vision of evangelical conservatism was, while partly true, very much incomplete. As George Marsden points out, many of Moody's allies, even Moody himself, tried to preserve the tradition of Christian social service; their supposed "anti-poor" ideas have tended to be exaggerated (Marsden 2006, 85). In addition, much of evangelical opposition to efforts at, say, improving race relations or economic conditions lies within modern evangelicalism's essentially anti-structuralist, individualist nature, which emphasizes promoting personal responsibility over social programs (see Emerson and Smith 2000, 104). One need only look at a sampling of Charismatic churches to see that evangelicals care about improved race relations. Visiting a Holiness or pietist evangelical church will often bring a similarly positive image of evangelicals' concern for the poor. In addition, the liberal master narrative, promoted by groups such as Americans United for the Separation of Church and State, which emphasizes mainline Protestantism's pristine record against fundamentalist and evangelical "reactionariness," tends to omit holes in mainline and secularism's record as well. Even at the time Lewis wrote, signs of mainline Protestantism's and secularism's own social inadequacies were evident. For instance, at the beginning of 1917 and throughout World War I, one of mainline Protestantism's main accusations against dispensational evangelicals was that they were *insufficiently* patriotic, even traitorous (Marsden 2006, 145–146). Similarly, though conservative interests were clearly dominant by the time Lewis wrote *Elmer Gantry*, as late as 1910, one might be able to characterize evangelicalism as not being particularly nationalistic, with an occasional progressive sentiment even expressed, though conservatism prevailed (207). This was the same era when one could see H.G. Wells supporting eugenics and Jack London combining rabid racism with a progressive socialist gospel (Wells 1933, 361, 394; Reesman 2009, 1–2). Therefore, while the mainline church and secularists can certainly be excused for their stereotyping of evangelicals, one should hardly blame evangelicals for returning the same favor.

The Early History of Damning

The late nineteenth and early twentieth centuries represented a transitional period for evangelicalism. When *The Damnation of Theron Ware* was published in 1896, fundamentalism was still an embryo, not truly born (at the very earliest) until the publication of *The Fundamentals* in 1910 (Marsden 2006, 118–119). Even then, it would probably be more correct to use the term fundamentalist only after it was officially coined in 1920 (119). Until the Scopes trial, undoubtedly some evangelicals still hoped they could retain control of some segments of the mainline Protestant denominations. As late as 1925, fundamentalists had the potential to gain control of the powerful northern Presbyterian and northern Baptist groups. Once the Scopes trial exposed evangelicalism to public ridicule, it was difficult for non-evangelicals to any longer take the movement seriously (191). The disappearance of the evangelical from public life became one of the great historical myths of the twentieth century, conforming to secular biases about the continued growth of human progress and the eroding of religious values.

Yet, when *The Damnation of Theron Ware* was published, evangelicalism was still taken seriously as a social phenomenon, though increasingly it was seen as theologically irrelevant. British novelist Miss Humphery Ward's *Robert Elsmere* (1888), a phenomenally popular novel in its day, bemoaned the death of God (Wilson 1999, 10), as did novels such as Mark Rutherford's *Revolution in Tanner's Lane* (1887) (Bennett 1997, 182) (both works probably at least slightly influenced Frederic's depictions of evangelical belief). Liberal Protestantism, though not a recent phenomenon in America, had only gained its ascendancy in the 1870s and 1880s (Marsden 2006, 24–25). Though liberal Protestantism was present in many denominations by the time of *Theron Ware*'s publication, the movement's American leaders were still mainly Congregationalists and, in so far as anyone defines them as Protestant, Unitarian (Dorrien 2001, 397–398). These beliefs slowly spread to other mainline denominations in the first quarter of the twentieth century (398). And in conservative denominations, the dominance of the saintly (but for evangelical theology, disastrous) D.L. Moody meant that a small spark of something approaching ecumenism remained in the evangelical church (Marty 1986, 209).

The Methodist movement, which along with Catholicism and philosophical pragmatism is the chief theological force in the novel, was going through tremendous social changes at the close of the nineteenth century. The denomination was no longer agrarian; more elaborate architecture was being employed in churches, and organ music was now being employed as well, contributing to a sense of growing aestheticism that some evangelicals, and even a few non-evangelicals (including possibly Frederic himself), may have seen as decadence. Older Methodist populist traditions, such as the camp meeting, the revival, and the love feast were beginning to disappear, almost certainly because they no longer conformed to Methodism's new bourgeois image. Education in seminaries now included higher criticism, and liberal Methodists were slowly gaining control over the denomination. However, a powerful anti-modernist movement of Methodists continued to nag at these modernizers through the close of the twentieth century (Myers 1994, 55).

The Damnation of Theron Ware did fairly well on its release. By December 1896, a year into the printing, there had already been nine reprints (Bennett 1997, 184). It is difficult to obtain sales figures for *The Damnation of Theron Ware* today, but it certainly does not sell as well; its rank on Amazon, as of April 11, 2012, was 754,202 (Amazon.com [2012]). Its critical reputation is a different matter. Oscar Wilde considered the work "very interesting" (Bennett 1997, 185). Theodore Dreiser noted in his diary that he had read the work, and both F. Scott Fitzgerald and Sinclair Lewis both mentioned the novel in their own novels (Bennett 185). It is probable that Lewis was at least slightly influenced by Frederic. Although neglected in the first half of the twentieth century, in the sixties some New Critic specialists in Frederic studies believed that a Frederic renaissance was in the offing, so highly regarded was the work by the New Critics; regrettably the novel never achieved that renaissance, though it continues to be well-regarded enough to merit a Penguin Classic edition (Klopfenstein 1997, 34–35). It is likely that the novel's critical neglect is more an accident, or a product of differing modern interests, than of any lack of regard for its artistic merits. Academics who read it, ranging from Catholics to evangelicals to homosexuals, frequently report enjoying the novel for its sophisticated discussions of art, sexuality, religion, and science. That the novel appeals to such a wide base of people indicates that it will likely retain at least some loyal following for years to come.

The Damnation of Theron Ware: *Sexy Catholics, Sexy Critics, Celibate Priests, and Clueless Evangelical Clerics*

The Damnation of Theron Ware is a work deeply concerned with the role of art in society. The novel tells the story of a young Methodist minister, Theron Ware, who slowly loses his faith under the influence of a Catholic Modernist priest (Father Forbes) and a rich Catholic aesthete (Celia Madden). The novel is notable for its even-handed depiction of Catholicism, extremely unusual at the time, and its mastery of subjects ranging from higher criticism to contemporary science. The conflict in the novel is multi-sided and need not be explained in detail here. Basically, however, the work uses Theron's moral disintegration, as he loses his faith, to comment on a number of trends in the late nineteenth century, including the rise of higher criticism and evolutionary theory, the growth of philosophical pragmatism, and artistic decadence and its relationship to evangelical belief. It is the latter subject with which this text is concerned, but it cannot be understood apart from its relationship with these other philosophical systems.

Theron represents a typical petit bourgeoisie social climber, who wants to transcend his social background and enter the realm of high culture and grace. He starts off the novel with a genuine love of Methodism, though an incipient materialism is already evident in his character. However, it does not take him long to confide, "I don't mind admitting to you that there is a good deal in Methodism — I mean the strict practice of its letter ... that is personally distasteful to me" (Frederic 1895 [hereafter cited as *DTW*], 122). Theron is alternately enticed by both higher criticism and high art; indeed, the modernism of the one feeds the modernism of the other in his mind. His experience, for instance, of the Catholic modernist theologian Ernest Renan's *Recollections of My Youth* (1863) has an aesthetic tinge: he describes it as "gentle, tender, lovable" (*DTW* 131). Theron, like many another evangelical aspiring to higher social status (Brian McLaren, for instance), glorifies the intellectual and artistic world as "a world of culture and grace, of lofty thoughts ... where men asked one another, not 'Is your soul saved?' but 'Is your mind well furnished?'" (132). For Theron, higher criticism embodies a kind of theological beauty, embodied in Renan's words, which very much matches the artistic beauty Theron discovers in his friend Celia. By contrast, Theron comes to detest the "shrill clamor" of Sister Barnum's singing and the "conceited and pushing note" that is the height of Brother Lovejoy's musical ability (130). Theron believes that "folks who sang with such unintelligence, and who threw themselves with such undignified fervor into the childish business of the bread and water, could not be formidable antagonists for a man of intellect" (*DTW* 148). Like modern Emergents, Theron believes he is that man of intellect able to transcend his culture for the "higher" things. In many ways, Theron's situation here mirrors that of African-Americans after Reconstruction and the colonial artists operating during this period. Theron has an inferiority complex about his own culture's achievements, seeing them as lacking. Beginning the novel with an appreciation for Methodism, Theron slowly loses the populist touch that made Methodism such a powerful force in nineteenth century America.[1] Theron's tragedy is that he sees this process of losing faith solely as enlightenment, or *illumination*, as Frederic originally titled Theron's process (and the novel) (Donaldson 1986, xi).

For Theron, the world of high culture can only lead to progress and social enlightenment. He contends, "The march of science must ... soon produce a universal skepticism. It is in the nature of human progress. What all intelligent men recognize today, the masses must surely come to see" (*DTW* 241). Evangelicalism, despite its reputation, has a long history of attempting to accommodate itself to modern thought. Much of the disastrous appeal of Common Sense Rationalism to eighteenth century evangelicals, for instance, was that it offered evangelicals an "intellectually respectable" method of propping up traditional moral and religious values, one that did not have to "appeal to traditional religious authorities" (Noll 1994, 87). Common sense philosophy combined with Baconian ideas of data interpretation provided the lens through which evangelicals viewed scripture (Detwiler 1999, 91). These ideas, essentially rationalist in outlook, worked well enough for those who had few doubts about the truth of the Biblical text to begin with. But for people of even such marginal intelligence as Theron, this interpretive schema simply did not make sense because it was built (they felt) on a tautology: "The Bible is true, and therefore we can trust it to give us truth." When the logic of this system began to collapse towards the end of the nineteenth century, many Christians simply lost their faith, unable to adapt to the changing theological currents of the time.

What makes Theron's position, like McLaren's today, problematic is that he assumes, as the Emergent Church does in its division between primitive moderns and advanced postmoderns,[2] that 1) the newer theology is always best and that 2) theological "progress" automatically equates with theological intelligence. Theologies that would have appealed to Theron's aesthetic, religious, and scientific sense were still available at the time: Horace Bushnell's adoption of Coleridge's moderate Anglican theological system, for instance, was only half a century old, and though somewhat perplexingly viewed as outdated by theological liberals of the day, still remained a powerful critique of the linguistic basis of religious belief (Dorrien 2001, 123–125, 174). Jonathan Edwards's more conservative theology, though considered outdated in the nineteenth century, had in many ways avoided the rationalist traps that would plague nineteenth century theology and turn evangelicalism into a religion solely of rationalist Biblical proof-texting (taking quotes out of context) and even more disastrous rational presuppositional apologetics (Noll 1994, 86). And Edwards, like Bushnell, valued the aesthetic sense, particularly in nature, writing treatises on it, such as *The Nature of True Virtue* (1765) (Johnson 1935, civ).

Therefore, there were some evangelical paradigms for viewing high culture at the close of the nineteenth century, though the Congregationalist roots of Edwards and Bushnell's thinking would probably have caused concern for a man like Theron. What alienates Theron from his culture's aesthetic sense is not that culture's shallowness, but the fact that he is actually seeing his own reflection in what he thinks is their shallowness. Though there is a slight note of ridiculousness to some of Theron's conservative evangelical nemeses, one can detect the obvious pathos Frederic feels for such people in Frederic's seemingly anti-evangelical depiction of Brother Pierce. Pierce warns Theron, early in the novel:

> We ain't had no trouble with the Free Methodists ... jest because we kept to the old paths.... Everybody can shout "Amen!" as loud and long as the Spirit moves him.... Someone was sayin' you thought we ought to have a choir and an organ. NO siree! No such tom-foolery for us!... Why, they say some folks are goin' round now preachin' that our grandfathers were all monkeys. That comes from departin' from the ways of our forefathers, an' putting in organs an' choirs, an' deckin our women-folks out with gewgaws, an apin' the fashions of the worldly [*DTW* 28].

Frederic's depiction here initially seems to mock evangelical belief. Evangelicals are opposed to all the things that the reader assumes artists like Frederic admires: music, beautiful women, high fashion, and (by logical extension) literature and the visual arts. Frederic allows the reader to keep this initial assumption for a good deal of the novel. Realizing that his audience would probably be composed of upper middle class and elite sophisticates like himself, well-versed in both contemporary visual and literary art, Frederic lures the reader into buying into their anti-populist, anti-petit-bourgeoisie prejudices.

Methodism, with its history of religious "enthusiasm," had long been a subject for mockery by cultural elites who disdained its "new revival measures" (Hatch 1989, 14). Though Methodism had for the most part shorn off its lower-class trappings by the late 1800s, its reputation for "anti-elitism," as well as its (to elites) "devolution" into Holiness and, later, Pentecostal beliefs still made its more conservative wing an object of ridicule (212). Frederic's audience, particularly Congregationalists, Unitarians, Episcopalians, and secularists, would have found the aforementioned scene symptomatic of the ridiculousness of Methodist artistic legalism, with its concern over proper church decorum and its rejection of stylistic innovation in church services. These groups would remember earlier fights, still present in some people's minds, about the appropriateness of novel-reading. Many evangelicals in the first half of the twentieth century saw fiction as "worse than useless" (C. G. Brown 2004, 96). Though this viewpoint had changed significantly by the second half of the nineteenth century (97), aesthetes of the late 1800s had some cause to feel resentment at what they saw as the restrictiveness of antifictive and anti-artistic evangelical beliefs.

But Frederic slowly shifts the reader's vision of the artist and hints that there may be more to Brother Pierce's iconoclastic philosophy than is at first supposed. Dr. Ledsmar, the voice of scientific reason in *The Damnation of Theron Ware*, is a particularly persuasive voice for artistic iconoclasm, commenting:

> All art, so-called, is decay.... When a race begins to brood on the beautiful—so-called—it is a sign of rot.... Take the Jews—those marvelous old fellows—who were never more than a handful, yet have imposed the rule of their ideas and their gods upon us for fifteen hundred years. Why? They were forbidden by their most fundamental law to make sculptures or pictures.... Now at last their long belated apogee is here; their decline is at hand. I am told ... the Jews are [now] producing a great lot of young painters and sculptors and actors.... That means the end of the Jews [*DTW* 80].

Ledsmar's depiction of the anti-artistic Jew, which is contrasted in the novel with the artistic Greek (represented by Celia), sees art as an essentially decadent and anti-rationalist force. For Ledsmar, the opposite of science is not religion, but art. If science represents all that is rational, then art represents all that is chaotic, irrational, and emotional. And indeed, Celia, the chief aesthete of the novel, is a flighty, emotional, and even cruel character, who is responsible, as much as Theron himself, for seducing Theron into his "damnation." Celia says of the Greeks that they have "absolute freedom from moral bugbears" and recognize that "beauty is the only thing in life that is worthwhile" (*DTW* 202). This aestheticism, of course, stands in stark contrast to Ledsmar's late nineteenth century rationalism, which calls for strict empirical verification of physical phenomena and therefore has little time for aesthetic abstractions, which are ultimately insolvable, perhaps pointless. Frederic's distinction between Jews and Greeks is almost undoubtedly a nod to Matthew Arnold's *Culture and Anarchy* (1869), in which Arnold preferred the "intuitive, intellectual, and imaginative approach" of the Hellenes (Greeks) to the "literal minded legalism" of the Jews (Wilson 1999, 261). Frederic, however, unlike Arnold, seems to prefer the Jew at least as much as the Greek. But Frederic's point is not simply to say religion is no worse than art. He suggests, more subversively, that science and religion have fundamental similarities that make them far more akin than the sciences ever will be to the humanities.

For Frederic, the root of this similarity lies in the commonly shared presupposition of nineteenth century science and evangelical Protestantism that the physical universe is knowable and a common respect for "facticity": in so much as we can ever know facts (science would be much more skeptical of most facts than religion), facts should be respected. Both science and evangelical Protestantism, as epistemes, value facts over feelings. Of course, Methodism, as a theological system, is much more emotive than rational. However, its emotiveness, unlike Celia's, is tied to a belief in objective moral truth, a belief that prevents evangelicals from ethically relativizing their every action. What damns Theron is that he accepts the relativism of Celia's Catholic aestheticism, without the secure theological grounding in Church history and tradition that allows Catholics to question such traditions while remaining morally grounded in a relativist age (see Urbanczyk 2006, 49–52, 54–55). Lacking such a tradition, Theron is damned (55). The ideal of "art for art's sake," without a tradition that knows how to merge the artistic with the sacred, turns simply to bankrupt materialism and artistic impoverishment. Theron, lacking the grounding to really distinguish himself as either a theologian or artist, ultimately simply becomes an "average kind of man," a corruption of this ideal (*DTW* 342).

The religious impulse, in Frederic's reading, is not simply antithetical to the artistic impulse; it is, in many ways, more principled. Celia herself finally points out the moral impoverishment that has resulted from Theron's fascination with the arts, and with the exoticism of Catholic belief (itself closely equated with the arts in *The Damnation of Theron Ware*):

> You showed me once ... a life of George Sand that you had ... bought — bought because you had just discovered that she had an unclean side to her life. You chuckled as you spoke to me about it, and you were for all the world like a little nasty boy, giggling over something dirty that older people had learned not to notice.... What you took to be improvement was degeneration. When you thought that you were impressing us most by your smart sayings and doings, you

were reminding us most of the fable about the donkey trying to play lap-dog [*DTW* 323].

Theron believes that in embracing the arts, he is entering a refined world; the liturgy of Catholicism, the relativism of theological modernism, the music of Chopin and the novels of George Sand are to bring him into a world of sophistication. He is to be culturally elevated above a people he now feels superior to. Celia implies that Theron's embrace of the arts is really just a form of class-climbing, one that forsakes the "honesty" of Theron's original nature and the "sincerity" of his "absurd religion" for materialistic hypocrisy (*DTW* 322). Theron is a latter-day Dimmesdale, but without the moral grandeur and terrible moral suffering of that religious hypocrite. Instead, Theron eases into hypocrisy, utilizing precisely that part of human nature (the arts) that the aestheticians of the nineteenth century thought most uplifted people. He is the donkey in Aesop's fables, unable to realize that while there is some honor in realizing one is a cultural donkey, there is none at all in trying to be a poseur artistic lapdog (Aesop [2012]; *DTW* 322). Aesthetes like Celia will not respect such poseurs, nor will the fundamentalists whom one leaves behind; and both will essentially be right in their assessment, for the goals of evangelicalism and the dandified aesthete are, at their core, irreconcilable. The aesthetes wanted art unbound by morality, but to be evangelical is to be, by definition, morality-bound.

Celia is saved from total destruction only because she comes from a religious tradition where the aesthetic and the religious impulses are fundamentally one impulse, not two. Celia's brother, Michael, similarly, points this out, when he notes, "When you go among others [Catholics]—you know what I refer to—you have no proper understanding of what their sayings and doings really mean" (*DTW* 298). The moral strength of Michael and his father Jeremiah Madden, grounded in their theologically conservative vision of Catholicism, is in marked contrast to Celia's pale imitation of Wildean dandyism and Theron's imitation of that imitation. Significantly, neither Jeremiah nor Michael are artistically or intellectually inclined. Jeremiah knew "nothing whatever" of books and "made only the most perfunctory pretense now and again of reading the papers" (86). Michael confides to his friends that he wanted to be a priest but did not have "the brains for it" (86), and is mentally inclined to respect even Theron's "education and talents" (297). Both men's theological conservatism is portrayed extremely sympathetically in the novel; Jeremiah Madden, in particular, comes off as almost a saint. By rejecting the aesthetic impulse, these men are able to tap into a deeper level of piety not available to those who have wedded the bankruptcy of the dandy ideal (art for art's sake) as a moral proposition with the equally disastrous propositions of philosophical pragmatism, which "reduced truth to utility" (Dooley 1982, 76), and higher criticism, which implemented such pragmatism at the theological level.

The conflict between religion and art, therefore, is an intrinsic element of *The Damnation of Theron Ware*. Those who stay within the conservative confines of their religious tradition are, by Frederic's estimation, intellectually limited, the tradeoff they pay for rejecting the arts and its philosophical bedfellow, higher criticism; it is this intellectual limitation that regrettably turns them into a spiritual proletariat. Similarly, though evangelicalism writ large has some cultural affinities with the science of the late nineteenth century, it tends to be more open to the emotional and irrational aspects of life than a Ledsmar or a T.H. Huxley would prefer. Evangelicalism, except perhaps in its Reformed form, lacked the scientific and pragmatist obsession with quantifying all emotive experiences; it was definitely not a faith that was comfortable with William James's *Varieties of Religious Experience* (1902). Faith, for evangelicals, had an effect on the real world; but it also transcended that world.

It was ultimately the this-worldly orientation of late nineteenth century aestheticism, higher criticism and science that caused evangelicals to condemn all three elements of contemporary culture as symptomatic of the decadence of what they termed modernism. But this theological shorthand elided significant differences between the modernist manifestations of these fields, particularly between modern art and modern science. Evangelicals tended to see both fields as an enemy. Dutch evangelical theologian H.R. Rookmaaker sought the "demise" of modern art, because it was based on "Enlightenment assumptions" (Siedell 2008, 157). Francis Schaeffer, similarly, was deeply concerned with modern art because it had lost its "hope of a unity of knowledge and a unity of life," instead presenting a "fragmented concept of reality" (Schaeffer 1976, 190); for Schaeffer this amounted to a betrayal of the Christian tradition, though he often expressed deep sympathy for individual modernists (see for instance, his comments on Van Gogh, p. 183). Such hatred was sometimes promoted by modern artists themselves. Tzara, for instance, mocked religion in the "Dada Manifeso 1918," though only in an aside (Tzara 2003, 253). Richard Huelsenbeck, an important figure in the early Dada scene who wrote a major survey of the early history of Dada in 1920, said that Dadaism was "atheist by instinct.... The Dadaist is opposed to the idea of paradise in every form, and one of the ideas farthest from his mind is that 'the spirit is the sum of all means for the improvement of human existence'" (Huelsenbeck 2003). For the Dadaists, religion, with its ordered, structured, codified system of beliefs, represented everything that their own chaotic, absurdist, and deliberately irrational beliefs opposed (Kleiner 2009, 393).

Yet, in so many ways, Dadaism mirrored early twentieth century evangelicalism, and particularly its later fundamentalist manifestations. Both philosophies tended to reject the idea of progress (see Kleiner 2009, 393, about Dadaism's rejection of progress); both philosophies also expressed a profound alienation from contemporary culture: Dada through its attempt to progressively deconstruct the basis on which art had previously been built, fundamentalism and dispensationalist premillennialism through their profound rejection of the "world" for the comforts of the church, a rejection that took on an increasingly anti-capitalist tinge as the twentieth century wore on (Boyer 1992, 250), despite the overall support among dispensationalists for some elements of American consumerism. *The Damnation of Theron Ware*, written before the formation of Cubism and Dadaism, could not of course predict how radically Dadaists would destroy the foundations on which high art stood. What it did note, however unconsciously, was that the relativization of aesthetic values that had gone hand-in-hand with the relativization of moral values would be a major source of conflict in the twentieth century.

This conflict is particularly seen in Celia, as the embodiment of the decadent ideal, wanting a "Greek" society in which "everybody was an intellectual aristocrat, where the Philistine was as unknown, as extinct, as the dodo" (*DTW* 194). Elements of Celia's vision of the artist survive to the present day. The Nietzschean artist hero has become virtually a cliché among aspirant artists: It was Hitler's self-myth (Spotts 2002, 11), as it was for Ayn Rand and Jack London (Landa 2007, 120,138). Modernists and Postmodernists argue that they no longer put the same stock in artistic creativity or originality. For instance, Craig Owens argues for a postmodern art whose goal is "no longer to proclaim its autonomy, its self-sufficiency, its transcendence; rather it is to narrate its own contingency, insufficiency, and lack of transcendence" (2003, 1025). Supporters of Baudrillard's theorizing on the "hyperreal" and Walter Benjamin's views of the radical possibilities of mechanical reproduction of the arts can be seen as following in this tradition. But the insincerity of such arguments is evident to even the most casual reader or art fan. Artists may no longer openly use terms such as "original" and "creative"; but almost no artist markets himself as derivative or conformist (with the possible exception of Warhol). Celia's glorification of the artistic genius, despite its similarities to Hitlerian rhetoric, Nietzschean philosophy, and ponderous Randian bombast, seems to have emerged triumphant in the twenty-first century. The cultural Philistine is universally derided, and even Reformed and Emergent intellectuals, the descendants of supposed cultural Philistines, now beg to be included among the aristocratic art elite.

All this, of course, would be fine, except for the fact that Duchamp and the Dadaists destroyed the basis on which artistic "originality" and "greatness" was based. Shakespeare is Stephenie Meyer is a monkey typing random letters

2. Romantic Realism 49

on a typewriter. If art is in the eye of the beholder, then it is hard to see by what standard the art world holds Arthur Danto to be a more preeminent cultural critic than the late derided Senator Jesse Helms. The modern reader, like Theron, is all in sympathy for Celia's derision of the Philistine, all the time ignoring the fact that the fundamentalist Philistine, in being skeptical of the Romantic, now Nietzschean, claims for artistic genius, actually is much closer to the spirit of Duchamp than the art world elite is. At the very least, these Philistines usually do not claim their own works are original, or creative. Instead, following in the steps of C.S. Lewis, they prize tradition and continuity of culture, realizing that originality is a buzzword of the twentieth century that may soon lose its meaning from overuse. Moreover, evangelical cultural Philistines, like the Dadaists, are populists (Lindsay 2007, 219) who scorn the growing elitism of a contemporary art world. Evangelical Philistines do produce kitsch — one need look only at Jack Chick tracts or the film *A Thief in the Night* (1972) to see the possible truth in that accusation — but, in this relativistic era, why is this kitsch any less interesting than *The Sound and the Fury* (1929), *Love in a Time of Cholera* (1985), or *Beavis and Butt Head* (1992–1997, 2011). On this, a modern Celia would have to be silent, for the eternal values and forms, the "Greekness" that undergirded her condemnation of artistic Philistines, is no longer operative.

Theron Ware represents two of the most enduring typologies of evangelicals throughout the last century and a quarter: the hypocritical minister and the uncultured rube, stereotypes that would be more crudely united in Elmer Gantry. Unlike Elmer, however, he does have aesthetic aspirations and a dimly utilized desire for beauty. He condemns the cultural Philistines, but is never quite able to escape their influence. This does not speak to any sense of ambivalence — Theron wishes desperately to belong with the Greeks — but instead denotes the aesthetically crippling nature of evangelical, and particularly Methodist, belief.

Modern evangelicals in the "cosmopolitan" (Lindsay 2007, 219) evangelical world are similarly trying to escape their "uncultured" background. Lindsay is tenuous in defining what the denominational affiliations of these cosmopolitan elites are. However, when it comes to contemporary elite evangelical art criticism, the dominant theological tradition is clearly Reformed, with a few Emergents. There is not a single significant identifiably non–Reformed or Emergent evangelical book on art theory that has been published in recent memory. The closest one comes to such a position is Daniel Siedell's *God in the Gallery* (2008), which significantly breaks with Schaeffer (Siedell 2008, 7), but is still largely influenced by Reformed scholarship (7–8). Of the 21 artists included in the anthology *It Was Good: Making Art to the Glory of God* (Bustard 2006), three fairly openly identified themselves as Reformed

Calvinists, while most of the rest were clearly influenced by Schaefferian (as well as occasionally Anglican or Catholic) artistic theory (349–355). Sandra Bowden, who writes the book's opening, is the president of Christians in the Visual Arts (CIVA), the most important extant evangelical arts organization, an organization that is heavily indebted to Hans Rookmaaker and Francis Schaeffer for whatever philosophy of aesthetics it has (Siedell 2008, 158). Rookmaaker's and Schaeffer's disciples, like Theron's, want to escape from the constrictions of artistic Philistinism; they, in a sense, no longer want to fit the typological classifications of anti-art evangelical pastors, censors, and parents that one sees operative in novels such as *Elmer Gantry* and *Go Tell It on the Mountain*.

What is missing from this theological system of aesthetic interpretation (particularly in Schaeffer) is the realization that fundamentalism's artistic legacy to modern evangelicalism should not be a source of embarrassment, but of pride. The large-scale fundamentalist adoption of dispensationalist theology has given evangelicalism a theological form that is itself an aesthetic statement about the world; some of the most powerful and sympathetic non-evangelical works about evangelicalism, such as the film *The Rapture* and the novel *We All Fall Down* (2006), play with central dispensationalist ideas about the Rapture, the Tribulation, and the so-called End Times. The various cultural legends surrounding such dark figures as the Antichrist and the Whore of Babylon and even darker objects such as the Mark of the Beast have established an incredibly rich mythological system that has powerfully affected the faith of millions and spawned a whole sub-genre of Rapture fiction and film (Hendershot 2004, 178, 182–189).[3] Some of the imagery used in these works, particularly in the infamous *Thief in the Night* series (1972–1983), with its guillotine condemning its heroine to hell (185), has drawn as much controversy as many a more well-regarded secular work, earning mentions by celebrity "artists" such as Marilyn Manson (187–188). Similarly, largely Arminian, often dispensationalist, Pentecostalism, despite the derision heaped on it by Calvinist theologians, has contributed its own unique genre to fiction: the spiritual warfare novel, a kind of Manichean conflict between heaven and hell set to fiction (for those interested, see Cox 1995, 281–284, which gives a liberal Protestant reading of the spiritual warfare genre's classic novel, *This Present Darkness*). Smarter evangelical novelists, such as Leif Enger, have utilized the creativity of dispensationalist and Pentecostal theology to enrich their own novels, playing with evangelicalism not simply as a religious ideology, but as a mythic system with its own rich cultural tradition, one that often shows its creativity more through the elaborate, perhaps implausible, theologies it constructs than through carefully argued logical presuppositions (the method favored by Schaeffer). This work argues that evangelicalism should, like Theron's evangelical enemies, reject the arts as much as possible, at least until the art world stops valuing products over people; however, in so much as Reformed Calvinists and Emergents continue to wish to embrace an aesthetic worldview, they could do worse than imitate their fundamentalist and Pentecostal cousins. Maybe in so doing, they would transcend the typology of the artistic rube or anti-art pastor that *The Damnation of Theron Ware* inadvertently started and advertently critiqued.

Ultimately, Theron's choice to see his own religion in aesthetic terms proves his damnation. He takes the advice of Sister Soulsby, his soul-stealing, pragmatic mentor, who suggests to him that Methodism is like a play, one in which Theron, through the arts and higher criticism, has suddenly gotten to see behind the scenes (*DTW* 171). Just because he sees behind the scenes, Soulsby claims, does not mean that the play "isn't beautiful and affecting, and all that. It only shows that everything in the world is produced by machinery.... The trouble is that you've been let in on the stage ... and you're so green ... that you want to sit down and cry because the trees are cloth, and the moon is a lantern" (171). Rather than call the audience's attention to the play's artificiality, its inauthenticity, it is better to "move along smoothly" (172). Religion becomes for Theron merely an artistic performance; and as the founding member of the school of evangelical artistic rubes, his performance is not adequate to the task. He can fool the Methodists of his congregation easily enough (230–231), he can even fool himself until the last possible moment, but he cannot fool the reader, who knows that Theron would have been better off never seeing the artifice of the drama he was in. Once that artifice was stripped away, damnation truly was the only artistic and spiritual path left to him. And in that damnation, Frederic implicates his readers as well, for they have enjoyed an artifice that seeks to caution against the very artifice it is portraying (Becknell 1991, 70). For Frederic, the battle between art and evangelicalism speaks not to the strength of the former phenomena, but to the spiritual emptiness of an age that has torn down its evangelical roots but left nothing in their place.

Elmer Gantry: *The Defining Artistic Image of Evangelicalism*

No artistic work, with the possible exception of *Inherit the Wind*, has done more to shape the contemporary perception of evangelicals than the novel *Elmer Gantry*. From the novel's genesis, it was immensely influential. Written by Nobel Prize–winning novelist Sinclair Lewis, *Elmer Gantry*, by the day after its publication, had already sold a hundred thousand copies, an immense number of sales during the late twenties. The novel remained the number-one bestseller for most of 1927. Its Signet edition continues to be published year after year, thanks in large part to its continued cultural relevance (Lingeman 2002, 301).

When the novel came out it received a great deal of criticism, both from the religious establishment of its day and from the artistic elite. Billy Sunday called for God to strike Lewis dead for his novelistic portrayal of evangelicals (Lingeman 2002, 302). Reverend John Roach Straton, whose desire to be a "Protestant pope" partly inspired Lewis's depiction of Gantry (266–267, 306), decried the novel as "figments of a disordered imagination" (303). Meanwhile, art critics largely derided Lewis's work. Interestingly-named art critic Elmer Davis, writing in *The New York Times Book Review*, argued that Lewis had sacrificed art for propaganda in making a "missionary tract" (304). Rebecca West argued that Elmer's mode of thinking on religion was no more complicated than Lewis's (304).

Today, the novel enjoys a mixed critical reputation. Lingeman considers it a "seriously, but not fatally flawed" novel (305). But as he points out, much of the shock — and much of the unreality — that the original critics of the book saw in *Elmer Gantry* seems less unbelievable 75 years later, in an age "of errant televangelists and evolution banning creationists" (307). And indeed, that assessment is largely accurate. While *Elmer Gantry* certainly has its flaws as an artistic work, and even as a portrayal of the evangelical community, it is certainly a fairer depiction of evangelical life than the notoriously inept *Inherit the Wind* or the rhetorically dishonest *Handmaid's Tale*, neither of which even bothers to understand the community it attacks. Lewis was well known for his preference for exhaustive sociological and literary research, and none of his novels (with the possible exception of *Arrowsmith*) was better researched than *Elmer Gantry*. Lewis consulted extensively with two pastors, a moderate Methodist, William Stidger and a more radical Unitarian, Leon Birkhead (268–269). He traveled hundred of miles out of his way just to observe the preaching of notorious fire-breathing pastor J. Frank Norris (271), and listened to the preaching of the great Aimee Semple McPherson, a fairly clear model (despite the occasional denial) for Sharon Falconer (273, 283). Lewis subscribed to numerous church papers and filled his rooms with more than two hundred volumes of theological works, which from the evidence present in *Elmer Gantry* he was clearly familiar with (274). He even held his own "Sunday school class" in which he good-naturedly but ruthlessly attacked what he saw as Christian pretense (275).

The enormous effort that Lewis put into his work is often apparent from seemingly offhand asides. For instance, when one of Elmer's Methodist parishioners asks him what he thinks of "John Wesley's doctrine of perfection" (Lewis 280), Elmer responds, "It's absolutely ... proven" but then wonders what the doctrine of perfection is (Lewis 1927 [hereafter cited as *EG*], 280). What makes this scene so hilariously funny to anyone with any knowledge of Methodism is that Wesley's doctrine of perfection is as about as central a doctrine to Methodist belief as one can possibly get. Elmer's ignorance of it therefore is both a great inside joke and a penetrating comment on Elmer's, and by extension the Protestant Church's, intellectual and moral bankruptcy. Further examples could be provided from the novel of Lewis's attention to detail and theological astuteness, but such a specific example should alone suffice to prove the sincerity of his desire to treat the evangelical community, if not respectfully, at least honestly.

What does need to be stated is how different Lewis's approach to research is from modern authors such as Tom Perotta, Theodore Roszak, and Margaret Atwood. Perotta, in studying evangelicalism, utilized mainly web research, reading the Bible every day and occasionally viewing a Christian website. The result, in his novels *Leftovers* and *The Abstinence Teacher*, is an embarrassing lack of understanding — or simple respect — for the culture he is dealing with, a respect he would likely show if he were dealing with a racial, ethnic, or non-Christian minority group (Perotta, 2007). Theodore Roszak, despite his obvious command of the social sciences, creates a faith community that blends *every* element of occasional stupidity that the evangelical community has come up with: People who support firebombing abortion clinics, support the Holocaust, condemn AIDS victims, and put their weight behind sadism (Archer Books, [2012]; Roszak 2003, 219–229, 291, 295). Even at the time *The Devil and Daniel Silverman* was published, such exaggeration was not only ridiculous but verged on being a conspiratorial reading of evangelical culture. Evangelicals were by the early 2000s beginning to put considerable political pressure behind AIDS research, not against it (though this support was hardly always purely motivated). Anti-Semitism was not only *not* a prominent element of evangelical theology; it was arguably no more present in evangelicalism than other theological systems. The German Confessing Church, for instance, with its combination of Neo-Orthodox and evangelical faith, arguably did a better job against the Nazi party than German liberal Protestantism (Lindsay 2007, 46–48; MacCullouch 2009, 941–943). And the relatively low number of murders committed against abortion providers (eight since 1993) (NARAL 2010, 1), despite evangelicals' belief that abortion was both murder and genocide, spoke more to evangelical apathy about abortion than genuine political commitment. Atwood's efforts were, predictably, better, but even she relied on creating a tenuous link between the Christian Right in America, Iranian theocracy, and the Puritans (Atwood 1986, 316–317). Such a connection was problematic, because most evangelicals were even more opposed to theocracy than were the brave (and numerous) Iranian political radicals who protested against Khomeini. The only explicitly theocratic system in evangelicalism, Reconstructionism, was routinely derided among evangelical intellectuals and lay members alike. In so far as Reconstructionist ideas did influence evangelical intellectual culture — and they did have an effect on a certain class of Reformed, and more rarely, Charismatic elites, such as Pat Robertson (Charismatic) and Francis Schaeffer (Reformed) — such influence was largely underground. Had any leader openly advocated theocracy, they would have found the rest of the church at their throats. Neo-evangelicals, pietists, and even many fundamentalists simply had no interest in supporting a theocracy, still less one founded by Pentecostal "heretics" and Presbyterian cousins of the Puritan persecutors of the Baptists. Atwood, like Roszak, stretches her credibility beyond the breaking point, and the result is a work that, if not artistically compromised, is suspect as any representation of supposed truth.

Lewis may offend evangelicals, but he took evangelical belief seriously. Few authors would ever match his commitment to artistic truthfulness. Insofar as evangelicals condemn him, they condemn merely what they see as a dark side of themselves: the movement's anti-intellectualism, its distrust for the aesthetic, its rampant materialism, and its political adventurism. But in such condemnations, evangelicals miss an opportunity to critically engage with the history of their theological tradition and its representation in literature. *Elmer Gantry*, as a novel, locates the poverty of evangelical aesthetic ideas, not so much in evangelical beliefs themselves (though these beliefs play a part), but in the social and economic poverty many conservative evangelicals endured. He thus acknowledges what later authors would seek to hide: evangelicals' place within the spiritual proletariat, oppressed by the spiritually capitalist forces of mainline Christianity and other non-evangelical groups.

For Lewis, it was this material poverty, when combined with the materialism of the twenties, that led to the aesthetic and cultural bankruptcy of the modern evangelical church. Look, for instance, at Lewis's description of Elmer's small town, rural church, located in a clearly (though not explicitly stated) impoverished community:

> The church provided his only oratory, except for campaign speeches by politicians ardent about Jefferson.... It provided all his painting and sculpture, except for the portraits of Lincoln, Longfellow and Emerson.... From the church came all his profounder philosophy.... If he had sources of literary inspiration outside the church — in McGuffey's Reader ... and he had a very pretty knowledge of the Nick Carter Series ... yet here too the church had guided him. In Bible Stories, in the words of the great hymns, in the anecdotes which the various preachers quoted, he had his only knowledge of literature [*EG* 32].

Elmer is the definitive artistic rube and preacher-hypocrite character type in all of American literature. Most depictions of preachers after *Elmer Gantry*, ranging from Reverend Brown in *Inherit the Wind* to Pastor Dennis in *The Abstinence Teacher*, have borrowed from this cultural mythology. But such depictions (*The Book of Bebb* [1971–1979] happens to be an exception) usually ignore this inconvenient passage. Whereas Brown's anti-intellectual fanaticism, for instance, has no cultural context, Lewis suggests that Elmer's lack of appreciation for the "finer things" in life may just possibly be a product of the fact that he has been denied those finer things of life by the social and class situation he finds himself in. The church, for Elmer, far from being a culturally denigrating institution, is the only place where he is exposed to anything approaching art (as traditionally defined) at all. Its art is clearly, by Lewis's standards, "inferior" art; one will not find Celia's Chopin or George Sand here.

However, the evangelical church at least exposes Elmer to a few moving Bible stories, to a basic understanding of oratory, to decrepit but functional church architecture, and to a literature a little better than the terrible Nick Carter books of his youth. Lewis here pointedly and subversively asks his readers whether they would have ended up any better than Elmer, had they not had access to the fine arts that now allow them to laugh at such religious rubes and fakes. The richer churches of the mainline denominations, however, as the spiritual capitalists of their times, had no interest in sharing their better understanding of the arts with evangelicals, who as a spiritual body lack a common cultural heritage with the artistic elite. Nathan Hatch points out that among modern "working and lower-middle-class Americans ... religion seems to be thriving" despite the fact that in "the realms of high culture — in the best universities, in the arts, and in literary circles — religious values are probably no more pervasive in the United States than in Europe" (1989, 211). Evangelicalism, as a populist belief system, undoubtedly represented cultural kitsch to those in the mainline churches who supported the arts, and in these backwoods evangelical churches themselves, there were simply not enough intellectual resources to feed the artistically starved Gantries of the world.

There is also a certain dignity in the barrenness of Elmer's church, one not found in the contemporary Congregational and Episcopalian churches of his day. While the richer, older denominational groupings invested in up-to-date architecture, up-to-date theology, up-to-date pastors, and up-to-date social concerns, Elmer's church is as barren as any Protestant construction one could imagine. Lewis was clearly aware of the relative aesthetic impoverishment of Protestantism vis-à-vis Catholicism. Elmer's fellow minister Frank Shallard, a former evangelical, is moved by a local Catholic church's "lofty roof ... curious shrines ... the mysterious door at the top of a flight stone steps" (*EG* 372). All these things "unloose Frank's imagination" and momentarily propel him to consider converting to Catholicism, till he discovers that "it [the Catholic Church] does not compel you to give up your sense of beauty ... or your pleasant vices. It merely requires you to give up ... your reason, your heart, and soul" (374). If *Elmer Gantry* is any indication, Lewis felt a deep ambivalence about the aesthetic "strength" of High Church Catholicism and Anglicanism versus the anti-aestheticism of conservative evangelical belief. While Lewis clearly ultimately sides with the cause of "artistic beauty," the roots of his own extremely brief foray into evangelical belief long stayed with him (see Lingeman 2002, 17, for a discussion of Lewis's desire to be a missionary). Lewis's works, more than almost any novelist of his era, show a (probably unconscious) disdain for the aestheticism of Wilde and Baudelaire (already then old news) and the modernism of Joyce and Woolf. This unconscious and never mean spirited distrust of the power of art was mirrored on the part of Joyce's and Gertrude Stein's modernist set with a snobbery towards Lewis that speaks little for either their supposed progressivism or their value to later art criticism (see Lingeman 2002, 232).

Lewis's works, however carefully he crafted them, always had a sense of brutality to them, a sense not so much of being ill formed, as much as of being unconcerned with aesthetic, rather than moral or political, effects. Being a disciple of H.G. Wells and Jack London (Lingeman 2002, 25, 32), Lewis's novels' power lay in what they revealed about society, not about (as is more the case in modernism) psychology. In this sense, Lewis's work tends to lean more closely to the Protestant anti-aesthetic than to the Catholic or Anglican high-church aesthetic of writers such as Joyce and Woolf. For instance, Horace Carp, an Episcopal-loving member of Elmer's Baptist seminary who later converts to Episcopalianism (*EG* 154) comments on the deeply anti-aesthetic Baptists, saying that they are a "horrible denomination — all those moldy barns of churches, and people coughing illiterate hymns.... The only church is the Episcopal! Music! Vestments! Stately prayers! Lovely architecture! Dignity! Authority!" (*EG* 90). However, Harry Zenz, an atheist pretending to be a believer so he can be ordained, prefers the Baptists precisely because they are intellectual "numbskulls" who allow ministers to get away with anything they want intellectually, so long as they are perfectly safe in the pulpit. By contrast, "there are some intelligent people in the Episcopal and Congregational Churches ... and they check up on you.... Oh no, Father Carp — the Episcopal pulpit for actors that aren't good enough to get on the stage" (91). Lewis here, with a keen eye to sociological detail, points out (as Zenz but not Carp sees) that the desire for high church experience is driven as much by class considerations as by aesthetic ones. Embracing the arts and high culture is a way of increasing one's cultural capital, and for both denominations and individuals, such cultural capital translates into economic and political power — the very aggrandizement of power to spiritual capitalists that this work proposes operates in mainline Protestant and secular narratives of evangelicalism. The more beautiful one's church, the more likely it will be invested with dignity and authority. Among American Protestants, therefore, an appreciation of aesthetic experience has usually translated into advantageous economic effects. For instance, in the Episcopal Church, as of 2006, 35 percent of Episcopalians made a $100,000 dollars or more (Pew Research Center 2007), nearly twice the national average. In general the more aestheticized mainline denominations, such as the United Methodists, Episcopals, and Presbyterian Church U.S.A., outperformed evangelical denominations economically (particularly when one takes into account the fact that the United Methodists have a large, often economically struggling, sub-section of African-Americans, which are practically a sub-church — segregated of course — within the church at large).

Compare this class-climbing Episcopalianism with the Baptist prude Brother Karkis, who at age forty-two had no knowledge of any book save "the Bible, revivalistic hymnals, a concordance ... and a manual of poultry-keeping.... He had never met a woman of the world, never drunk a glass of wine, never heard a bar of great music, and his neck was not free from the dust of cornfields" (*EG* 93). Or take Eddie Fislinger, a fundamentalist nemesis of Elmer's, who nevertheless undergoes almost exactly the same education that Elmer is forced to endure: "He had, partly from his teachers and partly right out of his own brain, any number of good answers to classmates who protested that he was old fashioned in belaboring domino-playing ... listening to waltz music, wearing a gown in the pulpit ... reading novels, transsubstantiation, and these new devices of the devil called moving pictures" (40). The point here is not to argue that Karkis or Eddie is beloved by Lewis. They are clearly not, and Lewis sees their censorious and ignorant nature as dangerous. But at the same time, Lewis is simply too smart a social observer to miss that this censoriousness, while contributing to their economic impoverishment, is also partly a byproduct of it, operating in a vicious cycle. For Fislinger, the result is that he ends up living a life of "depressing stinginess" (154). When Elmer visits him about a third of the way through the novel, he observes, "His own hotel bedrooms were drab enough, but they ... were as luxurious as this parlor with its rain-blotched ceiling, bare pine floor, sloping chairs, and perpetual odor of diapers" (154). The image of evangelicalism as leading to a stinking barrenness, free not only of beauty but of any real hope, is a powerful one; what Lewis seems to ask is whether such poverty would happen as often in more conservative evangelical churches, if they did not link the beauty of the Anglican or Catholic traditions with doctrinal concerns about transubstantiation, papal infallibility, and grace vs. works.

The typological characterization of the anti-art evangelical rube, embodied in the even more specific typology of the hypocritical pastor, finds its fullest expression in Elmer; however, these more minor characters point out that Elmer's life history is hardly unique. In an increasingly industrialized society, divided between the theological haves and have-nots, American cultural elites sow the seed of their own destruction. Rather than create a broad-based culture of intelligence, one in which the working class and the petit bourgeoisie can also enjoy the fruits of modern music, film, and literature, the elites seek simply to alienate those not refined enough to understand their taste.

Lewis, himself always an aspirant to higher social status, sides with the elites; he expresses a deep concern, for instance, about the rise of censorship of the arts (*EG* 392). However, Lewis seems to indicate that there may be more than a good deal of pretension on the part of the left as well. Phillip McGarry, a theological liberal friend of Frank Shallard, critiques Frank for liking:

> arguing more than you do patiently working out the spiritual problems of some poor, dumb, infinitely piteous human being that comes to you for help.... I know that if you could lose your intellectual pride, if you could forget that you have to make a new world, better'n the Creator's right away tonight—you and Bernard Shaw and H.G. Wells and H.L. Mencken and Sinclair Lewis (Lord, how that book of Lewis', "Main Street," did bore me.... It just rambled on forever, and all he could see was that some of the Gopher Prairie hicks didn't go to literary teas quite as often as he does!—that was all he could see among those splendid heroic pioneers)! [357].

Lewis loved all the authors mentioned here—he was close friends with Mencken, admired Wells tremendously (Lingeman 2002, 51–52), and was inspired by the socialist ideals of both Wells and Shaw (41). Clearly, therefore, he is in part mocking the petit bourgeoisie, particularly the readers of *Main Street* (1920) and *Babbit* (1922), who so derided him in the twenties. But at his heart, Lewis was a Midwesterner (462–463, 491), and therefore the satire is two-sided, directed not just at the anti-art rubes he hates, but at the artistic community that he was a part of (and as we have seen, alienated from). Thus Lewis can make fun of his own artistic efforts, seeing them as being partly motivated simply by a desire to offend small-town America and the petit bourgeoisie who are unable to enjoy the ennobled culture he now found himself a part of. The small person's theological dilemmas are ridiculous, and in a sense enslaving (*EG* 357); but they are symptomatic of a division between high and low culture, high and low art, one in which the common man no longer understands the "clevers" who dictate literary and cultural taste, but becomes a spiritual proletarian left to eat the cultural scraps left him by the spiritual capitalist artistic caste.

Lewis, as neither the most profound nor aesthetically sophisticated writer of his time, can see that the "ordinariness" of theological conservatives is symptomatic of his own ordinariness, of the essential ordinariness of his age, in which literary opinion is determined as much by "literary teas" and journalists such as Mencken as it is by genuine talent. The common man's opinion, never well respected, is now not only unwanted but positively derided. Words such as "controversial" and "subversive" became code-words, and sometimes substitutions, for terms such as "quality." This is not to say these new terms were wrong, or that the new censors were right in seeking to use coercive measures to block the sale of *Ulysses* (1922) or *Lady Chatterley's Lover* (1928). But it did mean that for Lewis, the petit bourgeoisie, particularly religious conservatives, needed to be listened to and gradually cultured, not just thrown to the side as the uncultured debris of the twentieth century.

The dangers of simply abandoning religious conservatives to their censoriousness are clearly exhibited in the gradual evolution of Elmer from uncultured roughneck to a pastor with designs on world dictatorship. Elmer is someone who has been

> compelled in college to read certain books, to hear certain lectures, all filled with flushed, florid polysyllables, with juicy sentiments about God, sunsets, the moral improvement inherent in a daily view of mountain scenery, angels ... ideals, patriotism, democracy, purity, the error of Providence in creating the female leg ... the beauty of domesticity, and preachers' salaries. These blossoming words, these organ-like phrases, these profound notions had been rammed home till they stuck ... ready for use [*EG*].

Like Theron Ware, Elmer's main aesthetic training is oratorical. Insofar as he reads, he reads only to increase his preaching skills. Therefore, his interest in the arts is essentially utilitarian: it is a means to an end. For Lewis, writing at a time when Kantian presuppositions about aesthetic disinterestedness were still socially operative, this would doubtlessly have been frowned upon. Though it was perfectly fine for Lewis to use art as a means to a career, it was not all right for Elmer to use books simply as tools, without any aesthetic or artistic function. The fact that Elmer is "compelled" to read these books indicates what to Lewis is the essentially coercive nature of religious rhetorical education. Emphasis is placed, not on beauty, nor on truth, but, as with Sister Soulsby in *The Damnation of Theron Ware*, in the pragmatic, cash value of one's oratorical skills. Elmer is eventually a successful oratorical artist, not because he speaks powerful truths or uses words of great beauty, but because his sermons sell, bringing him parishioners and power. Indeed, Elmer's most powerful sermon, repeated with minor variations throughout the novel, is actually a plagiarized version of one of the writings of the "notorious" atheist Robert Ingersoll (*EG* 61–62). Elmer is not concerned with where he gets his ideas, nor whether they are moral; he is merely concerned with what effect they have on his audiences. Elmer's essential artistic instinct, therefore, is essentially the same as Hitler's: he aesthetically objectifies human beings as things to be manipulated for dramatic effect.

When Elmer eventually gains a little bit of culture, his research into the arts is largely desultory and guided by sentimental considerations. He loves Dickens, for instance, but cannot stand the intellectualism present in Carlyle (*EG* 274–277). Even when he finds a good artist that he genuinely likes, such as Rudyard Kipling, he rejects the artist, precisely because "he found that he really enjoyed reading Kipling, and concluded that he could not be a good poet" (277). As Elmer apes the manners of his betters to advance into the religious elite (at this point in the novel, he is positioning himself to become a major influence in the Methodist church), he seeks also to ape their theological, cultural, and social ideas. Indeed, the only reason Elmer reads these artists is because his bishop, an aspiring writer with little talent, wants him to (250, 277). For Lewis, Elmer's sudden interest in the arts, like his adoption of evangelical rhetorical practices, is essentially utilitarian. Elmer is interested in art for its "use value" and therefore is unwilling to be taught by it, as ideally a Kantian viewer would wish to be. Therefore, when he develops artistic taste, the taste is (by Lewis's standards) all wrong.

Lewis suggests this essentially pragmatic attitude to art is dangerous because art is not always pragmatically useful either to the church or to the state. When it is not, powerful religious and sociopolitical forces can work to eliminate the exercise of artistic freedom. Frank Shallard, an unbeliever by the end of the novel, warns that fundamentalists will be a "new Inquisition" that supports a "new hunting of witches" (*EG* 376). The arts, when not useful to promote religion or the state, can be condemned in order to promote those same interests. A frequent target of censors, Lewis doubtlessly was wary of the growing efforts of both fundamentalists and the Catholic Church to censor politically and sexually unorthodox works (see Lingeman 2002, 306, for Lewis's views on censorship). As Lingeman points out, Lewis felt such efforts were anti-intellectual (306); but Lewis's point was actually even more ironic than this. For Lewis, evangelicalism's anti-artistic bent, as expressed through Gantry, was essential to the evangelical community's pursuit of political power. This dream is given graphic form in Lewis's short but crucial description of the National Association for the Purification of the Arts and the Press (NAPAP), an organization devoted to passing "a bill for federal censorship of all fiction plays and moving pictures, with a penitentiary sentences for any author mention adultery ... ridiculing prohibition ... or making light of any Christian sect or minister" (392). This organization, which Elmer sees as his path to political power, seeks purification through destruction. The art of conservative religious politics, therefore, is the art of condemning art. In so far as evangelicalism embraces oratory and other artistic skills, it embraces them only to destroy their cousins in other fields. Evangelical politicians and preachers, in particular, seek to regulate non-oratorical arts, because they represent, to Lewis, fields of potential free thought and expression that are immune to oratorical influence. Intellectuals and art lovers, such as Frank Shallard, represent a danger to evangelical social coherence because their love of the aesthetic allows them to transcend their social limitations. As Phillip Francis points out, "aesthetic experience" often plays a crucial role in moving individuals beyond or past evangelical or fundamentalist beliefs. For Lewis, therefore, fundamentalism, for its own survival, must reject the aesthetic; to not do so is to endanger the community's political and spiritual existence (P. Francis 2011, 9).

Indeed, Elmer's realization of his need to combine evangelical and censorious beliefs is the closest thing to a genuine aesthetic experience he has in the novel. Lewis mockingly calls this realization Elmer's "Great Idea" and wryly comments, "Newton pondering on the fallen apple — Paul of Tarsus comprehending that a certain small Jewish sect might be the new religion of the doubting Greeks and Romans — Keats beginning to write 'The Eve of St. Agnes'— none of these men transformed by a Great Idea from mediocrity to genius, was more remarkable than Elmer Gantry" (*EG* 393). NAPAP will serve as the launching board, by which Elmer will combine the Anti-Saloon League, the Vice Societies, which censor novels, paintings, motion pictures, and plays, the anti-evolution leagues and all the other anti-intellectual elements of the evangelical community (393). While Elmer's program embraces more than just the arts, it is the arts — specifically his opposition to almost all of them — that gives him the idea to unite all these organization in the first place. Anti-aestheticism is his muse; censoriousness is, for Elmer, an aesthetic experience, one with, for him, enjoyable connotations. Lewis warns his readers that for evangelicals, and in particular fundamentalists, censoriousness represents a deeply religious experience, one that brings them closer both to their ideal of aesthetic "perfection" (where there is no beautiful object at all, save God) and religious devotion (where God alone is worshipped and venerated). To an aestheticized, spiritually capitalist mainline church, as well as to secular writers following in that tradition's footsteps, this was not an ideological position they wished evangelicals to pursue.

Lewis's assessment of Elmer and of the religious community he represents is not so different, in the final analysis, from that of this study. But whereas Lewis had justifiable reason to see such anti-aesthetic pronouncements as reactionary, one could today just as easily see anti-aestheticism as a progressive force as a reactionary one. The transformation of contemporary art into mainly (perhaps merely) a product for investment has divorced contemporary and modern art from its (purported) grounding as a force of social resistance. Since at least 1933, when Hitler achieved power, art has as readily served politically utilitarian purposes as the rhetoric of Elmer and his friends; the difference, of course, is that while real-life fundamentalists were honest in their loathing for the aesthetic and their love of the censorious, and usually less prone to coercive measures to enforce censorship, secular totalitarianisms, whether of a Communist, Fascist, Nazi, or now, corporate nature, have freely used such tactics with impunity.

Doubtlessly some of these groups, particularly the Nazis, took advantage of religious groups' prejudices to advance an explicitly coercive agenda against the arts. However, the argument that evangelicals have done so is much more problematic. The preferred evangelical tactic of suppressing the arts has been to work through the democratic process, using (or being used by) politicians such as Jesse Helms and Pat Buchanan to advance their anti-art agenda. The artistic community's complaints about the "censorship" of Mapplethorpe and Serrano rather conveniently ignored the fact that the evangelical community's condemnation of the National Endowment for the Arts (NEA), as a publically funded institution, was meritorious in so far as the fact that evangelicals had as much right, in a democracy, to legislate their aesthetic opinions as any other group. Indeed, the almost monolithic association of the artistic community with the political left, itself something of an aberration in the long history of the arts, gave weight to the evangelical claim that the artistic community, and indeed the arts in general, were not really interested in engaging religious believers intellectually or simply fairly. Francis Schaeffer, like Joseph Stalin, Mao Zedong, and Hitler, had fanatic political opinions, which affected how he perceived aesthetics. And like Hitler, Schaeffer was fascinated with the arts. But the significant difference between Schaeffer and these men was that he did not seek to enforce his aesthetic viewpoints at the barrel of a gun. Indeed, when compared to such secular writers as Robert Heinlein, Ayn Rand, or H.G. Wells, Schaeffer's cultural politics were remarkably mild. And Schaeffer, in some ways, was more extreme in his cultural politics than most other evangelicals. While evangelicals do seek to censor at both a local and national level—for instance, Bill Bright attempted to buy the negatives of *The Last Temptation of Christ* (1988) so he could destroy the film (Lindlof 2008, 176)—it is definitely problematic to equate this kind of censoriousness, which is still essentially democratic in orientation, with that exhibited by, say, the

Nazis, who often mandated who could and could not paint, write, or sculpt by literal government fiat (Spotts 2002, 30–32).

To argue that the evangelical community is against the arts is a perfectly valid position to take, though with the increasing prominence of artists like Makoto Fujimura and Edward Knippers it is also an increasingly implausible one. But to argue that that censoriousness automatically equates to moral turpitude leaves unquestioned a number of logical presuppositions. Why, for instance, should evangelicals be expected to value the arts, particularly if (as we shall see) the arts community primarily seeks to alienate them? Furthermore, even if one accepts that the evangelical community engages in direct censorship, the groundwork that modernism has laid gives weight to the evangelical argument that on occasion, censorship is necessary. If all (or almost all) experiences can be conceptualized as in some sense aesthetic, then surely censorship cannot be the kind of absolute evil that rather unsophisticated aestheticians such as Lewis and Margaret Atwood portray it to be. Otherwise, one could not bomb the death factories of the Nazi regime (which were architecture and undertaken for an aesthetic purpose — at least according to Cohen [*Architecture of Doom*]), or ban snuff films (cinema), or prevent an artist from tying a dog to a wall and leaving it to die, or killing a couple of animals for a film; we would in all these cases be "destroying art." Modernism, which rightly fought censorship in its own day, now, through its relativism, makes censorship not only necessary, but inevitable.

This, however, does not mean that all evangelical censorship efforts are created equal. Lewis is clearly right to condemn the kind of censorship that Elmer wants to enforce because it is based on the same sense of "aesthetic absolutism" that characterizes Schaeffer's works, in which there is "good" art and "bad" art. For Schaeffer, art is intrinsically judged by "the message or worldview conveyed" (Hankins 2008, 128).The Schaefferian system, though better than Stalin's or Hitler's because it is not coercive, is essentially dictatorial; it assumes that one can know with certainty what "good" or "bad" art is, precisely by judging art on its message. The system I offer here does not make this mistake; rather than argue that art is either "good" or "bad," DDM theory argues that the whole pursuit of the aesthetic is, in the contemporary context, tragically flawed, first because Duchamp made such a pursuit both ridiculous and ethically flawed (What, after all, can't be art?) and second because the glorification of beauty that occurs in Schaeffer's worldview theory, and the glorification of wealth-through-art in the contemporary art scene and modern publishing industry, leads to a corresponding devaluation of the "ugly" (in worldview theory) and the non-elite (as in the contemporary art scene). Insofar as art becomes merely a tool of the rich (who now buy it up en masse) and the corporate and governmental elite, aesthetics ceases to be about art (as traditionally defined) and instead becomes what in reality art has always been, a method of exerting cultural influence and power. In Sinclair Lewis's era, it was still possible to view art as a provocateur; today it would probably be more correct to view it as a pacifying influence. In seeing the figure of Elmer Gantry, the anti-artist theocratic rube, as the embodiment of the corroding influence of American Philistinism within Protestantism, the contemporary art and literary communities ignore their own complicity in pacifying society. When the contemporary art and entertainment scene making over a trillion dollars (Singh 2011, xxi), one cannot avoid the fact that art is no longer trying to divorce itself from the market, if it ever had. In such a situation, the rejection and censorship of the aesthetic as entirely as possible in a world where every object is laden with aesthetic potential, is just as valid an ethical response as to simply delight in the new, the controversial, and the shocking. In the hands of evangelicals, art at least still has power, if only through its negation. In the secular world, even that power is now denied it.

3

Lonely-Hearted Fascists: The Evangelical Community in Disarray

By the early 1930s, the evangelical community was in disarray. The Scopes trial had unleashed an "outpouring of derision" (Marsden 2006, 184) on fundamentalists, leaving their forces disunited and lacking direction. Lewis's *Elmer Gantry* seemed to be the nail in the fundamentalist coffin (188), both a reflection of popular opinion and an important molder of contemporary cultural views on conservative Protestant belief. At about the same time, J. Frank Norris, one of the most prominent fundamentalists in the country, was accused of murder. Though acquitted, the publicity damage resulting from Norris's trial was substantial (190). By 1929, J. Gresham Machen, an important Reformed evangelical associated with the fundamentalist movement and perhaps the single most formidable intellectual supporting conservative Protestantism, had been prodded out of Princeton seminary, and had been forced to found his own denomination, the Orthodox Presbyterian Church (Marty 1991, 184, Marsden 2006, 192). Northern Baptists also faced theological defeat (Marsden 2006, 192–193), mainly because of poor organizing (193). As the new decade dawned, the evangelical community found itself in political disarray, marginalized and labeled as anti-intellectual and reactionary even by observers who had sympathy with the community (191).

Nor did the thirties seem to offer much hope for evangelicals seeking for renewed cultural influence. While more principled and intelligent leaders such as Machen were marginalized or retreated from public life, other more demagogic preachers and populist leaders took their place, most famously Kansan Gerald Winrod and Disciples of Christ minister Gerald L.K. Smith (Marty 1991, 265–268). While the power of the evangelical right still continued to provoke fear among some left-wing writers (notably Sinclair Lewis in *It Can't Happen Here*), many non-evangelicals came to see the movement as largely an irrelevancy. Many observers judged that "fundamentalism was rapidly declining and would soon die out" (J. Carpenter 1997, 13). Few would have predicted, as George Marsden points out, that the movement would ever "persist as a major factor in American life" (1991, 231). Evangelicals in this era had to fight hard against the general sense of spiritual and material emptiness produced by the modern era. The increasing dominance of mass culture, what Theodore Adorno called the "culture industry" (Macey 2000, 78), led to an ever more vapid American spiritual life. Interestingly, it was precisely the evangelical community, particularly fundamentalists, who rejected mass culture most vigorously in the thirties, forties and fifties. Many fundamentalists refused to let their children see movies, dance to jazz or rock (Henry 1947, 7–8), watch television or engage in other activities motivated by pop culture impulses. Such bans remained in effect in some denominations as late as the 1980s and 1990s, including (for instance) parts of the Pilgrim Holiness movement. Doubtlessly such actions were partly motivated by prudery, but they also represented a genuine distrust of popular mass culture, one that remains with evangelicals to this day. For evangelicals in the thirties, that rejection of mass culture left them feeling socially alienated, oppressed not so much by a specific theological group (though mainliners certainly played prominently in evangelical imagination during this era), but by a general cultural malaise; it also made evangelicals ideal ideological ciphers for artists wanting to make a point about mass culture.

Therefore, insofar as evangelicals and fundamentalists were portrayed at all, they were usually ciphers on which to fix particular representations of the spiritual life. Often, as say with Reverend Casy in *The Grapes of Wrath* (1939) or Semon Dye in Erskine Caldwell's *Journeyman* (1935), the goal was to create a generalized representation of religion, rather than a specific critique of evangelical belief. Meanwhile, in a different vein, Sinclair Lewis's *It Can't Happen Here* continued the social realist tradition he himself had established in the 1920s.

The major artistic accusation against evangelicals during this period was that they were an essentially fascistic force. There were reasons both for supporting and for rejecting this analysis. As David A. Rausch points out in *Fundamentalist-Evangelicals and Anti-Semitism* (1993): "Many fundamentalist-evangelicals [during the twenties and thirties] believed that a 'true Christian' could not be an anti–Semite! And the movement as a whole not only spotted the anti–Semitism of Adolf Hitler, but also believed that the Holocaust was indeed occurring at a time when more liberal religious movements were labeling such reports 'atrocity propaganda'" (1993, 94). On the other hand, as Rausch notes, "There were elements of the fundamentalist-evangelical belief system and popular attitudes that were extremely distasteful to members of the Jewish community" (99). Arno C. Gaebelin, for instance, not by a long shot the most anti–Semitic evangelical (indeed he would be more properly called a philosemite by his time's standards) nevertheless believed that "the Antichrist would be an apostate Jew" (112). Thus, Sinclair Lewis's major assault on evangelicalism as a fascistic theological system in *It Can't Happen Here* and West's more measured critique of Lonelyhearts as a "Mussolini of the soul" (1933, 52) in *Miss Lonelyhearts* expressed at once a realistic expression of secular concerns about evangelical anti–Semitic rabble-rousers such as Gerald Winrod and a xenophobic, bigoted critique of evangelicalism in that it only presented one, and likely not the dominant, side of evangelicalism's relationship to the Jewish community.

Written by Nathanael West, *Miss Lonelyhearts* is one of the most moving portraits of religious belief in the twentieth century, yet ultimately one of the most damning — not only in its condemnation of Lonelyhearts' Mussolini-like nature, but in his cipher-like representation of a man in existential anguish. West portrays an insolvable conflict between evangelical "saintliness" and the simple sordid materialism of the twentieth century; Lonelyhearts is in a sense mad, and his nemesis Shrike, often identified with Satan, may actually be the novel's protagonist as much as Lonelyhearts is (Jones 2005, 113).

Nathanael West would undoubtedly be remembered as one of the greatest American writers of the twentieth century had it not been for his tragic early death in 1940. Harold Bloom, while seeing West as an "uneven" writer, argues that *Miss Lonelyhearts* is a "remorseless masterpiece" that "excels *The Sun Also Rises* (1926), *The Great Gatsby* (1925), and even *Sanctuary* (1931) as the perfected instance of a negative vision in modern American fiction" (Bloom 2005, 1). *Miss Lonelyhearts* itself was well regarded upon its publication. Cultural luminaries such as Edmund Wilson, Dashiell Hammett, Erskine Caldwell, and even William Carlos Williams praised the novel (J. Martin 1970, 177). Reviews were overwhelmingly positive (191–192); only financial problems at West's publishers prevented the novel from becoming an absolute hit (192).

Lonelyhearts represents the first, and last, modernist representation of an evangelical protagonist in literature. Most works after *Lonelyhearts* returned to realism, or during and after the sixties, borrowed some sort of postmodern (or in science fiction, New Wave) sensibility. West, influenced by the avant-garde of his day (J. Martin 1970, 112, 125), creates in Lonelyhearts and Shrike characters that are emblematic of the spiritual emptiness of an age: Shrike, the cynic editor, and Lonelyhearts, the advice columnist. As Thomas Lorch has pointed out, Miss Lonelyhearts, in being an advice columnist, is in some sense an artist, but an individual, who though a success as a saint, "fails completely as an artist." Lorch argues that for West, "art is another means of achieving virtually the same ends" as religion (1967, 17). Thus, in Lonelyhearts we see the first modern depiction of the evangelical-as-artist character type, one that will later be repeated in *Portofino* (somewhat), *Blankets*, and *Peace Like a River*.

What causes Lonelyhearts to fail as an artist? In part, it is his very sincerity. He tells his friend Betty that "he sees that the majority of the letters [he receives] are profoundly humble pleas for moral and spiritual advice, that they are inarticulate expressions of genuine suffering.... He [Lonelyhearts] also discovers that his correspondents take him seriously. For the first time in his life, he is forced to examine the values by which he lives" (West 1933 [hereafter cited as *LH*], 32). Lonelyhearts in a sense takes his craft, and his readers, too seriously. For Lonelyhearts, art is about finding truth, about conveying it and reporting it accurately. He wants to give his viewers the "really real"; he believes that "Christ was the answer, but if he did not want to get sick, he had to stay away from the Christ business" (3). Lonelyhearts is torn between his desire for authentic Christian faith and a modern life that makes that Christ-figure increasingly implausible as time goes on. Lonelyhearts cannot recognize the essential absurdity and irony of modern life, in which life is both purposeless and ultimately governed solely by material concerns. While there is something, of course, slightly noble about Lonelyhearts's desire for a transcendent Other that he can relate to, that hope ultimately is, for West, comical. Lonelyhearts's nemesis Shrike points out the essential pretensions of his combination of the role of artist and aspiring believer: "I can walk on my own water. Haven't you heard of Shrike's Passion in the Luncheonette, or the Agony in the Soda Fountain? Then I compared the wounds in Christ's body to the mouths of a miraculous purse in which we deposit the small change of our sins" (7). For Shrike, as Beverly Jones points out, there is "no meaning in anything, especially suffering, and there is no escape from it in this or any other life" (Jones 2005, 115). By contrast, Lonelyhearts still believes there is some eternal value by which he use his art (e.g., his columns) to rescue those trapped in a sordid world. The essentially missionary aspect of evangelical belief, however, prevents Lonelyhearts from either being of genuine help to his audience, or creating life of lasting value. He is martyred, not so much by opposition as by his own message.

Lonelyhearts, as an evangelical artist, reduces Christ to (as Shrike puts it) "the First Church of Christ Dentist, where He is worshipped as Preventer of Decay" (*LH* 35). It is only Christ who can prevent society from decaying into a pursuit of pleasure, or art for art's sake (34), only Christ who can give existential hope for those trapped by the desire for suicide or drugs (35). As a preventer of decay, Christ presumably works against those cultural forces, like modernism itself, that many bourgeois Protestants saw as symptomatic of the general collapse of Christian society. Christ becomes the artist-warrior who, Hitler-like, swats down these threats to the bourgeoisie in exchange for absolute obedience. The essential dictatorial nature of Lonelyhearts's aesthetic vision is pointed out by Shrike: "Miss Lonelyhearts, he of the singing heart — a still more swollen Mussolini of the soul.... He has come here to help you with your moral and spiritual problems, to provide you with a slogan, a cause, an absolute value, and a *raison d'etre*" (52). West suggests the danger of developing an evangelical aesthetic system was that it codified absolute artistic values. It gave people slogans, symbols, and ideas by which they could inflict dictatorial policy. As a modernist who traveled widely and had himself met many important European modernists (see, for instance, J. Martin 1970, 84–92, for a description of West's time in Paris), West was almost certainly aware of the growing oppression of Modernist, particularly Expressionist, artists in Germany. Paul Schultze-Naumburg's explicitly anti–Expressionist comparisons of Expressionist paintings and deformities were in vogue in Weimar Republic Germany, and would later serve as a helpful propaganda foundation for further German depredations against the arts (not to mention the mentally ill and disabled) (Schultze-Naumburg 1993, 299; *Architecture of Doom*). In such an environment, the aesthetic ideals of evangelicalism, with its rejection of the intellect and of artistic freedom, and its outright censorious nature, would have been threatening to artists such as West. Evangelicalism, fascistic or not, in its censoriousness sounded too much like the Nazism of Germany.

Indeed, West hits here on one of the central problems of evangelical aesthetics over the last fifty years, which has been its tendency to center around an extremely small group of individuals, and take its aesthetic cues solely from such individuals, individuals who (sometimes) impose their viewpoints dictatorially. While the schools that the modernist turn in the arts gave birth to are virtually limitless — such as Dada, Expressionism, Abstract Expressionism, Magical Realism, Conceptual Art, and Landscape Art — evangelical aesthetics has been till recently quite limited in the artistic options available to it. Aesthetic theory has been overwhelmingly dominated by Francis Schaeffer, H.R. Rookmaaker, and the Inklings mythopoeic school of artistic criticism. This has been problematic because these intellectuals have become often the only voices heard in evangelical artistic debates. Rookmaaker's manifesto *Modern Art and the Death of a Culture* (1970), for instance, is often used as a "textbook for a variety of art history classes" (Siedell 2008, 158), despite its overly restrictive definition of what constituted proper Christian art (155). Schaeffer and the Inklings, meanwhile, have come to define evangelical "high culture," often with intellectually disastrous results. Schaeffer's "worldview" art system, based both on Rookmaaker's artistic theories and Cornelius Van Til's presuppositional apologetics (both of which have their roots in Dutch Calvinism), further dumbed down evangelical appreciation of the arts by encouraging most evangelicals to simply borrow Schaeffer's view on the arts as their own (this is hardly the fault of Schaeffer so much as the people who came after him). For those who escaped Schaeffer, there were always C.S. Lewis and J.R.R. Tolkien. While both of these novelists had quite interesting ideas on artistic expression, frequently the more unorthodox and non-evangelical ideas in their works were culturally expurgated out of evangelical discourse.[1] As West foresaw, the pronouncements of the "Mussolinis of the soul" could potentially have great power among the spiritually searching.

The problem was that this spiritual searching made vapid artists such as Lonelyhearts the "priests of twentieth century America" (*LH* 44). The sentimentality, the lack of honesty about the human condition, and the dictatorialness of Christian belief that West places at the center of Lonelyhearts character, all contributed to constructing an increasingly conformist culture. The bromides, the artistic Eucharists, that the Lonelyhearts could offer out simply were inadequate to deal with the sense of social alienation that twentieth century individuals faced. By contrast, the modernist aesthetic recognizes the essential desire of "the downtrodden ... to hang onto life and enjoy their puerile amusements, not ways to suffer and die" (Jones 2005, 119). The working class does not want to be elevated by Christian belief or by modernist aesthetic views, but seeks only to listen to that jazz, watch Andy Hardy movies, and dance till the early hours of the morning. Modernism does not offer the answer to the spiritual crisis of the twentieth century, but at least it does not try to pretend there is an answer. Lonelyhearts, by contrast, seeks to provide that answer through a mythic system that West believes can no longer operate in a modern context.

Miss Lonelyhearts—ironically, considering West's deep love of the arts—seems to warn against the unification of the arts with religion. A couple of anonymous characters comment: "Well, that's the trouble with his [Lonelyhearts's] approach to God. It's too damn literary—plain song, Latin poetry, medieval painting, Huysmans, stained-glass windows and crap like that.... What I say is, after all one has to earn a living. We can't all believe in Christ, and what does the farmer care about art? He takes his shoes off to get the warm feel of the rich earth between his toes. You can't take your shoes off in church" (*LH* 14–15). Lonelyhearts approaches God through the aesthetic, and the radical division between the intellect and the spirit that nineteenth century developments in the arts, theology, and science seemed (incorrectly) to make necessary, deny this path to modern Christians. The line "One has to earn a living.... We can't all believe in Christ, and what does the farmer care about art?" (15) is evocative; it suggests that in a cash society, continued belief in both Christ and art is a liability that the contemporary world simply cannot afford. Art has become a "church" and one cannot take one's shoes off in something that has now become holy. Modernism, particularly Dada, sought to dethrone the essentially churchfulness of artistic development and bring it back into the real world of real things, the ready-mades of Duchamp and the factory-produced works of Warhol; ironically, modernist art became just as "churchified" as the realist and naturalist schools that it so scorned. West's essential point is still an apt one — Lonelyhearts's love of "Latin poetry" and "stained-glass windows" as emblematic of a religious artistic traditionalism pointed to an essentially classicist, even medieval, view of the arts. Not only is a love of such arts at variance with the spirit of the modern age, it is essentially incompatible with his own Protestant background, a background that is deeply iconoclastic.

For West, Lonelyhearts's aesthetic impoverishment is symptomatic of the general failed union of artistic and Christian belief. Christ, Shrike tells Lonelyhearts, is "the Miss Lonelyhearts of Miss Lonelyhearts" (*LH* 6). In Christian belief, he is the original failed artist, the Messiah who just couldn't get his creation right and had to die as a scapegoat to atone for what God did. For two millennia, Christian art had managed to ignore its long-awaited apogee, its exposure as an aesthetic form with no internal spiritual meaning. With the rise of Darwin and higher criticism, and the corresponding gutting of the core of Christian belief, that apogee was at last at hand. Christianity could no longer expect to have aesthetic or even cultural dominance, because the grounds on which it had based its rule — its rich iconography and symbology (crucifixes, stained glass windows, etc.) — no longer invoked the same feelings of sublimity, fear, and power that they once did. Christ was now an empty signifier, and it was the "rich earth," not Christian belief, that held the key to what the modern world could artistically make out of itself, if anything.

The Jesus of *Miss Lonelyhearts* is no longer on the cross — quite literally, as Miss Lonelyhearts has taken him off that cross and nailed him like a pig to the wall (*LH* 8). Lonelyhearts has played with the "name of Christ" (9–10), but never let it come alive, because it is a "hysteria, [a] snake whose scales are tiny mirrors in which the dead world takes on a semblance of life" (9). That Lonelyhearts ends up succumbing to the faith of his childhood is a story not of redemption, but of artistic damnation. He has failed to find a way of navigating between the "deadness" of the world he lives in (9) and genuine aesthetic achievement. Instead, he makes the fatal deal with religious hysteria, and becomes trapped in his own sainthood, a victim of a religious delusion that has the potential not simply to corrupt him, but to hurt those who benefit from his artistic "works" (his columns).

West, as a Jew living in an intensely anti–Semitic decade, can hardly be blamed for seeing the seeds of artistic totalitarianism within the Protestantism of his day. Indeed, whether it was expressed in bourgeois Germany, America, or in the slightly less repressed United Kingdom, the desire to maintain control over the arts remained a central impulse of this era. What West did not see, and could not, was how modernism, particularly when evolved into its current postmodern pluralism, would later make possible the re-emergence of Christian classicism as a challenger to a modern art that disciples of Rookmaaker and Schaeffer believe has "marginalized" "Christian art and the Christian artist" (Siedell 2008, 157). Today, groups such as Christians in the Visual Arts and the Coalition of Christian Colleges and Universities serve "as part of an alternative institutional framework for interpreting and legitimizing Christian art" (157). As Daniel Siedell points out, advocates of Christian art often deliberately work to destroy the historical connections to artistic tradition that unite modernism with previous schools of literary and artistic expression (157), seeing this as a way of delegitimizing modern art in both the popular and, more importantly, political eyes of 20th century America. The concern expressed by both Lewis and West that Protestantism was increasingly absolutizing its aesthetic values is absolutely true; however, these values were never, whether in Germany, Britain, or America, truly iconoclastic in the sense that the DDM approach would support.

From the standpoint of Dialectical Dispensational Marxism, ideally one strips the world of as much of the glorification of art as possible — not simply replacing classicism with Modernism (Modernist movement), or Modernism with classicism (as in Christian worldview theory), or Expressionism with Romanticism (as the Nazis tried to do). Like modernists such as Duchamp, Dispensational Marxism expresses disdain for the "religion of art" (Tomkins 1996, 32). But a DDM approach would argue, in opposition to absolutizing aesthetic philosophies such as the worldview movement and Nazism, that the total destruction of aesthetic impulses one does not like, besides being pointless and unethical, is ultimately simply impossible. Expressionism and Dada are not only art when transcribed to a canvas or a Brechtian play; they are art when they are within the mind as well. As such, the only way of defeating these impulses is through persuasion. Kill one Expressionist, and another will simply take her place. To use a cliché, one cannot "kill an idea"; today, even ideas can be art. The coercive censorship of Mapplethorpes, Serranos, and Picassos can ultimately not work, since one is not killing the art, but simply killing its visual manifestation. As long as artists remain alive, their "subversive" visualizations of the aesthetic will remain with them, inside their brains if nowhere else. Since, despite non-evangelical perceptions to the contrary, the vast majority of evangelicals are averse to killing artists, and since the suppression of the visual arts is only possible with the suppression of non-evangelical thought patterns at the neurocognitive level, coercive censorship at a governmental or even corporate level seems neither Christian nor pragmatically effective.

3. Lonely-Hearted Fascists

Dispensational Marxism is different from Nazism and worldview theory in that when offered the choice between form of art A versus form of art B, it does not choose A or B, but neither. Dispensational Marxists are simply not interested in creating an aesthetic dictatorship in which Adolf Hitler, Francis Schaeffer, or even modernists such Duchamp rule with an artistic iron fist the tastes of the masses. Instead Dispensational Marxism asks people to examine how much of their lives is ruled by aesthetic impulses that deny the value of non-human, "non-beautiful," or non-elite life. Ideally, the world would allow for the appreciation of beauty without a corresponding lapse in respect for the life behind that beauty, or put into that beauty. In practice, though such respect is frequent, almost ubiquitous, at the individual level, it is almost non-existent at the level of capitalist and national interchange. In 2010, for instance, U.S. DVD rentals and sales accounted for some $14 billion dollars, most of which were for fictional films, a genre that must be at least reluctantly, and quite possibly not even reluctantly, be considered art (Lieberman [2011]). Christie's International *alone* accounted for *$5.0 billion dollars in art sales in that same year* (Artdaily.org [2012]). For a Dispensational Marxist art critic, the problem with art today lies not in the dominance of modernism (as in worldview theory), or solely in the union of capitalism with the arts (as more perceptive modernist and postmodernist critics have pointed out), but in art itself. Structuring a world into the "tasteful" and the "ignorant," the "daring" and the "conformist," the "worldview supporter" and the "secularist" or whatever other distinction one wishes to make, art today simply serves as another social mechanism by which governments and corporations can divide us into groups of "us" and "them," all the while prompting people of similar economic and even spiritual interests to avoid noting their real cultural affinities with each other. But even worse, the "art world," whether it is the huge contemporary art scene or the much more marginalized but still impressive evangelical art world, seems to be concerned more with status and increasingly extreme bids for ever-increasingly grotesque amounts of money than with actually helping out the people who produce the "art" that most concerns our daily lives: shoes, clothes, furniture, silverware, and so on. It is those artists, not Andres Serrano, who are economically marginalized. It is those artists, not Cindy Sherman, who are brutally censored for speaking out for better workplace and living conditions to create the art that we all need simply to survive. And it is precisely those artists that do not get any respect. It is those artists, not people dipping sharks in formaldehyde or "shoplifting for their art," that deserve more artistic respect; the bankruptcy of modernism does not, as worldview supporters suggest, lie in modernism's aesthetic relativism, but rather in its refusal to take that relativism to its logical conclusion and make Ford autoworkers,

Mexican migrants, Asian Walmart assemblers, and Arabian carpenters into the truly respected artists of the twenty-first century. The failure of both worldviewers and modernists to consider the value of this more pragmatic form of artistic expression speaks to the continuing validity of West's prognostications about the state of materialized religion and materialistic art at the midpoint of the twentieth century. The times may have changed, but the spiritual emptiness of that turbulent century haunts us till this day.

It Can't Happen Here, *Can It?: Sinclair Lewis and Evangelical Artistic Fascism*

Sinclair Lewis's second major commentary on evangelical religion was *It Can't Happen Here*, a prophetic tale about the takeover of the United States by fascists. At the time Lewis wrote the novel, his career was on the downturn. Recent novels by Lewis, such as *Dodsworth* (1929) and *Work of Art* (1934), failed to earn Lewis the lasting critical acclaim of his earlier works (Lingeman 2002, 336, 398). Lewis's increasing problem with drinking had also hurt his career (398); though many of Lewis's later works would be praised for their progressive social views (see in particular 505–508 on the accolades Lewis received for *Kingsblood Royal*'s [1947] pro-black arguments), *It Can't Happen Here* was his last highly regarded novel.

Lewis was inspired to write the novel in part by his wife Dorothy Thompson. Thompson had from a very early point of the Nazi regime warned Lewis of Nazism's histrionic, subversive powers. Indeed, Thompson directly compared Hitler to the leading American evangelicals of her day, William Jennings Bryan and Aimee Semple McPherson (Lingeman 2002, 398–399). Thompson's interview of Louisiana governor (later senator) Huey Long, a figure widely feared to be a harbinger of American fascism, also shaped Lewis's analysis of how fascism could arise in America. Lewis did not so much fear actual Nazis as he did a wide variety of populist leaders, who could perhaps coalesce around someone like Long. At the time this was not an unrealistic position: Thirties rabblerousing politicians ranged from such now-derided figures as Father Coughlin to more respected Americans such as the fascist-leaning isolationist Charles Lindbergh and the idealist socialist Upton Sinclair (400–401). Lewis hypothesized that a union of Christian religion, capitalism, and populist rhetoric could sweep a corporate state into power (401, 404). A phenomenally successful novel, *It Can't Happen Here* sold 94,000 copies in its trade edition and was a bestseller (408). Its long-term cultural influence can be particularly seen in the science fiction television miniseries *V* (1983), which basically retells Lewis's story line for line, but using aliens as the fascists (Donavan 2011, 135). *It Can't Happen Here* is also a rather obvious influence on

Phillip Roth's *Plot Against America* (2004), whose plot closely resembles that of Lewis's novel, and also possibly the critically acclaimed British film *It Happened Here* (1966), which had a similarly dark view of collaborationism in the face of Nazi and fascistic oppression. As late as 2009, with the second *V* series' first airing, *It Can't Happen Here* has shown its considerable cultural longevity.

It Can't Happen Here tells a rather simple story. The main hero of the novel, Doremus Jessup, is a sixty-year-old reporter of independent, vaguely liberal politics and equally vague Unitarian religious heritage (Lewis 1935 19–20, [hereafter cited as *ICHH*], 21, 117). Jessup, a man in many ways not unlike a more timid version of Lewis himself, is forced to slowly turn against an increasingly repressive U.S. government run by a charismatic politician, Buzz Windrip. Windrip skillfully combines a variety of populist promises with a fascist model economy and a militaristic foreign policy position to gain power over the country, which he rapidly turns into a version of Nazi Germany.

Lewis's biographer Richard Lingeman argues that the fairly obvious model for Windrip is Huey Long (Lingeman 2002, 404). I would argue that in addition to Long, another obvious model was evangelist and aspiring politician Gerald B. Winrod, whose name and politics are both similar to Windrip. Winrod was a well-known figure in the thirties, detested by liberals for his anti–Semitism and attempts to unite evangelical Americans into a force in support of Nazism (Marty 1991, 265–267). Considering the rather conflicted, and by no means always negative, view of Jews held by evangelicals during the thirties (Rausch 1993, 94, 99), Winrod's plan held little real chance for success, but in his time he entered into alliances with considerably more powerful and influential anti–Semites, such as Father Charles Coughlin (Marty 1991, 267). With the success of Winrod and fellow racist evangelical Gerald L.K. Smith during the thirties it was a reasonable, though probably wrong, assessment for Lewis to see the Protestant right drifting towards Nazism (for Smith's influence, see 267–269).

Whether or not Lingeman is in agreement with my analysis of Winrod's influence, he clearly does see the combination of evangelical religion and fascism in the novel, remarking that Buzz Windrip "sounds very much like Elmer Gantry" (Lingeman 2002, 402). Although Windrip speaks well of many religious traditions, he makes it clear that he is no fan of higher criticism, the liberal boogeyman for the religious right of his day; Jessup at one point equates "Holy Roller" orgies with Windrip's "jungle hysterics" (*ICHH* 119), further emphasizing the evangelistic tone of the political leader. Like both Elmer Gantry and Gerald Winrod, Windrip's goal is a nationalized, fully united Protestantism (Lingeman 2002, 402; Marty 1991, 265–267). Windrip, however, is more politically savvy than Gantry and more politically cunning than Winrod, masking his allegiances until it is too late for either the right or left to effectively combat them. And the most powerful tool that Windrip has, the tool that unites him with the aestheticized fascism of Hitler and the fundamentalism of Bryan and Winrod, is his oratory.

Windrip's artistic skill lies in his ability to woo audiences. To Doremus Jessup's fellow political reporters, Windrip is

> an actor of genius. There was no more overwhelming actor on the stage, in the motion pictures, nor even in the pulpit. He would whirl arms, bang tables, glare from mad eyes, vomit Biblical wrath from a gaping mouth; but he would also coo like a nursing mother, beseech like an aching lover.... But below this surface stagecraft was his uncommon natural ability to be authentically excited by and with his audience, and they by and with him [*ICHH* 70].

For Lewis, Hitler's oratorical power tied him with both the aesthetic world, via acting, and the spiritual world, via preaching. Both of these fields, rather than seeking to represent reality, as Lewis's naturalist hero Jack London did or Lewis's more sociologically modeled fiction attempted to do, instead sought to distort reality through artifice and illusion. As a writer, Lewis, like London, was singularly devoid of cant. His fiction frequently criticized even Lewis's own subject position (*EG* 357), and he was as brutally realistic about his centrist liberalism's foibles as he was discontent with the right-wing and left-wing radicals of his day. Windrip's manipulation of audiences, therefore, spoke not simply to the worst part of human nature, but the worst part of religious and aesthetic life as well. Windrip was the master obfuscator who could make you think that he "was Plato, but that on the way home you could not remember anything he had said" (*ICHH* 70). Lewis had a definite respect for the actors who stuck to acting, and he could even be tolerant of religious leaders such as Frank Shallard who stuck to religion and only religion, but he could not brook the kind of mad oratory of a Bryan or a Windrip. It rang too falsely of the rhetoric of the "Common Man" (71) and the kind of lockstep patriotism of industrialists and Rotarians in Lewis's earlier novel *Babbit* (Lingeman 2002, 403). As Lewis had repeatedly pointed out, first in *Main Street* (1920), then in *Babbit*, *Elmer Gantry*, and *It Can't Happen Here*, the union of patriotic oratory, capitalism, and religion was inherently dangerous.

What makes the situation in *It Can't Happen Here* so much more threatening than that promoted by the cosmic everyman Babbit is that Windrip is the "Common Man twenty times magnified by his oratory, so that while the other Commoners could understand his every purpose, which was exactly the same as their own, they saw him towering among them, and they raised hands to him in worship" (*ICHH* 71). Windrip, in other words, has Babbit's salesmanship skills, but raised to a demonic level, where he becomes a figure of practically religious adulation. And here too one can see Lewis's essential problem with preaching and oratory as art forms—their tendency to turn their practitioners into figures of religious veneration. Evangelical artistry, even when it was successful, produced exactly the wrong kind of art: the art of the dictator.

In pointing out the essentially artistic nature of fascistic oratory, Lewis also pointed out, without perhaps meaning to, the essentially aestheticized worldview of fascism. As Frederic Spotts, the most perceptive critic of Hitler's artistic views, has pointed out, Hitler's speeches were "the most potent expression of his artistic talents" (2002, 44). Hitler manipulated audiences through a number of mechanisms. Some of these mechanisms were quite simple— tricks of movement and mannerism, his natural vocal abilities, a "psychic ability to connect with an audience and mesmerize it" (45). But Hitler's aesthetic manipulation of his audiences went far beyond such simple tricks. Meeting places were selected with great care so that they would always be over-filled, giving an impression of strength. Hitler had special equipment installed in his speaker's podium that allowed him to alter lighting (47). Hitler's use of extreme lighting effects, particularly Albert Speer's famous "cathedral of light," was legendary (57). The total effect was that fascism essentially became not simply aestheticized politics, but aestheticized religion. As Spotts points out, what "Hitler provided was ritual in place of belief, or ritual as belief.... In ceremonies adapted from Catholic practices, ritual was not so much an outward expression of belief as a mode of producing it.... Such theatrocacy was participatory ideology." In an increasingly post–Christian, post-religious Europe, fascism served as a way of uniting an ideologically diverse people through a shared aesthetic experience. Participatory art, for the Nazis, was a means of solidifying group cohesion and expressing power (61).

Lewis's analysis of fascism is not quite as sophisticated as Spotts's. He tended to concentrate on fascism's book-burning tendencies, while somewhat ignoring fascism's actually fairly deep ties with certain more traditionalist art forms (*ICHH* 218–219). But Lewis did point out how American evangelicalism's essentially populist aesthetic sense could be manipulated through political hymns and allusions to famous literary figures. Windrip, for instance, appeals to a wide variety of (mostly) second-rate authors to prove that he is an intellectual figure (102). Windrip's list is meant to convey both his cultural conservatism—his favorites include such respected figures as Longfellow and Plato—and his general ignorance of any post-realist literary tradition (his list of favorite writers does not include any modernists or naturalists). This is immediately contrasted with the more secular Doremus's reading, which though also somewhat conservative and old fashioned, consists of much more generally respected works, such as *Moby Dick*, Swinburne's poetry, *Pride and Prejudice*, and *Vanity Fair* (102). Lewis unconsciously here confirms Bourdieu's, as well as Dispensational Marxism's, analysis of taste: Doremus, hailing from an upper-class denominational background (Unitarianism), seems to have an inherently superior taste to Windrip, whose religious background in the Campbellite evangelical churches is decidedly lower class and populist (117). Doremus's taste allows him to appreciate the finer things in life — art, good conversation, a charming mistress — but it does leave him somewhat lacking in his ability to connect to people of differing social stations, particularly his handyman Shad Ledue, who turns into his main fascist nemesis by the end of the novel. Ledue, a shiftless figure with few redeeming qualities, falls easy prey to the mix of fascism, evangelical populism, and jingoism that characterizes Windrip's Corpo state.

The actual art produced by Corpo supporters tends to be a mixture of hyper-evangelical religiosity and hyper-militarism, particularly "Bring Out the Old-Time Musket," Lewis's send-up of the "Battle Hymn of the Republic," which reads in part:

> Dear Lord, we have sinned, we have slumbered,
>   And our flag lies stained in the dust,
> And the souls of the Past are calling, calling,
>   "Arise from your sloth — you must!"
> Lead us, O soul of Lincoln,
> Inspire us, spirit of Lee,
> To rule all the world for righteousness,
> To fight for the right,
> To awe with our might,
> As we did in 'sixty-three....
> See, all the world is crumbling,
> Dreadful and dark and dire.
> America! Rise and conquer
> The world to our heart's desire! [*ICHH* 54–55].

Windrip's propaganda team here is masterfully obfuscating. Not wishing to offend one section of the nation at the expense of another, Windrip's team decides to glorify both the Union and the Confederacy as the heroes of sixty-three, promoting a sense of mutual national solidarity. This of course makes little sense, since whatever one's interpretation of the Civil War, it is doubtful that both sides could have been fighting for the "right" in such an ideologically divisive conflict. Windrip's team, however, draws on America's deeply religious connection to the Civil War, the time of the nation's last sustained major revivals (see Noll 2002, 422–438, but especially 424, on Civil War revivals), because the intense religiosity of the conflict, and the religious hagiography associated with both Lincoln and Lee, makes the conflict an ideal mechanism by which to manipulate evangelical public opinion. Nor is Lewis unrealistic here. The Civil War continues to remain a reliable artistic tool by which to manipulate the evangelical masses. For instance, the Civil War film *Gods and Generals* received support from prominent members of the evangelical community, or their organizations, upon its release (Turner [2012], Monroe 2003, Phillips 2003, Waliszewski 2003), despite its appalling racist revisionism concerning that conflict. Furthermore, the Civil War's status as a sort of mutual crusade for both right and left points to the need for Windrip's own followers to become evangelical crusaders in support of American values. Knowing that high and modernist art would not fly in America — as it did not in Germany — Windrip's regime relies on America's equivalent of a German *volkisch* artistic philosophy: America's narrative of fall and redemption, hitched to a narrative of manifest destiny. How one can be working for righteousness while seeking to rule the world is not asked by Windrip's followers, just as America's righteousness was not too closely examined by Julia Ward Howe when she wrote "The Battle Hymn of the Republic" (*EB*, "Julia Ward Howe"). Patriotic art, for Lewis, besides being bad art, tends to give its audiences a very distorted worldview. It is therefore ideal art by which to control a population.

Windrip is influenced by a number of writers, three being particularly significant. The first is Bruce Barton (*ICHH* 60). Barton was one of the most famous Christian figures of the 1920s. An advertising man, he wrote a number of successful books that, as Martin Marty puts it, reduced "the gospel to advertising-copy prose" (Marty 1991, 45). Barton was widely seen as embodying the materialist spirit of the twenties (45) and probably served as a partial inspiration for the dreadfully bad advertising poet Chum Frink in Lewis's novel *Babbit* (Lingeman 2002, 176). Barton's form of populist materialism and apathetic Christianity, lacking either the honesty of the Christian Right or the social gospel values of the principled Christian Left, clearly repelled Lewis. His union of the wallet and the cross represented the moral bankruptcy of a country that no longer really believed in the Christian values it was espousing.

The second interesting figure that Windrip enjoys is William Dudley Pelley, the founder of the Silver Shirts (*ICHH*, 60). Pelley was the founder of the notorious Silver Shirts organization, a fascist group that enjoyed very visible and fairly widespread support during the late twenties and early thirties. Martin Marty has characterized it as an "exaggerated version of ... 100 percent Christian Americanism," a similar movement popular in the early twenties (Marty 1991, 263). Pelley, though not part of the Protestant mainstream in any meaningful way, played off anti–Semitic fears in the thirties and attracted many Southern supporters (263–264). Pelley's writings combined the populism of a Windrip or Huey Long with the anti–Semitism and religious fervor of a Gerald Winrod and proved a major inspiration for the characterization of Windrip (263–265).

The third writer that Windrip invokes is more obscure: anticommunist Elizabeth Dilling, characterized by Glenn Jeansonne as the "most important woman to emerge on the far right in the 1930s" (1997, 10). Lingeman quite realistically suggests Dilling might have been the inspiration for the character Adelaide Tarr Gimmitch (2002, 404), one of Windrip's most fanatic supporters and the convention singer of "Bring Out the Old-Time Musket" (*ICHH* 54). Dilling's views were somewhat more ecumenical than Winrod's—she did have sympathy for conservative Catholics, for instance—but she was firmly on the side of conservative Christianity, including conservative Protestantism, so long as it supported her fanatically anti–Communist and anti–Semitic viewpoints. Dilling is quite significant because she was an admirer of such prominent fundamentalist figures as Gerald Winrod, G.K. Smith, and W.B. Riley (Jeansonne 1997, 10–28; see 14 for Dilling's views on fundamentalist ministers).

Lewis characterizes Mrs. Gimmitch as an anti-union rabble-rousing member of the Daughters of the American Revolution, and points out that organization's repeated tendency to turn into a hyper–Christian, hyper-patriotic version of the Ku Klux Klan, with the racism and anti–Semitism of that organization rather thinly (often non-existently) veiled (*ICHH* 4–7). Gimmitch, like Windrip, focuses on an anti-aesthetic vision of American culture, though engaging in artistic activities like oratory and singing. She complains, "We don't want all this highbrow intellectuality, all this book-learning. That's good enough in its way, but isn't it, after all, just a nice toy for grownups? No, what we all must have ... is Discipline—Will Power—Character" (6). Gimmitch claims to have a common man's vision of American culture while actually she is deeply trapped in an egocentric self-centered worldview that emphasizes the selfishness of laborers in wanting reasonable wages (6). She is the flip side of Shad Ledue. While Ledue, to Lewis, is selfish in wishing to appropriate the middle class's wealth without any effort (88,140), Gimmitch is even more selfish in not allowing the laboring class any share of the economic pie.

Lewis here points to how fears of communism, combined with hyper-religiosity, worked against both middle-class and working-class interests in the thirties, neither class being much served by the rhetoric being thrown about by their minders. Jessup rightly realizes, "There is no [political] solution! There will never be a state of society anything like perfect" (*ICHH* 110).

For Jessup, it is precisely the dangerous idealisms of the thirties—fascism, communism, and fundamentalism — that present the most danger to a civilized society. Jessup reflects that perhaps the "most vigorous idealists have been the worst enemies of human progress instead of its greatest creators" (116). Though this viewpoint is in part informed by Lewis's own relatively privileged position on the social food chain, it also reflected a very real tendency, possibly inherited from his mentor Jack London, to be suspicious of utopian programs. For Lewis, conservative America's idealist ideological form was fundamentalism, and because he felt fundamentalism was aesthetically impoverished (see *EG* 31–32), it was likely to produce an anti-intellectual culture very amenable to fascist influence.

For Lewis, in the final analysis, the combination of fascism and fundamentalism led to the kind of mass media, single-issue politics that was later actually promoted by the Christian Right. Windrip says of the Silver Shirts and William Dudley Pelley, "These fellows have Messages and we haven't got time for anything in literature except a straight, hard-hitting, heart-throbbing Message!" (*ICHH* 60). While the Corpo government's plan actually has fifteen planks (60–61), it is promoted through simplistic advertising and oratory that seeks to enthrall the masses with easy-to-understand slogans. Windrip realizes that the American public is not primarily concerned with thinking for itself, but in being thought for and taken care of by a government that will give it whatever it wants. The simpler Windrip's message, the more direct it is, the more likely it is to appeal to a fundamentalist audience that is used to colorful but anti-intellectual and anti-artistic sermons by the likes of Riley and Winrod. The only proper art in the new state is the art that serves the state's message — that is, the art that serves the state. In this sense, in some ways Windrip's regime is even more culturally conservative than Nazism, which could sometimes tolerate dissenting viewpoints or ethnic groups if Hitler or Goebbels was particularly moved by what was being expressed (see especially Spotts 2002, 84–85, for Hitler's artistic "exceptions" for Jews or relatives of Jews whose art he found aesthetically pleasing).

Lewis felt that evangelical politicians such as Windrip fundamentally disrespected the intellect of their audiences, including fellow evangelicals. Windrip writes in his book *Zero Hour*, "An honest propagandist for any Cause, that is, one who honestly studies and figures out the most effective way of putting over his Message, will learn fairly early that it is not fair to ordinary folks — it just confuses them — to try to make them swallow all the true facts that would be suitable to a higher class of people" (*ICHH* 180). Windrip believes that ordinary people do not want facts, do not want to be given a fair understanding of either the national or global situation. His cynicism is the natural cynicism of any practitioner of *realpolitik*; what makes it so deadly is that he hitches this cynicism to both an idealistic political movement and a conservative economic agenda. By doing so, he hurts his own followers while promising to help them. What is important for Windrip is not the message being conveyed, but that his audience believe in it. Lewis realized, as few of his contemporaries of any political allegiance seem to have done, that politicians and political leaders were first and foremost users, whether they were communists, fascists, fundamentalists, or liberals. What Lewis saw that none of the followers of these movements did, was that the best intentions of idealists would always work against them; political leaders were first and foremost concerned with maintaining and exercising power, second with appeasing their most prominent supporters, and only peripherally with appeasing their base.

Lewis's vision of evangelicalism, then, is ultimately a tragic one. The evangelical dictator will have all the anti-intellectualism of the Nazi state and his art will, like Nazi art, be of a generally inferior quality. But evangelicalism is even worse than Nazism in that it deliberately works against the aesthetic sense of life at every level. Nazism, whether Lewis acknowledged it or not, had a much more complicated and ambivalent view of the arts, at least among its leaders, many of whom prized the arts in many ways, even as they repressed some of Germany's greatest artists, writers, and musicians (see Spotts 2002, especially chapter 10, "The Modernist Enemy," 151–168). An evangelical Hitler, for Lewis, wouldn't even rate as diabolic: he'd simply be a lout, a despot on the level of Genghis Khan, as imprecise in his killing and political views as he was in his artistic ones. For Lewis, even evangelical evildoers are second-rate.

It is hard to fault Lewis for the conclusions he came to about the Christian Right of the 1930s. Lewis did severely overvalue the aesthetic sense's capacity to create "moral" people. Most of his characters, not just Doremus and Windrip, seem to be classified as heroes or villains mainly by their choices in books and/or by their support for liturgical and liberal churches (with the more liturgical and liberal churches generally producing the more refined, book-loving characters in the novel). And Lewis can certainly seem somewhat dated in his portrayal of the working class. But these faults are counterbalanced by Lewis's very real concern, powerfully expressed, about the dangers of uniting a populist aestheticism, whatever its views of capitalism or even spiritual capitalism, with a populist, evangelical political movement.

It would perhaps be an exaggeration to say that Francis Schaeffer is the fulfillment of Lewis's cultural nightmare. Schaeffer, after all, was appalled by racism, and his main mentor on aesthetic theory, Hans Rookmaaker, lost his dearly beloved Jewish fiancée to the Holocaust (Gasque 2005, 69; Schaeffer 1976, 114, 128). The problem is, however, that worldview theory copied many of the artistic assumptions of Nazi aestheticism, particularly Nazism's dislike of modernism and glorification of "eternal" (in the words of the fictional biopic of Hitler, *Max*), some might say Platonic, artistic values (Spotts 2002, 151–168, 399–400). Translated into an American context, worldview theory therefore provided a potential seedbed for a Christianized fascism that selectively embraces Schaeffer's later, more conservative theology, without coming to terms with the much more liberal vein of Schaeffer's thought. Fortunately, except for extremist Reconstructionists and dominionists, few evangelicals have seemed genuinely interested in true fascism; however, a growing number of evangelicals have been interested in, as Jeff Sharlet terms it, the "fascist aesthetic" (Garfield 2007). Christian youth movements, particularly Battlecry and Joel's Army, have become incredibly adept at using fascist-like symbolism, regalia, and flags to promote ostensibly Christian ideals. Schaeffer's political philosophy provided the talking points for these latter-day proto-fascists, while Schaeffer's artistic philosophy is now used to promote ideas of cultural conquest that bear only passing resemblance to anything Schaeffer actually taught. Schaeffer was everything Lewis did not see in evangelicalism — an intellectual, sometimes progressive, a lover of the arts and European culture. But ironically, in creating the worldview movement that so proudly proclaims his name, Schaeffer again pointed to the continued prescience of Lewis's artistic vision. Progressive and moderate evangelicals can only hope that later generations of evangelicals will turn the tide against those who continue, by their actions, to defame Schaeffer's legacy.

Conclusion

After *It Can't Happen Here*, conservative evangelicalism and fundamentalism for a time passed from public view. Though still acknowledged somewhat in Southern literature, particularly the fiction of Flannery O'Connor and protest novels such as Richard Wright's *Native Son* (1940), evangelicalism took on largely negative connotations in literary discourse, when it was mentioned at all. Even as evangelicalism slowly evolved out of its fundamentalistic impulse, the secular world continued to view it as a backward, largely reactionary mindset against modernity. The ability of modernists such as Nathanael West and social realists such as Sinclair Lewis to deal sympathetically with evangelicalism was gradually lost, as writers retreated to largely formulaic presentations of evangelical belief. Feeling imperiled by Macarthyism and the growth of conservative influence in the country, the artistic community struck out at evangelicals as the scapegoat for the United States' rightward turn. Justified or not, that reaction would come to define secular artists' reaction to evangelicalism for the next half-century.

4

The Fifties: Creativity and Creationists

In the late 1940s, evangelicalism began to re-emerge as a political force, thanks in large part to the efforts of Billy Graham (W. Martin 2005, 29–31). In the fifties, Graham rallied around him a host of new neo-evangelical leaders, particularly Carl F.H. Henry, who distanced the new evangelicalism from both the old evangelicalism and fundamentalism (Marty 1996, 438). The founding of *Christianity Today* in 1956, birthed by Graham's influence (Ellwood 1997, 133–134), gave evangelicals a respectable theological periodical to rival, if never surpass, the mainline Protestant *Christian Century*. Unnoticed by the evangelical mainstream, Francis Schaeffer firmly rooted himself in Europe during this period and founded L'Abri, an organization that would influence many young evangelical leaders by offering a more intellectualized alternative to traditional evangelical belief than they had then been exposed to (Hankins 42, 55). Fifties America, with its anti–Communist values and its general (some at the time said universal) support for "traditional values," seemed to promise a return to an idyllic evangelical past. Liberal churches were retreating to a more conservative neorthodoxy; outside these churches an "evangelical mood was rising" (Ellwood, *Fifties*, 134). During the fifties, the Southern Baptists were the fastest growing denomination, building 631 churches in 1953 alone. Other signs of evangelicalism's rise "included the popularity of Billy Graham, *Christianity Today* ... and even enthusiasm for C.S. Lewis, that perennial favorite of U.S. evangelicals" (Ellwood 1997, 134). The return to utopia was not to come, but to this day, many evangelicals still see the fifties as a golden era in American culture.

Within the evangelical movement, tensions between neo-evangelicals and fundamentalists would create fractures that would never really heal. Billy Graham's outreach to liberal Christians, exemplified by his interest in the World Council of Churches and his eventual (qualified) support for Martin Luther King, angered many fundamentalists (as well as Southern evangelicals of all stripes) (Marty 1996, 151; W. Martin 2005, 44). By the mid-fifties, Schaeffer would also distance himself from the more fundamentalist groups within the Reformed tradition that he had allied himself with (Hankins 2008, 50–53). While these breaks were undoubtedly painful to both men, their efforts paved the way for an evangelical movement that would be more socially and politically engaged.

In hindsight, this slow re-integration of evangelicals into American life can be seen as a disaster for evangelicals, and for the country they inhabit. Decades of conflict over issues such as gay marriage and abortion have left deep tears in the national psyche and exposed the evangelical community to both justified and unjustified derision. Worse, by re-integrating evangelicals into secular life, and (eventually) encouraging evangelical children to adopt secular artistic styles (especially in music), educational aspirations, management methodologies, and political skills, leaders such as Graham and Schaeffer unintentionally promoted the secularization of evangelical culture, robbing it of precisely those anti-materialistic, anti-worldly attributes that helped maintain a guard over evangelical children from non-evangelical influences. Fifty years later, with the rapid growth of the Emergent Church, the growing vocalness of the New Atheist movement, the draining away of important artistic voices such as Jeanette Winterson, Octavia Butler and Craig Thompson from evangelicalism to alternate spiritual paths, there can be little doubt that Schaeffer's and Graham's goal to again make evangelicalism intellectually respectable damned itself through its own success. Faced with a church that appears irresponsive to the concerns of the poor and racial minorities, young evangelical intellectual leaders now often abandon their heritage rather than deal with the mental turmoil such a conflicted and confusing upbringing brings.

Much turmoil, therefore, could have been spared, had fundamentalism and neo-evangelicalism stayed united during the forties and fifties. Fundamentalism's traditionally cultural separatism, though often rooted in selfishness, was better adapted to help the evangelical movement survive in the long term. As one of the two main spiritually capitalist forces of the fifties (the other being the mainline church), the neo-evangelicals tasted the fruits of power that had been denied fundamentalists, Pentecostals, and Holiness churches for a quarter century. After some disastrous missteps with Harry Truman, Graham quickly united himself with establishment political leaders such as Dwight Eisenhower and Richard Nixon (W. Martin 2005, 41). Nor was Graham adverse to helping out Democrat leaders, such as Lyndon Johnson (31). The important thing for Graham was not what party held the power, but how the power was used to advance his (and therefore, Christianity's) agenda. Though Graham eventually somewhat retreated from politics after his ill-timed alliance with the Nixon administration (146–147), his removal from the political equation simply left the door open for more radical evangelical political engagement, with more Machiavellian leaders such as Jerry

Falwell, Pat Robertson, James Dobson, and D. James Kennedy becoming the dominant forces in evangelical politics. With Graham's removal from the political equation and Schaeffer's death in 1984 (Hankins 2008, 228), there was no one to put the break on the evangelical movement's descent into a cultural Armageddon that to this day has not halted the inevitable advance of gay rights, restored prayer to the public schools, or more than marginally improved the "situation" for fetal "life."

But this is hindsight. There is no way that Graham could have predicted the cultural forces he would unleash; indeed, during the fifties he was probably as much a moderating force on religion as a repressive one. And Schaeffer's influence was even more ambiguous. Though Schaeffer was instrumental in uniting pro-life politics with the evangelical church — a union that was not at all certain in the early seventies — he also supported causes such as environmentalism (W. Martin 2005, 238–239; Hankins 2008, 228), and was, if his son Franky's admittedly biased account is to be believed, fanatically anti-racist and much more tolerant of gays and lesbians than most *secular* people of his generation (Franky Schaeffer 2007, 77). Indeed, Schaeffer's and Graham's situation was far from unique. C. Everett Koop, who helped fuel the anti-abortion craze that gave birth to the culture wars, later found himself on the receiving side of evangelical anger for (vigorously) supporting the rights of Americans to receive safe-sex education in the hope of halting AIDS (W. Martin 2005, 249–257).[1] The tragedy of neo-evangelicalism — which is a tragedy in which all America now shares— is that the neo-evangelicals did the wrong thing for the right reason. A separatist fundamentalism and secularism could have stayed at peace. But once cultural engagement was again dictated, conflict was inevitable. What the final results of that conflict will be, no one is yet able to tell.

In the fifties, however, the main cultural conflict in America was not over abortion or gay rights; it was about communism and racial integration. And the evangelical community found itself the target of African-American and progressive intellectuals who saw its anti-intellectualism as a recessive feature of the American character. Many evangelicals would unite against communism (Ellwood 1997, 38–39), some against civil rights (W. Martin 2005, 78–79), and in the process ignore the internal danger that neo-evangelicals and the Reformed movement were beginning to pose for evangelical cultural coherence.

Go Tell It to the Artist: James Baldwin and the Tragedy of African-American Aesthetic Expectation

James Baldwin's *Go Tell It on the Mountain* was published in 1953 to mixed reviews (Boyd 2008, 35). Today it is considered a classic. Critic Lev

Grossman rated it one of the 100 best novels of the twentieth century (2005). It has inspired a film version (*Go Tell It on the Mountain*), and with the success of Baldwin's other works, such as *The Fire Next Time* (1963) and *Another Country* (1962), has ensured Baldwin a permanent place in the American literary canon.

Go Tell It on the Mountain was written at a tumultuous time in African-American history. Living under the Eisenhower administration, with a president with a rather dim view of civil rights (Marty 1996, 382–383), the political situation was tense. The army had only recently been fully integrated, professional sports had only had black athletes for six years, and the sweeping social changes that Brown vs. Board of Education were to usher in were still a year away. But Baldwin saw, as anyone but the blind could see, that change was inevitable: the only question was whether it would come through non-violent protest, violent protest, or a combination of both. While *Go Tell It on the Mountain* is set in the mid 1930s, the concern with then-contemporaneous civil rights issues, such as the continued threat of racial violence in the South, is evidenced through depictions of black families cowering in their homes, afraid of lynching parties (Baldwin 1953 [hereafter cited as *GTIM*], 63). While Baldwin's cultural critique of white racism is not as well developed in *Go Tell It on the Mountain* as it is in *Another Country*, the former novel shares with the latter work a deep concern with how the arts relate to race.

Baldwin's work is significant to this study because it represents the first African-American attempt to articulate the relationship between aesthetically-minded African-Americans and the evangelical church. Baldwin's work highlighted significant differences in how black evangelicalism perceived both the role of the church and the relationship between aesthetically- and non-aesthetically-minded evangelicals.

One difference between black and white evangelicals that is absolutely vital in understanding *Go Tell It on the Mountain* is how black churches interpret the concept of freedom. Academics C. Eric Lincoln and Lawrence Mamiya have pointed out, "For whites freedom has bolstered the value of American individualism.... But for African Americans freedom has always been communal in nature" (Lincoln and Mamiya 1990, 5). As the two authors point out, whites too often try to associate one way of being that is true for all African-Americans, appointing each black as a representative of their racial group (5). The problem with such a supposition, when it comes to the novels under discussion here, is that Baldwin's views of religion are much different from Octavia Butler's or Toni Morrison's. While there are some general aesthetic tendencies present in these works — most notably a persistent prophetic critique of white culture — Baldwin's work should not be mistaken for that of these later writers, nor for that of such contemporaries as Ralph Ellison or Richard Wright. His vision is complicated by a much closer initial identification with his evangelical identity than even, say, Butler, as well as his later identification with the gay community.

Go Tell It on the Mountain is partly an autobiographical tale. Baldwin's father David, like Gabriel, was a terror (Boyd 2008, 4). The elder Baldwin was a common laborer (18), raising Baldwin in the Baptist tradition, but Baldwin did not have a major religious experience until he came under the spell of Pentecostal preacher Rosa Artimas Horn (Hardy 2003, 4–5). Horn's church of almost 3,000 fed many people during the Great Depression. She campaigned against dance clubs and pool halls, gave radio addresses and sparked a rivalry with cross-town rival Father Divine, an important African-American religious figure in New York during this period (5). Baldwin, in his later works, would compare his early preaching efforts in the Pentecostal church to theatre, showing how aware he was of the potential — and for him, negative — aspects of evangelical artistry (5–6). Baldwin himself claimed that it was his love of writing and literature that would later push him out of the evangelical church (7). Yet, in the terrors and dramatic hypocrisy of that church, Baldwin found much "rhetoric, rhythm, and song" that "captured his personality" (8).

Baldwin's novel was the first major African-American novel to depict the "diasporic" evangelical type — that is, an ex-evangelical who is leaving or has left their community, either for secularism or another form of religious belief. Baldwin' concerns in *Go Tell It on the Mountain* are multifaceted: in part, he depicts the disintegration of an African-American family under the oppression of a racist socioeconomic and cultural system. But other thematic interests are present as well, particularly a careful attention to mapping out the aesthetic limitations of African-American life during the 1930s. The novel sets up a conflict between young John Grimes (a thinly veiled autobiographical stand-in for Baldwin) and his father Gabriel; partly a generational conflict, partly a religious conflict, this conflict also has distinctly aesthetic dimensions, with Gabriel playing the black equivalent of the artistic rube.

John is a young African-American longing to escape from the impoverishment of his community. He feels that his only escape is to "become a Great leader of His people." John is "not much interested in his people and still less in leading them anywhere, but the phrase so often repeated rose ... like a great brass gate opening outward for him on a world where people did not live in the darkness of his father's house, did not pray to Jesus in the darkness of his father's church, where he would eat good food, and wear fine clothes, and go to the movies as often as he wished" (*GTIM* 12). For John, therefore, the church seems, at least initially, an aesthetically limiting place; it leaves him in aesthetic darkness. While the world's culture — white culture, largely — is a world of the arts, a world of beauty, the culture John lives in is "darkness." The term is, of course, both aesthetically and symbolically telling. It can be equated to John's skin, but also to the material lack of "fine clothes" and artistic forms like "movies" within the black church. The world of that church limits John's aesthetic options, because he is unable to gather either the rich artistic inspiration that the Harlem Renaissance provided nor the only marginally more limited aesthetic joys that could be derived from black popular culture at the time, such as jazz. Though the church John attends provides more than just theatre, as Clarence Hardy suggests about Baldwin's own church (Hardy 2003, 8), it is limited by the social conditions imposed upon African-American church culture in the thirties. That culture, often deriving from Methodist roots, often now (as in Baldwin's case) Pentecostal in allegiance, tended to appeal to only one side of a person's spiritual and aesthetic character: the emotional.

This is not a comment simply on the African-American church, but on Pentecostal and Methodist culture in general, which have long, particularly in the former tradition, preferred emotion to rationality, feeling to logic. To this particular church observer, this is one of the greatest strengths of the Pentecostal church, particularly in a postmodern era that distrusts the rationalist ideas of mainline and Reformed Protestantism.[2] But in the modernist era, which still had memories of a nineteenth century when rationality and logic were king, it is understandable why an ambitious African-American such as John Grimes would want to avoid being labeled as "irrational" or "emotional." After all, whites had used the emotionality they found in black churches as a frequent excuse for stereotyping black church experience, indeed black aesthetic experience. Even today, Christian writers such as Hubert Spence associate rock with African and African-American musical styles, and then by extension Satanism (2011, 137), while evangelical music critics have made it something of a personal quest to eradicate even contemporary Christian music (CCM) because of its association with African tribal beats (Howard and Streck 1999, 33–35). These kinds of opinions, which have existed in evangelicalism since at least the fifties (when Baldwin was writing *Go Tell It on the Mountain*), exhibit a kind of thinly veiled racism, in which words such as "tribal" or "jungle music" (a frequent pejorative used against rock in some of the churches this author has attended) substitute for more open expressions of racial hostility. For someone like John, the darkness of an African-American church consisted largely of its inability to offer any wider artistic or cultural vista from which he could observe the world around him, at least without being labeled a nonhuman being with a "junglified" artistic heritage. By his wish to become the "Great Man" for his people, John expresses the desire to transcend artistic nullity — the empty, bare, "dark" nullity of his church's aesthetics — for the richness he sees in the white world.

But John's dilemma is complicated by the more communal nature of African-American religious experience. Unlike a white evangelical, in saying no to his church he is also saying no to his racial identity. Because the African-American church is such a focal point in the black community, John realizes that he is rejecting more than just a religion. Thus, where a white ex-evangelical would tend to feel anger or condemnation towards a community as restrictive as John's, John's own position is more ambivalent. He longs to be fully a part of the community (to embrace "Forever and forever, and beyond all question, the way to go") (*GTIM* 75) — hence his dramatic (though probably temporary) conversion at the end of the novel — but he feels that he has "no right to sing or to rejoice" (56). For African-Americans, church is a cultural, as well as a religious identity; a form of identification that white evangelicals would only belatedly discover once they found out (again belatedly) that they were no longer the majority group in America.

John's most powerful aesthetic identification at this age is with the dominant white culture that oppresses him. Upon looking at the grandeur of "white" New York, he reflects:

> In the narrow way, the way of the cross, there awaited him only humiliation forever.... The way of the cross had given him a belly filled with wind and had bent his mother's back; they had never worn fine clothes, but here, where the buildings contested God's power and where men and women did not fear God, here he might ... clothe his body with wondrous fabrics rich to the eye and pleasing to the touch. And what of his soul.... To hurl away for a moment of ease, the glories of eternity!... These glories were unimaginable — but the city was real [*GTIM* 28].

John's experience of religion is that it is impoverishing. It literally has the emptiness of air, something blank and, unless carried to New York by Duchamp, not considered an aesthetic object in the 1930s. By contrast, the dominant white culture seeks to challenge "God's power" on his throne. Its aesthetic goal is that of Babel-makers, and like Babel-makers it is corrupt, enslaving, and awe-inspiring in its aesthetic hubris. If the church is to offer any aesthetic fulfillment, it will be in the "glories of eternity," glories that are invisible to the naked eye in this life. The material world, the world one can see, is "rich to the eye and pleasing to the touch"; by contrast the "glories of eternity" are "unimaginable." Reality can only be located in that which one can physically sense; to talk of an aesthetic object available only to the imagination, an abstraction that cannot even be truly thought about outside of anthropomorphic terms, requires more faith than John is capable of exercising. Spirits, trinities, gods, are ethereal ideas; the world of John's aspirations, where he can touch "fabrics rich to the eye," is one in which the material aspirations of a generation of African-Americans are made physically tangible to them. If the church cannot, therefore, pragmatically help John, it ceases to lose any social utility or religious usefulness, except insofar as it provides John with a community support system.

Such a viewpoint may seem cynical to white evangelicals; such a reaction to the realities of African-American religious experience ignores how often white evangelicalism's own spiritual motivations are socioeconomic. If John's glorification of material things is a form of idolatry (in Christian terms), it is an idolatry only made possible by those who constructed those same buildings that challenged God: in other words whites, many of whom are evangelical Christians. It is easy not to worship the golden cow, when one is receiving daily manna from heaven. For African-American evangelicals such a path has seldom been open; it is therefore not surprising that for a young African-American, keenly aware of the sensuous, the beauty of this world is to be preferred to the beauty of the next.

Baldwin juxtaposes John's longing for a more fulfilled, aesthetic experience of the world with Gabriel's deep suspicions of beauty and anything approaching an artistic approach to church-life. When thinking of some elder church members he knows, Gabriel reflects: "They seemed to him so lax, so nearly worldly.... Though they preached with great authority, and brought souls low before the altar ... they did not give God the glory, nor count it as glory at all; they might as easily have been ... highly paid circus-performers, each with his own special dazzling gift.... And this ... frightened him. He did not want ... to hold the gift of God so lightly" (*GTIM* 103). Gabriel's suspicions about the natural theatricality of the church are, of course, Baldwin's as well. Neither the writer nor the fictional character has much use for the church as simply a kind of performative ritual. Yet Gabriel does not reflect that his own life is similarly such a performance, a constant effort to appear holy to appease the desires of his mother, or to trick his first wife Deborah. Gabriel recognizes the clownishness of the church, but does not withdraw from it, and in consequence becomes the clown himself, the circus performer who seeks to spiritually actualize through rhetoric what he cannot do through action. Baldwin warns here against the dangerousness of seeing church as simply, and only, a performance. Much as Sinclair Lewis did in *Elmer Gantry*, Baldwin here finds the church (the black church, specifically, but evangelicalism in general as well) to exist in a space where too often aesthetic performance is mistaken for divine inspiration. If a clown can pretend to be Christ's servant, then why cannot Christ himself just be an enormously sophisticated mountebank himself?

Baldwin critiques the iconoclastic impulse as being essentially motivated by self-righteousness, subliminally charged with sexual guilt. Having impregnated Esther, a woman he is not married to, Gabriel feels a deep sense of rage, but directs it more at his community's popular culture and art than at himself:

> They [his people] had all turned aside ... to fall down before idols of gold and silver, and wood and stone, false gods that could not heal them. The music that filled any town or city he entered was not the music of the saints but ... infernal, which glorified lust and held righteousness up to scorn. Women ... stood night after night, twisting their bodies into lewd hallelujahs in smoke-filled, gin-heavy dance halls, singing for their "loving man" [*GTIM* 135].

For Gabriel, the very things that attract his son to the world repel Gabriel himself. But Gabriel, rather than seeking to use his iconoclasm as a way of uniting his community or as a means of principled anti-materialist rejection of modern cultural practices — ragtime, bluegrass, and dance-halls, for instance — uses his anti-artistic ideas merely to suppress his step-son's spiritual and mental development. The constant danger that iconoclasm faces, a devolution into simple anti-intellectualism — a devolution that the anti-art movement, in so far as it was iconoclastic, avoided — ensnares Gabriel. For Gabriel art merely represents the dangers of lucre and sexuality, dangers that he himself is tempted by, but is afraid to grasp for himself and unable to take without guilt.

And this is a crucial point, because different evangelicalisms operate in different ways, particularly white and black evangelicalism. For white evangelicalism, its recent love affair with intellectualism and aesthetics has been a disastrous event for American culture. Most of the intellectuals and art critics produced by this love affair — for instance, apologists such as William Lane Craig, Lee Stroebel, Josh McDowell, Francis Schaeffer, and Os Guinness — are just smart enough to keep those who are faithful in line, while having a disastrous impact on evangelical intellectual life. Craig, Strobel, McDowell, and Guinness promote apologetic arguments that are rehashed and largely discredited versions of the kind of arguments used by more sophisticated evangelical thinkers at the beginning of the century. Aestheticians such as Schaeffer and Rookmaaker, meanwhile, keep Christian art theory largely in bondage to anti-modernism, even as much more sophisticated art theorists and artists, such as the artist Mako Fujimura and academic Daniel Siedell, struggle with contemporary members of the evangelical arts community (notably Douglas Campbell) to move beyond simplistic "heretical modernist" versus "artist of faith" binaries (Siedell 2008, 160, 184–185).

For black evangelicals, the situation is different in several respects. First of all, conservative theology is much less equated with conservative politics in black evangelical culture than in white. Therefore, while black evangelicals tend to be more politically conservative than the progressive tradition in African-American Protestantism, they are still far more liberal than white evangelicals (Lincoln and Mamiya 1990, 228–229). In white evangelicalism, a greater embrace of the aesthetic aspect of religion does not necessarily lead to more liberal political positions. Relatively non-artistically inclined traditions, such as the Holiness movement and Pentecostalism, arguably have as good, or better, a social record than, say, the various Reformed churches, which pride themselves on their intellectual achievements and at least claim (often unconvincingly) to be supporters of the arts. By contrast, while one cannot easily posit any causal or connective link between a greater sympathy to beauty and more progressive political views among African-American Protestants, it is not hard to imagine such a link. Right-wing white evangelicalism has produced relatively few socially engaged artists, even among those who have left the movement. Ex-evangelicals such as Craig Thompson, Jeanette Winterson, and Franky Schaeffer tend to emphasize aesthetics and beauty in their works to the exclusion of politics, perhaps because the traditions they grew up with were so overwhelmingly didactic. When their art occasionally verges into political matters or critiques of evangelical belief, as does Schaeffer's, the result is often disastrous. By contrast, even the most unsophisticated African-American critiques of evangelical belief, such as Octavia Butler's *Parable* series, play quite deeply with the spiritual traditions they engage and the politics those traditions engender. Whether it is Richard Wright critiquing Adventist culture, W.E.B. Dubois commenting on black church life, or Toni Morrison magnificently dissecting the roots of fundamentalist belief in *Paradise* (1997), black authors are able to make their novels politically relevant without sacrificing them to the didacticism that ruins most white evangelical (and diasporic) work.

Therefore, anti-art iconoclasm, as exemplified in Dispensational Marxism, has more mixed benefits for African-Americans than it does for whites. On one count, the perversion of the art world, particularly the entertainment industry, is of more vital concern to African-Americans than anyone else. Though "high" art, particularly literature, has played a fairly noble role in African-American history, it is not without its paradoxes. *The Klansman* (1905), considered an important novel in its day, led to both the notorious film "classic" *Birth of a Nation* (1915) and directly through that film to the rebirth of the KKK (Wade 1987, 138–139, 144–147). Popular art, however, has had a decidedly more negative influence on African-Americans. Popular art that African-Americans actually invent — jazz, rock, rap, graffiti, etc.— is typically viewed as social poison by the white establishment, till some white kids co-opt it as their own. One need not dislike Eminem to realize that his vaunted position in the rap world is as much a product of his race as it is of his (admittedly genuine) talent. Meanwhile, the genre of Will Smith, Martin Lawrence, and Tyler Perry films manages to give a corporatized version of what African-American life is like, a vision aided by highly selective reality TV programs, such as *Hardcore Pawn* (2010–present) or the *Jerry Springer Show* (1991–present), that tend only to show the most economically impoverished—and therefore emotionally volatile—members of white and black working-class communities. Getting rid of art, at least popular art, might not seem like a bad idea to African-American intellectuals looking at a white culture that has continuously artistically distorted African-Americans as an alien and monstrous Other in pursuit of its own aggrandizement of political and spiritual power (the very foundation of spiritual capitalism).

But Baldwin rejects the iconoclasm that both his father and this work suggest, and for (at the time) a very sensible reason: the danger of leaving art solely as the provenance of whites. Baldwin skillfully portrays the pitfalls of succumbing to iconoclasm or anti-intellectualism by a brief vignette in the relationship between Richard, John's biological father, and Elizabeth, John's mother. Richard takes Elizabeth to visit the Museum of Natural History and the Metropolitan Museum of Art. Richard is very much a portrait of what Baldwin sees himself as, or to be more accurate, what he potentially could have become—an art lover who aspires to greatness but is weighed down by economic and social inequality. Richard tries to explain to Elizabeth what he sees in the art museum, but she "never grasped" what he "tried to tell her." Elizabeth "could not find, between herself and the African statuette or totem pole, on which he gazed with such melancholy wonder, any point of contact. She was only glad that she did not look that way. She preferred to look, in the other museum, at the paintings" (*GTIM* 167). Elizabeth, like Gabriel, ends up feeling ashamed of her aesthetic heritage, despite the rich contributions African and African-American art had even then made to music, rhetoric, and even Cubism (Nash 1989, 164). Therefore she does not identify with the African statuary but with the other paintings ... and this is where Baldwin takes a knife cut worthy of the finest assassin at the cultural pretensions of the white artistic community. For the context of the passage suggests that the other museum—the museum with the supposedly "real" art—is the Metropolitan. Black art is therefore simply classified as "natural history"—a relic of a culturally "primitive," evolutionarily unsophisticated past. While white art is to be contemplated, black art is not to be recognized as art, but simply as a relic of an obsolete or unsophisticated prehistoric age.[3]

For the art museum world, white was and in many ways continues to be the definition of beauty. This reflects wider trends in society promoting white models, clothing lines geared almost exclusively to whites, hair salons that cater only to white female tastes, and publicity machines that go into high gear whenever a white, preferably blond, female, is kidnapped or a white child raped. Elizabeth is seeing far more than just a statuette. She is seeing the evisceration of her own image, the destruction of black feminine identity and black beauty in order to idolize the white body. Her joy that she does "not look that way" leads her to value images that, by the standards of modernists, contemporary Christians, and anti-racists, are no more "objectively" beautiful than she is. Elizabeth, therefore, has bought into the kind of "absolutized" aesthetic tastes, the division of the world into "beautiful" (e.g., white) and "ugly" (e.g., black) art, that the modernists had already labeled irrelevant by the early twenties (when this scene is set). Baldwin warns his readers how powerfully aesthetic standards are shaped by racial prejudice and hints that perhaps aesthetics itself, as least when defined as a theory of beauty, is powerfully determined by racist considerations. Therefore, the spiritual capitalist force operating in black culture during both the 1920s and 1950s is different than that operating in white culture; that force is the totalized system of white racism that envisions blacks, including black Christians, as "uglified" subhumans.

Elizabeth's reaction to the arts, therefore, is one of fear. She is unable to understand Richard's fascination with them. She knows it gives him "a kind of bitter nourishment ... that the secrets they [the artworks] held for him were a matter of life and death. It frightened her ... she felt that he was reaching for the moon and that he would ... be dashed down" (*GTIM* 167). To Elizabeth, the arts represent a dangerous path, because white culture has already predetermined what societal place African-Americans will have, and that position is one that will exclude any but the most rudimentary (to whites) forms of artistic expression. Richard, in trying to rise above his circumstances and become, if not the Nietzschean artist, at least the Nietzschean self-educated lover of the arts, risks suppression by the white community. And in fact, he does end up dying — a suicide — after being falsely imprisoned for a short time by police (171–176).

Richard's death reminds his African-American readers that if they do not enter the arts, the academy, and other fields till then controlled exclusively by whites, it will be white science, white literature, white painting, and white sculpture that determine how future generations of African-Americans are viewed. Richard's angry question, "Ain't we got to be educated, too — to live with the [white] motherfuckers?" (*GTIM* 166) indicates that he himself is aware of this dilemma. The only way he feels African-Americans can get respect from whites is by equaling them culturally, by knowing "everything them white bastards knew" (168). But that is only possible if African-Americans can gain a foothold in powerful ideological apparatuses such as the art museums, the publishing industry, and the schools. Richard's tragedy is that he comes too soon — but through him, he gives birth to John, generating through that most basic act of creation the cultural legacy that will pass beyond his father.

John does get "saved," but his salvation is an ambiguous one. Clarence Hardy III has argued that ultimately it is very hard to tell how Baldwin would wish us to interpret John's conversion (2003, 10). It can be argued with equal force that John's conversion is a damnation, or a redemption. Hardy himself argues, more complexly, that with the conversion, John "becomes his own person. The process enables John to establish an autonomous personality separate from his father's influence and control" (20). Hardy's position is, to my mind, the most likely, but it does not go far enough. Not only does John's conversion provide him with autonomy, it also points the way to his eventual liberation from traditional Christian belief. He tells his friend Elisha, "No matter what happens to me, where I go, what folks say about me, no matter what anybody says, you remember — please remember — I was saved. I was *there*" (*GTIM* 225). John's words clearly suggest that people will have something to say to him, that he will be doing things that other people in his church will disparagingly talk about. It also indicates, through the use of the past tense, that John may anticipate a time when he will not be part of the church, when he will not be saved. Salvation here becomes a metaphor not for a spiritual experience but for a union with one's religious and racial community. As Hardy points out, John seeks to make peace with his step-father so he can transcend his influence (Hardy 2003, 20); yet there is no greater symbol of that influence in John's life than the church he attends. By transcending the patriarchal father, John paves the way for a future ascension over the head of a much greater Father (*GTIM* 144). Through John, Richard's desire for a culture where blacks and black art can be just as well respected as the white "motherfuckers" is given some small semblance of peace. But whether John will ever fulfill the aesthetic potential within him is not revealed. The reader can only hope that he takes the road of his real father, the Nietzschean hero, and not the Gantrian path of his step-father.

Much of the power of *Go Tell It on the Mountain* lies in how richly Baldwin interposes little pieces of artistic information — a comment about a vase or a photograph, or a song, for instance — in his grander image of a black evangelical church gone off the rails. Baldwin's work laid the foundation for a black literary aesthetic analysis of evangelicalism that differed markedly from non-evangelical and ex-evangelical portrayals of white evangelicalism. Baldwin's work, though concerned about the censorious, ultimately reminds his white readers that such censoriousness is the inevitable by-product of a racist, classist, and homophobic artistic environment. Elizabeth's self-censorship,

Gabriel's rejection of the aesthetic, speak to the now-shared iconoclastic values of black and white culture. Baldwin doubtlessly had some hope that art could mitigate some of the effects on the black community of these societal plagues. He may have failed to take into consideration how often the arts are used for societally or politically repressive aims. But for black artists, evangelical or not, rejecting the aesthetic is cultural suicide. There are no separatist enclaves in Idaho or South Carolina for African-Americans to retreat to, no place in the country where black children will not be exposed to white-imposed standards of artistic and physical beauty.

Insofar as any African-American evangelicals, therefore, wish to adopt the Dispensationalist Marxist model proposed here, they should remember that the primary advantage of it to the African-American community is that such a model deprivileges distinctions between "good" and "bad" art, "taste" and "crudeness," "high" art and "low" art. Since there is real reason to suppose that black art will be typified as low art no matter how deserving of "high" status it is (witness how long it took even obvious canonical authors such as Harriet Jacobs and Richard Wright to be accepted as "real" writers), there are definite benefits in adopting the Dispensational Marxist position. But there are also more risks here to African-Americans than to whites, because while white evangelicals can be oblivious to artistic developments outside their community and still maintain cultural cohesion (indeed, will more likely do so), blacks are in danger, in such an abandonment of the cultural arena to whites, of leaving room for the most grotesque of cultural stereotypes to go unquestioned. Therefore, the DDM model, though it could be applied to black religious culture productively, must take into account the differing social, political, and artistic situation of the African-American community. Otherwise, a rich theological tradition, with its own unique ideas on aesthetics, is in danger of being lost to the concerns of the less politically, culturally, and theologically developed artistic ideals of white evangelicalism. That fate would do neither community any good.

Inherit the Wind: *McCarthy, Mencken, and the Cultural Meaning of the Scopes Trial*

Inherit the Wind has done more to influence secular views of evangelicalism than any other text, save *Elmer Gantry*. The play, a retelling of the Scopes Trial (despite its claims to the contrary), was produced under the heightened influence of McCarthyism. Whereas previous commentators on the Scopes trial had viewed it primarily as a "media spectacular," fifties historians saw the Scopes Trial as emblematic of the same kind of anti-intellectualism that produced the McCarthy hearings (Larson 1997, 239).

Without a doubt, the target of the play was not fundamentalism per se, but the McCarthyite forces then operating in America (239–240). Playwrights Jerome Lawrence and Robert E. Lee were deeply concerned with the "blacklisting of writers and actors" (240). Thus, for Lawrence and Lee, the scientific heroes of the play—Henry Drummond and Bertram Cates—become the stand-ins for artists. Both scientists and artists, as intellectuals, must form common ground to resist the anti-intellectualism that is at the heart of American culture. The analysis of evangelicals in the play, however, merely confirmed both the mainline Protestant and secular stereotypes of evangelicals during this era.

Reviewers were not favorably impressed with *Inherit the Wind*, faulting it for its historical inaccuracies and lack of charity to the fundamentalists of Dayton. But the play has remained popular through the last six decades. The original stage version ran for three years, spawning first a touring version of the play, and later a film version starring prestigious actors Spencer Tracy, Frederic March, and Gene Kelly (Larson 1997, 243). The play is frequently invoked when the Creation Science or Intelligent Design movements try to (yet again) interject creationism into the public schools. The play has sparked three made-for-TV movies and two Broadway revivals, has been responsible for ten Tony Award nominations and four Academy Award nominations, and has sold literally millions of paperback copies alone (Guterman 2008, 567).

The play's popularity is not hard to understand, at least among those who consider themselves intellectuals. Scopes and Drummond, as the scientific and scientific-legal stand-ins for the artist-hero character type, allow readers an easy identification with the heroes, especially for contemporary artists and intellectuals who retain a deep suspicion of the evangelical community. Cates, with his simple naivety and "down home" American values, appeals to the desire of the artistic community to be at once superior to, and at one with, the communities they live with, a position both the mainline and artistic spiritual and materialist bourgeoisie aspired to. Drummond, by contrast, appeals to both the liberal desire to let everyone live in pluralistic peace (seen through his highly symbolic slamming of *The Bible* and *On the Origin of Species* [1859] together) (Lawrence and Lee, 1955 [hereafter cited as *ITW*], 129), and to a simultaneous, and highly contradictory, desire to "terminate with extreme prejudice" the fundamentalist movement and its creationist supporters.

Ishay Landa has perceptively noted that there is a "transition from the nineteenth century to the twentieth" in the perception of the hero within popular culture. A new "heroic model" emerges in the twentieth century, which is partly rooted in Nietzschean ideas (Landa 2007, 1). The idea of the romantic genius, the broad overcomer of religious stigmas, so often associated with Nietzsche, is in full display in both Cates and Drummond. In Cates that hero is embryonic, but in Drummond he is fully formed: the learned, science-loving intellectual who conquers the play's audience with his rhetorical deftness and florid prose.

It is significant, therefore, that the intellectual Drummond refers to both his supporters and detractors in artistic terms in his most significant peroration in the play. When asked if he finds anything holy, Drummond replies:

> Yes! The individual human mind. In a child's power to master the multiplication table there is more sanctity than in all your shouted "Amens!," "Holy, Holies!" and "Hosannas!" An idea is a greater monument than a cathedral.... Darwin moved us forward to a hilltop, where we could look back and see the way from which we came. But for this view, this insight, this knowledge, we must abandon our faith in the pleasant poetry of Genesis [*ITW* 93].

To Drummond, humanity can only reach its potential if unchained from antiquated ideas. Through Darwin, humanity manages to climb to the top of a hilltop, leaving behind the people who came before. While the pleasant poetry of Genesis will remain, it will remain, as just that, poetry. It can no longer have any eternal meaning as "truth," because the basis on which that truth was built has been made obsolete by the Darwinism that Cates teaches. What becomes important in Drummond's worldview is the power of individual human subjects to alter their world through thought. Whether it be an artist, a scientist, a sculptor, or any other intellectual, the goal is the same: to carve out of the world, through force of mind, an idea as monumental as a "cathedral." As Drummond puts it, "Progress has never been a bargain. You've got to pay for it" (93). Progress is for Drummond a contractual process between the intellectual *ubermensch* and the *canaille*. In return for the populace's support, artists, scientists, and other intellectuals will give the populace advances such as "telephones," plays such as *Inherit the Wind*, and the benefit of their wisdom (93). In return, however, the public have to abandon their own personal beliefs, no matter how cherished or essential for their culture's survival.

Secular intellectuals such as Richard Dawkins, Sam Harris, and Daniel Dennett would no doubt have little problem with this. Dawkins, for instance, classified religious indoctrination as a form of child abuse (2006, 315–325). However convincing Dawkins's point may be — and there certainly is a lot to be said in favor of it — it ignores the fact that religion operates culturally as well as theologically and spiritually. Therefore, when intellectuals such as Drummond and Cates ask a community to forsake sacred traditions in the name of "science" or "progress" or (as for Lawrence and Lee) "art," there are damages to the cultural fabric that the intellectual community ignores or even deliberately exacerbates. Historically, Western civilization has been ever ready to use the motifs of "artistic," "religious," or "scientific" progress in order to attack a weaker culture or subculture. This, of course fits into the Nietzschean paradigm, since such intellectuals are concerned primarily with their own dominance, their own achievement of "overman" or "*ubermensch*" status, rather than with the survival of the community. As spiritual or materialist capitalists concerned primarily with gaining power for their pet ideologies, worldviews, or artistic and scientific theories, these intellectuals have neither patience nor respect for the cultural traditions that have united spiritual communities for hundreds of years.

But even if one comes at *Inherit the Wind* from a Dawkinsian point of view, Drummond and Cates's belief in the social ideal of progress and its correlation to great thinkers, is odd, since of all the ideas in the play this is the most at odds with Darwin. Rachel, Cate's girlfriend, exhibits the strangely Lamarckian character of Cates's and Drummond's thinking. Rachel tells Cates:

> A thought is like a child inside our body. It has to be born. If it dies inside you, part of you dies, too! Maybe what Mr. Darwin wrote is bad. I don't know. Bad or good, it doesn't make any difference. The ideas have to come out — like children. Some of 'em healthy as a bean plant, some sickly. I think the sickly ideas die mostly, don't you, Bert? [*ITW* 124–125].

Lawrence and Lee's casual use of sociobiological metaphors here is quite strange. The idea that progress is an "intended product" of Darwinian law has been largely discredited by modern Darwinians (Bowler 2003, 163). The use of ideological metaphors to convey biological ideas was not exactly a very sophisticated form of cultural communication at mid-century. It had given birth to Social Darwinism, eugenics, and Nazi race biology, none of which had much use for the ultimately anti-racist implications of evolutionary theory in its modern form. Indeed, for some fundamentalists, particularly those coming from the premillennialist tradition, the evolutionary "survival of the fittest" mentality of the German army during World War I was directly responsible for their opposition to evolutionary theory (Larson 1997, 35). Prominent eugenicists noted "a tie between antievolutionism and opposition to eugenics" (28). The rather inconvenient point that fundamentalists often had, by most moderns' standards, ethical if hardly scientific reasons for disputing evolutionary theory was completely lost on Lawrence and Lee. The fact that Darrow "claimed to understand modern biology but mixed up Darwinian, Lamarckian and mutation-theory concepts" (72) is expressed, but only through Drummond's similar ignorance in the play, an ignorance that the playwrights clearly share.

As typical fifties intellectuals, Lawrence and Lee put a high value on the mind and intellect, as the expressions of a higher state of evolutionary consciousness. "Sickly" ideas, "sickly" plays, "sickly" novels all die, while the healthy ones remain. This idea would be perfectly plausible, except that intelligence does not necessarily imply that a species or even an individual is better adapted to survive. There is no proof that rational ideas are more evolutionarily adaptive than non-rational ones; indeed, the success of religion, despite some of its rather obvious rational disadvantages as a survival mechanism, calls into question the whole glorification of intellect as a survival trait. And here, the equation of the artist-genius with the scientist-genius, as the bedrocks of spiritual bourgeoisie sanity against the fundamentalist proletariat, would seem even more inept, since whatever supposed survival advantages are offered by science, the only evolutionary advantages anyone has plausibly attributed to art is that through wasteful spending, the fit individual shows his or her genetic desirability as a mate (Dutton 2009, 155–162).

Nevertheless, Lawrence and Lee persist in depicting Cates and Drummond as destroyers of fundamentalists words, for the greater beauty to be found in the words of science and anti–McCarthyite art. Drummond tells Cates and Rachel, "You murder a wife, it isn't nearly as bad as murdering an old wives' tale. Kill one of their fairy-tale notions and they call down the wrath of God, Brady, and the state legislature" (*ITW* 50). Drummond, like many products of the late Victorian debates between science and religion, disvalues myth as an approach to truth, seeing "fairy tale notions" as being the product of religious demagogues like Brady and censorious government bodies, such as like state legislatures. Such simplistic black-and-white divisions between truth and error, myth and belief, highlight the essentially religious component of secular identity within *Inherit the Wind*. Secular characters' beliefs often have as little rational basis for them as the religious characters they oppose.

But more crucially, Lawrence and Lee's fascination with killing "fairy tales" ignores the essential myth-making identity of dramatists themselves. A play is nothing if not a facsimile of the real. By its nature it delights in artifice — in the fake moons and trees that Theron Ware so abhorred in religion. Lawrence and Lee deliberately create myth in *Inherit the Wind*, positioning the play in a timeless place: "'Not too long ago.' It might have been yesterday. It could be tomorrow" (*ITW* preface, n.p.). Yet their beloved Drummond, the symbol of liberty, reason, and intellect in the play, is himself a myth destroyer with little love for either the artistic greatness of scriptures, or those scriptures' abilities to convey, in spite of whatever errors might be in them, profound spiritual, ethical, and literary truths. By confining truth to simply the factual, Drummond (and by extension Lawrence and Lee) limit themselves to a rather impoverished vision of what constitutes a fulfilling intellectual or spiritual life.

Drummond's anti-mythic impulse obviously would conflict with one of the oldest of evangelically approved schools of aesthetic interpretation: the Tolkien-inspired mythopoeic school. What becomes significant about *Inherit the Wind* is that it represents the crucial transitional text when the non-evangelical work moves from being mainly a commentator on the myths of evangelical belief (as in *The Damnation of Theron Ware*, *Miss Lonelyhearts*, and *Go Tell It on the Mountain*) to taking an active interest in trying to kill off those same myths through the efforts of the artist-intellectual himself. After *Inherit the Wind*, films such as *Elmer Gantry* (1960) and *Privilege*, and novels such as *The Handmaid's Tale*, the *Parable* series, and the *Portofino* series all aspired to be the giant evangelical myth-killer; the persistence of evangelical belief in the midst of these (with the notable exception of *Privilege*) often rather unsophisticated critiques of evangelical culture speaks to a growing secular inability to successfully artistically confront evangelicalism without resorting either to clichéd stereotype or outright historical inaccuracies. Evangelicalism's increasing sophistication as a provider of a sustaining, if implausible, cultural mythos, one with many attractions in an increasingly uncertain world, ensured that few of the movement's critics accurately assessed its strengths. Even fewer non-evangelicals proved themselves conversant with the dangers that that culture posed, either to themselves or to evangelicalism itself.

For Lawrence and Lee, the problem with evangelical belief is that it is anti-intellectual, and therefore deeply opposed to the arts. Drummond neatly encapsulates this viewpoint when he angrily protests to Bryan, "All I want is to prevent the clock-stoppers from dumping a load of medieval nonsense into the United States Constitution" (*ITW* 47). For Drummond (and even more for the H.L. Mencken stand-in, Hornbeck), evangelicalism is the bad form of "medievalism," one that produces Luddite clock-stoppers; by contrast the arts and sciences produce that quintessential medieval product of aesthetic grace, the "cathedral." While science is truth, evangelicalism is fairy tales, and nonsense; being nonsensical, it therefore loses value in an increasingly secularized, rational society ordered by the industrialized clock motions of capitalists, both spiritual and economic. Such an appeal, of course, is perfectly understandable in the context of the time in which *Inherit the Wind* was produced, when paranoid McCarthyite fears were giving a very bad name to the emotional side of human nature, particularly the tendency of the human species to engage in witch hunts and heresy-huntings at the slightest whim.

The problem with this approach is that neither evangelicalism nor fundamentalism were anti-rational. Rather, they were built on the Common

Sense philosophy of the Scottish Enlightenment (Marsden 2006, 14–17, Detwiler 1999, 31). As George Marsden points out, Common Sense philosophy "continued to appeal to Americans into the nineteenth century ... because it provided a firm foundation for a scientific approach to reality." Common Sense philosophy above all "provided a rock upon which to build this [science's] empirical structure" (Marsden 2006, 15). Insofar as the fundamentalists of the twenties (and the fifties) engaged in proof-texting practices, they were following a system that to them was as grounded in solid philosophical foundations as the most empirically rigorous science. The key idea in this theological system, based on Baconian inductive method, was that

> the Bible provides categories and standards to classify facts.... God created the world and ... revealed [Himself and his divine order] to humans in the Bible. Humans apply these categories and classifications to the data. Disagreements about particular facts disappear when we see the data within the context of God's creation and plan for humanity. Those who do not observe the data using ... divine categories simply misperceive the world [Detwiler 91].

Therefore insofar as Lawrence and Lee diagnosis fundamentalism as anti-intellectual, they misrepresent the essential theological dilemma fundamentalism faced in the twenties and continues to face today: the problem is not that fundamentalism is irrational, but that it is rational — actually far too rational — in the wrong way. While non-fundamentalist evangelical traditions have to a limited extent escaped getting hung up on issues such as biblical proof-texting and the consequent devotion to rationalism, fundamentalism remains trapped within an inductive trap of its own making. What Lawrence and Lee saw was not the birth of an old irrationalism, but the final death of an older rationalist form as a scientifically respectable way of interpreting scientific truth. A greater attention to why the clocks were stopping might have allowed Lawrence and Lee to more accurately predict "what time it was" in fundamentalism; such predictions, in the fifties, were sorely needed.

One cannot conclude discussing *Inherit the Wind*'s view of the arts without at least mentioning the character who most closely resembles an artist: The epigram-wielding Hornbeck. Hornbeck is a quite ambiguous character in the text; Drummond claims to dislike him (*ITW* 127), yet if the reader is supposed to as well, Lawrence and Lee make such dislike a hard sell. Most of the play's brilliant lines — the quips for which the play is long remembered after being read or seen — derive from Hornbeck: "Cynical? That's my fascination. I do hateful things, for which people love me, and lovable things for which they hate me. I am a friend of enemies, the enemy of friends" (33). Hornbeck realizes that his role as a reporter makes him essentially a paradox in contemporary America, someone who is loved and detested equally —

sometimes causing both reactions within one individual. Certainly the younger sympathetic characters in the play, Cates and Rachel, have ambivalent feelings about Hornbeck, never quite sure what to make of him. Hornbeck's cynicism within the play becomes a corroding influence, laying bare the lack of civility that exists between the secular left and the religious right. But by portraying the left wing as having far more sympathetic individuals on its side — Nietzschean science-loving heroes such as Cates and Drummond — while denying such protagonists to the religious right, Lawrence and Lee clearly imply which side of the culture wars they fault for the conflict.

Nevertheless, Hornbeck — and the rabid atheistic fanaticism that he represents — do come in from a beating from Drummond, who charges that Hornbeck "never pushed a noun against a verb except to blow up something" (*ITW* 127). Hornbeck's flaw as a writer, a flaw that Lawrence and Lee hope not to share in, is to use words as weapons, rather than tools of healing. For Hornbeck, the use of language, which is after all his art, is an essentially aggressive act. Unlike Drummond, his linguistic usage lacks pity or compassion. While Drummond mourns the death of Brady, Hornbeck observes, "Let us leave the lamentations to the illiterate! Why should we weep for him? He cried enough for himself" (125). Lawrence and Lee warn that a left-wing rhetoric divorced from the kind-hearted sympathy of Cates, Rachel, and Drummond can degenerate into the kind of pseudo-racist, anti–Semitic bilge that characterized H.L. Mencken, the model on which Hornbeck is based.

What then is the ultimate meaning of the last stage direction, in which Drummond puts the Bible and *The Origin of Species* side by side (*ITW* 129)? As has been suggested, part of that act represents a desire to placate liberal, probably mainline Protestant, Americans, the quintessential spiritual bourgeoisie, by creating a place for a unified culture, one that devalues the Bible as factual truth but values it as poetry. At another level, however, the act symbolizes the union of the scientific with the literary. Poetry, in the modern era, must be united to a rational mission, a mission that can only be exemplified by rigorous adherence to Darwinian ideas. Insofar as one does not follow the path of Darwin, one ceases to be an intellectual. Drummond laments that Brady looked "for God too high up and too far away" (128). For the modern artist, with God off his throne, humanity must take His place. Art becomes the substitute for religion, and art itself becomes the force of the spiritual capitalists that promises a bright utopian future. Lawrence and Lee are aware of the inadequacy of humanity for this exalted position. Even Rachel does not want to think that humanity came from "apes" (124); with humanity's anthropocentrism gone, the road to the hilltop where the God Nietzschean sits will be a hard one. But that road will not be followed if religious believers do not forsake religion for the sciences and the arts.

Inherit the Wind's continued vitality as a culturally popular ur-text concerning evangelicalism speaks to the enduring power of stark late-nineteenth-century divisions between science and religion, divisions popularized by vigorous agnostics such as T.H. Huxley (Larson 1997, 17, 18, 21). It is unlikely that such divisions will ever be fully overturned; both religious believers and non-religious scientists sees the "Othered" community that "opposes" them as being emblematic of everything that is wrong with contemporary society. Yet it is surely ironic that perhaps the most famous text on evangelical belief, the text that puts so much value on scientific truth versus religious lies, dispenses so liberally with any attempt at historical verisimilitude. The real-life Scopes was never in danger at all. There is some doubt as to whether he even actually taught evolution. His case was put up as a test trial by the ACLU and was not even instigated by creationists (Ruse 2000, 112). William Jennings Bryan, far from asking that Scopes be penalized for his crimes (as in the play), opposed attaching financial penalties to anti-evolution laws (*ITW* 116; Larson 1997, 242). The play's vision of Bryan, though true enough in its depiction of his fanatically held religious beliefs, gives short shrift to his radically left-wing politics, which deeply alienated him from the right-wing politicos of his day (Larson 1997, 37–41).

Of course art is not about verisimilitude, any more than religion is simply about facts. Nor do Lawrence and Lee claim to portray history accurately (*ITW*, preface, n.p.). In the final analysis, *Inherit the Wind* and fundamentalist interpretations of both that text and the Scopes Trial itself are engaged in the same mythic reconstruction of the past. But these mythic reconstructions, so powerful within their originating communities, mean little to those who come from an opposing viewpoint. In the battle over history, what matters is not truth, but what narrative one happens to prefer. This is a "truth" that the non-evangelical community and evangelicals continue to fail to recognize.

Elmer Gantry *in Color: The Hypocrite Rube on the Silver Screen*

Like *Inherit the Wind*, the film version of *Elmer Gantry* represents a transitional piece in American literature. Like that work, the film seeks to account for contemporary cultural conflicts by casting revivalist religion as an enemy. The opening to the film proclaims: "We believe that certain aspects of Revivalism can bear examination — that the conduct of some revivalists makes a mockery of the traditional beliefs and practices of organized Christianity.... We believe that everyone has a right to worship according to his conscience but — Freedom of Religion is not license to abuse the faith of the people" (*Elmer Gantry*). Unlike the courageous original novel, which targeted organized religion in general, including mainline Protestantism, Catholicism, evangelicalism, and New Thought, the film settles for a rather standard mainline Protestant narrative of Revivalist Christianity, complete with faith healing, barking evangelical believers, and courageous moderate pastors fighting off the clichéd truisms of Elmer Gantry and Sharon Falconer. "Examination of revivalism" is probably too strong a term for what goes on in *Elmer Gantry*; the film's depiction of evangelicalism is closer to the surface-level depictions of ignorant rural hicks in *Inherit the Wind* than to the detailed sociological analysis of the causes of evangelical belief that occurs in the original novel. The faith of revivalists—evangelical faith—becomes a "license" to abuse the more "honest" and staid beliefs of mainline, Catholic and older evangelical churches. Revivalism, being indecorous, represents a faith that is no longer appropriate for moderns.

When *Elmer Gantry* came out in 1960, it was enormously successful, winning three Oscars, including a Best Oscar for Burt Lancaster's depiction of Elmer Gantry (Los Angeles Times 2009). The film continues to be critically well received, with an extremely high rating of 96 percent on Rotten Tomatoes, one of the premier Internet film review sites (Flixter, Inc. [2012]). As a cultural artifact, it represents the final collapse of reserve regarding depictions of evangelical culture. Mainstream literary depictions of evangelicalism during the sixties, such as *At Play in the Fields of Our Lord* (1965), for the first time portrayed evangelicalism and religion almost entirely in a negative light. Such portrayals walked hand-in-hand with the questioning of religious fundamentalism found in the *Dune* series, and gave way to a generalized critique of the "sins" of all Christianity by the late sixties, most powerfully dramatized in British films like *Privilege*, *The Devils*, and *The Wicker Man*. While American filmmakers and novelists could never drum up quite the level of anti–establishment anger (nor aesthetic rigor) found in Watkins's *Privilege* or Ken Russell's *The Devils*, they did contribute *The Planet of the Apes* series to contemporary religious dialogue, a series that was at once irreverent and profound in its coopting of evangelical cultural idioms for ends of which the evangelical community did not approve. Therefore, the long-term cultural effects of the film *Elmer Gantry*, along with the film version of *Inherit the Wind* (which opened the same year), opened up a space for dialogue about religion that had been unavailable in the fifties. Evangelicals, unfortunately, were not admitted into this space, and the attempts to separate evangelicals from the American religious mainstream can be seen in the film's stark division of religion between revivalists and true believers.

What is the place of the artist in this new, more liberal world? *Elmer Gantry* hints at the changing role of the artist-intellectual by agreeing, in more modest terms, with the analysis of *Inherit the Wind*: The artist is the champion of society, the defender of the spiritual bourgeois community against irrational evangelical belief. In *Elmer Gantry*, the artist-intellectual is represented by Jim Lefferts, who instead of being a tired atheist (as in the original novel) is an intrepid reporter. Elmer and Jim, as in the novel, have a complicated relationship. Several times, Elmer almost ruins Jim's career, yet Jim, being the big-hearted atheist he is, forgives Elmer. Elmer says of Jim that he is "brilliant and witty. Uses words like a stiletto. He learned his trade from Mencken and Ingersoll, Sinclair Lewis, a lot of other atheists" (*Elmer Gantry*). The writer, for Elmer, is in fundamental opposition to the revivalist. He learns his trade from atheists; the writer with media pull, such as Jim, is even more dangerous, because he can spread anti-evangelical words like assassins' blades into the heart of every potential believer. The media threatens, by its power, to get into the same racket as the church, and potentially be as effective. Elmer's comments here are unintentionally revealing, for if contemporary popular culture has any analogical reference point outside of its own domains, it is religion. With many popular culture followers taking these phenomena as seriously (or semi-seriously) as they take religion, the power of religion has been lessened.[4] The transition of cultural authority from religion to mass media marks a site of both anxiety and tension. On one hand, *Elmer Gantry* praises those in the arts and mass media who fight for a more enlightened, less anti-intellectual culture. Yet the hucksterism, side-show nature of the revivalism in *Elmer Gantry* suggests that the filmmakers were aware of the dangerous power that revivalistic religion could have when united to mass media tools such as radio and television.

Jim, as the champion of a new, emboldened secularism that is making common cause with mainline Protestants against the evangelical hordes, sees revivalism as a degradation of the essential role of the preacher:

> What is a revival? Is it a church? Is it a religion? Or is it a circus side show, complete with freaks, magic, and rabble-rousing? Why does a revival attract thousands? To see a miracle, to be saved from a lifetime of sin in five minutes? To be entertained, cured, and cuddled in quick, painless salvation? We're a fertile land for corn, beans ... rumble-seat sex and revivalism [*Elmer Gantry*].

Jim's analysis of evangelical religion is not all that different from Sister Soulsby's in *The Damnation of Theron Ware*. Evangelicalism is essentially a drama made manifest, complete with fake scenery, fake lights, and very fake actors. But whereas Soulsby wants to improve the quality of the performance so that people can, in fact, be "cured" and "cuddled," Lefferts sees such "easy believism" as a cheapening of religious faith. For Jim the power of the Bible is that it is a book of "beautiful poetry and wisdom" (*Elmer Gantry*). But by reducing the scriptures to simply a circus side-show performance, one takes out of religion both its greatest religious and aesthetic possibilities. The union of religion with dramatic performance is something that obviously deeply disturbed Richard Brooks, the talented screenwriter and director who adapted *Elmer Gantry* to the silver screen. The minister and actor have too much in common. Both claim to be artists yet are engaged in an action that is fundamentally salesmanship — to sell a religion, or a movie. Both pretend to be what they are not, in order to achieve their aims. Thus, for both minister and actor, artifice is the nature of what they do; they cannot help but be what they are not. Religion demands of pastors and priests that they be more than any being can possibly be, living representatives of God on Earth. Acting makes similar demands, except that for actors, the more wild their simulacraic representation of life is, the more their audiences seem to eat it up. Society's seeming double standard in accepting the representational aspects of the dramatic while denying the representational elements of preaching is clearly evident to Brooks. But whereas art, for Lefferts (and for Brooks) does not typically descend into rabble-rousing, preaching very much can.

Yet Jim's analysis of what constitutes true religion shows the bias of a generation raised to believe in the supremacy of mainline, seminary-educated theology. He remarks that Sharon has no degree from any theological institution or sanction from any church (*Elmer Gantry*). Sharon attempts to justify herself by pointing out that "neither Peter or Paul or any of the other apostles" had such training. Lefferts counters:

> They ... lived with the Son of God, were taught by him.... What gives you the right to speak for God?... How did you get his approval?... Did God speak to you personally?... Where in the New Testament does it say that God spoke to anyone except His Son? But it does say in the First Corinthians "Let your women keep silence in the churches" ... "It is a shame for women to speak in the church" [*Elmer Gantry*].

Significantly, Lefferts appeals to traditional hierarchical distinctions between differing groups of Christians to mark out what constitutes theological and cultural superiority. Mainline and secular ideas are superior because they come from professional seminaries and respected churches, which are not likely to promote any sort of populist or culturally subversive theology, whatever their claims to the contrary. By contrast, the ideas of revivalists are transmitted through those who are not theologically educated — presumably of a lower social class — and through women, people long denied agency in American church life. Thus revivalism appeals to what is most indecorous for mainline denominations, denominations that were at the time of the filming of *Elmer Gantry* just beginning to struggle over issues such as female ordination and sexism in the Bible. Ironically, revivalism, particularly the Pentecostal revivalism that Sharon seems to represent, is simply too progressive for a man like Jim Lefferts, still trapped in mid-twenties assumptions about gender difference. These lines significantly do not appear in the original novel; it is doubtful that Sinclair Lewis, a progressive, if cynical, promoter of women's rights in novels such as *Main Street* and *Anne Vickers* (1933), would have ever uttered them. Instead, it is the film industry and *not evangelical religion* that panders to popular cultural prejudices in its depiction of the "hysterical female revivalist"; Pentecostal preachers, the spiritual proletariat in its most simple and oppressed form, are in this case ironically the champions of the downtrodden, while the left-wing Brooks is anything but.

But in a wider sense, Jim's role as cultural arbitrator of what constitutes true religion became a role that the mass media, the artistic establishment, and art-loving academics increasingly took on as the century progressed, as the power of spiritual capitalism shifted to a new spiritual bourgeois class, partly mainline Protestant and partly secular. Jim assumes that it is his role to be the protector of the public peace, to keep it safe from the soiled religion of the revivalists. He laments that there is "not a law in any state of the union, protecting the public from the hysterical onslaught of revivalists" (*Elmer Gantry*). It would be difficult to conceive how such a law could be formulated without infringing on the First Amendment rights of reporters such as Lefferts, or filmwriters such as his creator, Richard Brooks. That does not, of course, prevent Brooks from clouding the issue. Instead of provoking a debate on how religious traditions are defined by issues of class and gender, Brooks merely accepts the dominant assumptions of the mainline Protestant church, with its anti-populist, (then) anti–Charismatic, and anti-agrarian prejudices. Even the depictions of Sharon's audiences, which could be charitably described as lower working class, and less charitably described as "hicks" or "rednecks," speak to the divide Hollywood wanted to create between the establishment church (mainline Protestantism and sometimes Catholicism) with the outsider church (evangelicals). But by casting evangelicals as outsiders, Hollywood motivated evangelicals to create their own alternative film and television industry, a decision that had long-term consequences in the culture war.

The film's only (belated) awareness of differing class conditions occurs when Elmer tells a fellow socially respectable revivalist, Bill Morgan, "You're a five dollar textbook. Me, I'm a two-cent tabloid newspaper. You're too good for the people. I am the people. Sure I'm common — just like most people" (*Elmer Gantry*). Yet the use of Lefferts, as well as several mainline pastors, as cultural arbitrators of what is and is not respectable religion clearly notes that in religion, as in all things artistic, the "common person" is mocked even as he is praised. Lefferts points out the devastating effect rich evangelists have over their flock, in which they are allowed to "elicit money without accounting for how it is used" (*Elmer Gantry*). This analysis is confirmed by another pastor who argues, "Religion is not a business and revivalism is not a religion" (*Elmer Gantry*). Religion is something that is too high and holy—too upper class, in fact—to be divorced from the everyday sordid concerns of regular common people, concerns that often deal with cash. One need not be a sociologist to note the enormous success that business-oriented Christianity has had with the common people for many years. Both black and white evangelicals flocked to Norman Vincent Peale, to Joel Olsteen, and more recently to more multicultural purveyors of the faith of the wallet such as T.D. Jakes, to obtain both spiritual and material benefits. The fact that the theological groups most opposed to prosperity preaching tend to be, not coincidentally, the most prosperous—such as mainline Protestants and Reformed Christians (among evangelicals) (Pew Research Center 2007)—speaks to how divorced both more tradition-bound theological groups and the Hollywood arts community are from the everyday experience of the poor, who long for a quick fix to pervasive social imbalances that the spiritual bourgeoisie themselves create. If Elmer is vulgar, it is only because richer men like Lefferts and Bill Morgan have made him so.

Conclusion

With the widespread success of the film versions of *Inherit the Wind* and *Elmer Gantry*, depictions of religion were finally freed from the cultural conservatism that dominated popular culture in the inter-war and early Cold War period. As a result, many struggling novelists in popular genres such as science fiction and horror were now able to explore serious theological themes without fear of running afoul of the censors. This produced an explosion of great religious works in these genres, ranging from *The Exorcist* (1973), *Carrie* (1976), *Rosemary's Baby* (1968), and *The Wicker Man* in horror to *Planet of the Apes*, *Privilege*, and the *Dune* series in science fiction. As humanity moved to an unknown technological future, its depictions of religion now took on a fantastic tinge; yet this fantasy, ironically, included some of the most profound ruminations on religious belief that the postmodern world would ever give society. The Age of the Fantastic had begun.

5

The Age of Fantasy

Between 1960 and 1984, the evangelical movement underwent great changes, changes that were inspired in part by the intellectual elite of the movement, with a little prodding from neo-conservatives. Evangelicals were shocked by the social upheavel of the sixties, particularly the election of Catholic president John F. Kennedy, the growth and power of the civil rights movement, the banning of prayer in the public schools (W. Martin 2005, 47–54, 78–79, 85–86), and the growth of the counterculture. Some evangelicals retreated inward, prophesying apocalyptic scenarios based on premillennial dispensationalist theology (Hal Lindsay being merely the most prominent example) (Boyer 1992, 6). But evangelicals at first did not know what to do with the counterculture or the New Left. Some evangelicals, such as Bill Bright, Norman Vincent Peale, and Billy Graham, made hesitating steps into the political mainstream: Bright led a semi-secret campaign to co-opt Berkeley's student left, Peale campaigned against John F. Kennedy, and Graham aligned himself with Nixon in his 1968 election campaign. But these steps were often halting; Graham, for instance, famously backtracked after the disastrous revelations of Watergate (W. Martin 2005, 52–54, 93–94, 97, 145–149).

It was the evangelical intellectual elite, most prominently Francis Schaeffer and Rousas Rushdoony, that prompted evangelicals to enter back into political involvement. Rushdoony gave the evangelical movement a "political theology," while Schaeffer gifted evangelicalism with a "Reformed theology of culture" (Detwiler 1999, 15–16). Rushdoony's influence has tended to be overstated in recent years because of his founding of the Reconstructionist movement, which supports a "theonomic order" which would "make homosexuality, adultery, blasphemy ... and incorrigible behavior by disobedient children subject to the death penalty"; few evangelicals would openly support Rushdoony, and it is doubtful that he has more than fractional support among his Reformed base, let alone among evangelicals as a whole. However, it cannot be denied that Rushdoony powerfully influenced such major evangelical leaders as D. James Kennedy and Pat Robertson, both of whom interviewed him on their television programs; some of Pat Robertson's nineties theological and political moves can clearly be traced to Reconstructionist influences (W. Martin 2005, 353–354).

Schaeffer, however, was the dominant intellectual influence in this period. Schaeffer's wide-ranging intellect encompassed film, art, theater, and government, and motivated evangelicals to engage with culture (W. Martin 2005, 159–160). Schaeffer's presuppositional ideology, when transferred to politics, led to an aggressive engagement with cultural issues such as abortion (Detwiler 1999, 159). By reawakening the evangelical intellect, Schaeffer paved the way for a host of evangelical thinkers, primarily from the Reformed tradition, to take up arms against secular culture, or in the milder cases, critique it: there was Jay Adams, who argued for an end to Christianity's uneasy truce with psychology (see Adams 1970, 1–10); Gary North, who argued for a new form of Reconstructionist economics (W. Martin 2005, 353; see also Franky Schaeffer 2007, 333–334); C. Everett Koop, who was the chief evangelical guru on the abortion issue, till he lost his credentials with the right for vocally supporting AIDS victims during the eighties (W. Martin 2005, 249–257); and Mark Noll and George Marsden, who created an evangelical historiographical tradition that quickly became as respectable as anything coming out of Harvard or Yale.

Thanks in part to Schaeffer's influence, Jerry Falwell decided to try to prompt the evangelical movement to engage in politics during the late seventies and early eighties (W. Martin 2005, 202–204). By the time the Age of Fantasy had ended, evangelicalism, still less fundamentalism, could not be seen as a relic of the cultural past. The movement instead was looked on by secular novelists such as Margaret Atwood with a degree of dread.

But in the Age of Fantasy, novelists and filmmakers still primarily saw the Christian right as a dead, decaying tradition that either must bend to the popular will or alternately cynically manipulate the masses to gain its power. Again, the artist character type played a prominent role in this cultural critique. The *Apes* series utilized the scientist-hero stand-in in a role quite analogous to that played in *Inherit the Wind*; however, the *Apes* series' ultimate rendering of fundamentalist belief was far more nuanced, even ironic, than *Inherit the Wind*. Many of the fundamentalist apes' critiques of human culture and human nature in that series paradoxically turn out to be true, while the glorified remnants of human technology, particularly the Doomsday Bomb in *Beneath the Planet of the Apes*, lead to destruction. In *Privilege*, the artist character type is used even more directly; the movie directly predicts the growth of a Christian culture industry that exploits mass media stars to further governmental and religious agendas. *Dune*, the most profound text on fundamentalist belief ever written, uses a fictional messiah on a fictional planet, to comment on how the basic teachings of religion, the mythopoeic creations of the messiahs themselves, become corrupted by their followers, so that what starts as theological and intellectual creativity soon becomes radicalized to support a conservative agenda. And *Stranger in a Strange Land*, though somewhat paving the way for the negative theocratic dystopias of the eighties, was also a penetrating analysis of the relationship between evangelicalism and creative artistry, as well as another commentary on messiahhood in our times.

Before turning to *Stranger in a Strange Land*, it should be noted how much the creative, intellect-expanding tenor of sixties culture affected depictions of evangelical belief, often in surprisingly positive rather than negative ways. The late sixties and early seventies saw a host of movies and novels within the science fiction, fantasy, and horror genres that dealt with religion, including *Rosemary's Baby* (1968), *The Exorcist* (1973), *The Devils, Clockwork Orange* (1971), *The Wicker Man*, *The Omen* (1976), and *Carrie* (1976) being only some of the most famous. Most of these films, particularly the British ones, were skeptical of traditional religious authority, yet this skepticism usually led to sympathy for their religious subjects, or at least to respectful, as opposed to mocking, derision. *The Wicker Man*, for instance, hauntingly evokes the downfall of Christianity in twentieth century Europe and its replacement with pagan philosophy (Grant 1997, 1012–1013); the end of the film, in which the devout Anglican Sergeant Howie is burned alive by the modern pagans, is one of the most powerful scenes in the history of horror cinema, topped only by the even more horrific torture scenes of Catholic rebel Urban Grandier in *The Devils*. *The Exorcist* (for Catholics) and *The Omen* (1976) (for both Catholics and Protestants) both deployed quite positive imagery of Christians battling against an increasingly secularized age. Thus, the skepticism of sixties and seventies authors and filmmakers, particularly among the British, led not to an immediate condemnation of evangelical belief, but to an engaged cultural analysis of the evangelical tradition.

Stranger Things Have Not Been Known to Happen: Robert Heinlein and the Birth of the Science Fiction Evangelical Messiah

Prominent French critic Michel Butor commented in 1967 that science fiction is "the normal form of mythology of our time" (Ellwood 1994, 309) As Robert Ellwood has pointed out, the science fiction sagas of *Star Trek* and *Star Wars* (as well as other series, including *Doctor Who* and *Perry Rhodan*) provided a unifying mythos for an age that had lost its ability to believe in the traditional myths of its past. Science fiction became a prominent, powerful genre in the sixties, speaking to an age that had grown weary of the misdeeds of previous mythic-religious systems. But even in an age of spiritual searching and science fiction success, Robert Heinlein's *Stranger in a Strange Land* was unique: it was a foundational text of the counterculture and served a nominal role in the formation of a new religion, the Church of All Worlds (91–94, 309). More infamously, Charles Manson modeled his cult of female worshippers around *Stranger in a Strange Land*. *Stranger in a Strange Land* had already by 1979 sold millions of copies, gone through at least 48 printings, and won a Hugo award for best science fiction novel (Franklin 1980, 127).

The success of the novel is not hard to account for. Like most of Heinlein's fiction, *Stranger in a Strange Land* is a fast paced, compelling read. It tells the story of Valentine Michael Smith (usually referred to as Michael or Mike), a messiah figure who returns from an alien-inhabited Mars at the order of the Martians. Much of the novel addresses, with great talent, the difficulty of understanding alien cultures' (both human and non-human) differing linguistic and thought patterns, as Michael desperately tries to come up with the words necessary to convince humans of their need to learn the Martian language (which may save humanity from destruction). Heinlein's mastery at conveying complex philosophical points to teens and young adults made him a kind of more modern Ayn Rand (Franklin 1980, 127). Heinlein, as a writer, tends to "induce very strong reactions," both positive and negative, which either way helps sell his novels. Politically he has been labeled everything from a conservative to an anarchist to a libertarian to a fascist (5). All these labels have some element of truth to them, but Heinlein was a writer who transcended any one philosophical school, even if the libertarian bent was perhaps the strongest element present in his writing.

Heinlein's somewhat complicated connection with the right wing of American politics makes his work an intriguing counterweight to the leftwing, non-evangelical analysis of evangelicalism. Heinlein's biographer William H. Patterson Jr. has characterized Heinlein as a "deeply spiritual person, but he [Heinlein] had never had any attraction to the creeds and dogmas of any church, Christian, Buddhist, Shinto, or Pagan — none of them." Heinlein's religion "was America" (Patterson 2010, 239). Heinlein's critique of evangelicalistic churches in *A Stranger in a Strange Land* is a somewhat more complicated critique of evangelical culture than was generally present in the fiction of his time, partly because of this conservatism, and partly because the evangelical stand-in religion in *A Stranger in a Strange Land*, the Fosterites, depart from the contemporary evangelical doctrine of the time in several important respects.

The Fosterite cult of *Stranger in a Strange Land* is characterized as non-Christian by H. Bruce Franklin in *Robert Heinlein: America as Science Fiction*

(1980), but as Franklin concedes, Fosterite belief is really a mere update of an older faith (134), which seems to be pretty clearly evangelical Christianity. As Franklin points out, Heinlein uncannily saw the rising up of non-Christian mass cults in the 1970s; what is less apparent is that there were Christian cults that also took on distinctly Fosterite overtones, most notoriously the Children of God, a movement derived from Christian teaching that used pedophilia and prostitution as religious practices (Niebuhr 1993, Kaye 2007, Goodstein 2005). Patterson has noted that Heinlein objected to the theatricalization of religion, particularly the "monkey antics" of some of the religious teachers of his day (antics for which evangelicals were famous) (Patterson 2010, 238). Significantly, H. Bruce Franklin has pointed out the essential carnivalistic nature of Fosterite revivalism. As Franklin observes, "Instead of denouncing the commercialism of their time, the Fosterites wallow in it as their element, interspersing their hymns with door prizes and commercials" (1980, 135). Clearly, therefore, for Heinlein, a central problem with contemporary religious practice was that it had turned religious worship into simply an effort in "aesthetic appreciation" rather than in meaningful belief (Patterson 2010, 238). Spirituality, for Heinlein, could work in tandem with aesthetics, but it could not be replaced by aesthetic practice. Fosterite religion "pieced together time worn tricks, gave them a new paint job, and were in business.... Hitler started with less and all he peddled was hate" (Heinlein 1961 [hereafter cited as *SSL*], 256); Reverend Foster, founder of the Fosterite faith, had "an instinct for the pulse of his times stronger than that of a skilled carnie sizing up a mark" (*SSL* 289). For the Fosterites, religion was about product promotion as much as it was about saving souls—but the product being sold is happiness, a life free from "guilt and fear" (256). Though outside the church there is sin, practically any act, from church gambling to sex orgies, is permissible within the church itself. Heinlein, with a keen eye on American evangelical religion (indeed American religion in general), saw that it was evolving from a "God-oriented" religion to a "me-oriented" belief system. For churches to survive in the new religious marketplace, they would have to adapt themselves to the egotistic gospel of the sixties and seventies, with its emphasis on individualism and self-expression.

Though only a few evangelical groups made as direct a change as the Fosterites, since the publication of *Stranger in a Strange Land*, many churches have begun loosening rules on female "dress codes," rock music (previously deemed too sensual), and other minor markers of supposed non-Christian identity, such as hair length. The casino-like atmosphere of the Fosterite church, complete with its own slot machines (*SSL* 243–244, 257), is very much like the entertainment-based model of church worship that has been promoted by such evangelical luminaries as Bill Hybels and Rick Warren. For

Heinlein, religion is many things, but the essentially entertaining nature of Fosterite services, though not in itself wrong, tends to contribute to a kind of emotionalism that makes "monkey tricks" inevitable.

In Heinlein's eyes, religion as solely an aesthetic experience has a falseness about it, because ultimately it is built on emotion rather than thought. Mike's religious movement, the Church of All Worlds, is described by one of his followers as "a church in every legal and moral sense. But we're not trying to bring people to God; that's a contradiction, you can't say it in Martian. We're not trying to save souls, souls can't be lost. We're not trying to get people to have faith, what we offer is not faith but truth — truth they can check. Truth for here-and-now" (*SSL* 347). For the Church of All Worlds, religion is about truth, primarily. Truth is found through rationality, through the learning of the Martian language (403) and is a construct interpreted through the linguistic context in which it is operant. For Mike's followers, the only means of obtaining truth is to learn the language in which true things can be told. The evangelical faith of the Fosterites fails in this regard because, though it shares some of the ritual of the Church of All Worlds, it lacks the linguistic logic of that religious body. The concepts of the Church of All Worlds can't "be thought about without the [Martian] language" (403), and the evangelical Fosterites lack the language of rationality, of control over science and matter that are necessary for an intellectual, respectable religion, and thus must resort to theatricality to gain converts.

In many ways, then, Heinlein's critique bears similarity to Sinclair Lewis's analysis of evangelicalism's essentially anti-intellectual nature, a point later also made in *Inherit the Wind*. But Heinlein, like many science fiction authors, is subtler in both his condemnation of evangelical religion and his analysis of its spiritual problems. Unlike Lewis, for instance, Heinlein envisioned evangelicalism evolving from an overly sexually repressive religious movement to an ardently eroticized one. Today there is some evidence that this may indeed happen, with a booming evangelical sex toy industry and Christian organizations such as XXX Church and JC's Girls all promoting a more liberated, though not by evangelical standards immoral, form of Christian sexuality (*Missionary Positions*; *Pussycat Preacher*; Radosh 2008, 272).

Like Lewis, Heinlein detests the theatricality of the evangelical church; unlike Lewis, however, who only subtly took on evangelicalism's modernist and postmodernist "opponents" (speaking in Schaefferian terms here, not my own), Heinlein was quite open in his hostility to these groups. Jubal Harshaw, Mike's human mentor, admits that most representations "of the Crucifixion are usually atrocious.... But a poor portrayal is as effective as a good one for most people. They don't see defects; they see a symbol which inspires their deepest emotions.... The crummiest plaster crucifix can evoke emotions in the human heart so strong that many have died for them. The artistry with which such a symbol is wrought is irrelevant" (*SSL* 324). For Heinlein, Christian art, despite its kitsch nature, is at least partially on a path to greatness, not because it itself is good, but because the story it represents is so emotionally powerful. Christian art, at its shallowest, calls up reservoirs of emotion that (to Heinlein) remain untouched by modern art. Modern art is "pseudo-intellectual masturbation ... it's up to the artist to use language that can be understood. Most of these jokers don't want to use language you and I can learn" (325–326). Christian art, including the theatricality of Fosteriteism, is ultimately superior to modern art because it is at least a form of communication. For Heinlein, modern art does not reach that level. It obfuscates and serves to set up a barrier between people. Jubal does not want to hide himself from his reader in a private language (326), but instead wishes to use his art to emotionally move his audience. Heinlein's critique of modernism as essentially an unmoving, cold system of thought would find echoes in, for instance, Francis Schaeffer's similar analysis of the works of Duchamp and John Cage in *How Should We Then Live?* in which Schaeffer testily (if truthfully enough) remarks "Duchamp realized that the absurdity of all things included the absurdity of art itself" (1976, 190, 196). Heinlein therefore would seem a somewhat unwilling ally of the Christian Right's artistic critique of modernism. For him, the problem with Fosterite (and Christian) artists is not that they try to move their audiences (which he preferred to the purportedly unmoving aspect of modernism), but that they do so for what are inherently religious purposes.

Yet Heinlein undercuts his critique of evangelical Fosterite beliefs in order to point out that even rational religion must sometimes use irrational means to maintain its ends. Ironically, Michael partly designs his church following the Fosterite model (*SSL* 289–294, 332, 340), especially in its Gnostic layers of leadership, with only a select few reaching the elite status, an inner circle within the inner circles (340). For Heinlein, a few will attain exalted spiritual status; the rest are marks, chumps (274), who are incapable of true enlightenment. As critic H. Bruce Franklin has pointed out, this is a common theme throughout Heinlein's works:

> either the elite saves the day ... or society succumbs to the ignorance and folly of the masses of common people. His [Heinlein's] concept of revolutionary social change imagines something created by an elite for the benefit of the people.... He seems incapable of believing that progressive social change could come through the development of the productive forces and consequent action by the exploited classes themselves [1980, 34].

For Heinlein, whether the Church of All Worlds or Fosteriteism wins, the masses will ultimately be compliant with their new masters. Their only decision is which master to follow. Heinlein's well known cynicism is evident here—for the grand master of science fiction, like many of the libertarian and conservative science fiction authors writing around his time (such as H. Beam Piper, John Campbell, Ayn Rand), the masses were meant to be led and had no agency of their own. Thus, for Heinlein, in a tragic sense, whether a variant of evangelicalism or non-evangelicalism emerges triumphant is immaterial for the common people. Either way, they will be believing in an illusion (since only the inner circle of Mike's religion gets the full truth) (*SSL* 340). The Church of All Worlds can only give its salvation to the intelligent, to those gifted enough to learn the Martian language (403); Fosteriteism, as well as the other evangelicalistic belief systems within *Stranger in a Strange Land*, relies on men being "too stupid to count sheep" (403). The Church of All Worlds, by contrast, promotes a gospel of intellectual exceptionalism.

In *Stranger in a Strange Land*, the borderline between faith and reason is a thin one. One of Mike's carnie friends remarks on Mike's magic act: "What else does a chump want? Mystery? He wants to think the world is a romantic place when it damn well ain't. That's your job ... only you ain't learned how. Shucks, son, the marks know your tricks are fake ... only they'd like to believe they're real, and it's up to you to help 'em. That's what you lack" (*SSL* 274). The irony, of course, is that all Mike's theatrics are real; he can levitate people and make them disappear. But it is his initial alienness, his very lack of ability to understand human artifice and illusion, that makes him such a poor magician, and which he must overcome if he is to be an effective messiah. The difference between Mike and Christ is that where miracles are the key to Christ's message, for Mike they are merely the means. He uses his theatrical skills to induce prospective members into the church and then determines which members are capable of learning the Martian language and the Gnostic truths it teaches (332, 339–340). Though Michael uses illusion and artistry to bring crowds in, the only way to truly enter the faith is by understanding truth. And truth, like everything else for Heinlein, is ultimately something that only the elite can own. In this, despite his common ideological affinities with evangelicals, he very much follows the ideological assumptions of the spiritual bourgeoisie of the sixties, especially mainline Protestants.

Heinlein's analysis of religion is perhaps less penetrating than many other science fiction writers, such as Frank Herbert. Yet Heinlein was ahead of his time in fully articulating the flip side of the repressed evangelical—the evangelical erotic. His vision of the arts was more reflectively skeptical than Lawrence and Lee's cheery-eyed optimism. But most importantly, Heinlein's Valentine Michael Smith set the standard for science fiction messiahs, a standard that a few years later was surpassed by a series of almost unfathomable intellectual depth: *Dune*.

Dune: *The Mythopoeic Messiah*

The core of the *Dune* series is the six novels written by Frank Herbert. The plot of the entire series as it evolved over nearly twenty years is too detailed to be related here. The core story of the first three novels—*Dune* (1965), *Dune Messiah* (1969), and *Children of Dune* (1976)—involves the rise of the Atriedes family from a marginal, hunted noble family who rule the planet Dune to the dominant political and religious force in the universe. Paul Atriedes (later referred to by the name of Muad'dib) starts as the naive heir to the ducal possessions of the Atriedes, then becomes a hunted opponent of the Harkonnen family who re-occupy Dune, before finally defeating the Harkonnens and the Corrino dynasty that backs them up. Paul defeats the Harkonnens through a number of factors, not least of which is that he recruits the local Fremen tribes to be his warrior followers. However, in the process he becomes a figure of religious veneration to them because he possesses the gift of prescience, the ability to literally see the future. Paul gains this prescient ability by his addiction to mélange (also referred to as "spice") a powerful substance that has many potential desirable side-effects, including long life and, more importantly, the ability to fold space with one's mind, allowing interstellar travel. Because spice is the only substance that allows interstellar travel (the use of computers is forbidden for both pragmatic and religious reasons), it is the most coveted product in the *Dune* universe. By re-taking Dune and threatening to destroy all the spice deposits on the planet, Paul Atriedes ends up holding the universe hostage by its reliance on one resource, and forces the other ruling houses of the Imperium to do his bidding.[1] The Fremen, who now see him as their messiah, then spread out in a galaxy-wide jihad that spreads both terror and Paul's religion throughout the universe. The later books of the series (*Children of Dune* onwards) portray the efforts of the descendants of Mua'dib, particularly his son Leto II, to undo the damage the jihad has done, while retaining some of the enhanced human abilities and philosophical wisdom of the Atriedes line.

The political makeup of the *Dune* universe is incredibly Byzantine, and it is impossible to describe all the forces at work in it. The most prominent political entities, however, are the Tleilaxu, a human race of hermaphrodites with the power to create gholas (resurrected human beings); the planet Ix, which controls much of the technology in the universe; the Bene Gesserit, an order of female mystics who mold much of the religious tradition of the *Dune* universe (though they are interrupted in this, to a certain extent, by both

Paul and his son Leto II); the Spacing Guild, which controls galactic travel and transport; and CHOAM (Combine Honnete Ober Advancer Mercantiles), a massive galactic corporation. The Bene Gesserit, the Guild, and the Tleilaxu tend to be the most important of these groups, though by the end of the final book in the original *Dune* series (*Chapterhouse Dune*), only the Bene Gesserit continue to maintain extensive power.

The *Dune* series represents one of the most phenomenally successful and critically acclaimed science fiction series of all time. By 1988, *Dune* had sold at least 10 million copies. Herbert's novels frequently formed a core part of science fiction courses. *Dune* won the Nebula and the Hugo awards, science fiction's most prized literary marks of distinction. In a 1975 *Locus* poll, *Dune* was voted the all-time best science fiction novel, and over the last thirty years, only Orson Scott Card's *Ender* series (1985-present) and Dan Simmons's gargantuan *Hyperion* saga (1989–1997) can claim to have even approached that height (Touponce 1988, 119).[2] *Dune* is frequently seen as the science fiction equivalent of the fantasy epic *The Lord of the Rings* (1954–1955), and though not as famous as that series, it is dearly beloved by a host of fans. The original *Dune* saga inspired a number of sequels and prequels by Frank Herbert's son Brian and sci-fi novelist Kevin Anderson, as well as a critically panned feature film version by David Lynch and two somewhat more well-regarded miniseries that covered the first three novels of the original book series.

The analysis here will focus on the similarities between the roles Paul Atriedes and Leto II take in their societies and the role of the mythopoeic sub-creators in Tolkien's aesthetic theory, who create "secondary worlds" much as God creates the primary world (Tolkien 1994a, 150, 161, 165). Paul Atriedes and Leto II represent the dangerous part of sub-creation, the potential for mythmakers—whether they be religious, political, or artistic—to become trapped by their own mythos. Tolkien saw the Gospels as "a fairy story, or a story of a larger kind which embraces all the essence of fairy stories…. But this story has entered History and the primary world…. The Birth of Christ is the eucatastrophe of Man's history" (179). Tolkien realized the artistic nature of the biblical story though he saw it as resulting from the story, not from the telling, since, as he put it, "the Author of the story was not the evangelists" (179). For Tolkien, therefore, the Gospels were a wonderful artwork because they were outpourings of God's manifest creativity, which had the even greater benefit of being "true myth" (i.e., actual history). That myth ultimately liberates humankind and allows God to be fully worshiped for who He is; there can be no final defeat of Christianity. *Dune*, by contrast, has a much darker view of the benefits of myth-creation. Leto II, writing for posterity, emphasizes this in his *Stolen Journals*, when he points out that his enormous god-like powers (which include being able to access

5. The Age of Fantasy

ancestral memories) allow him to both understand past myths and create new ones: "If you know all of your ancestors, you were a personal witness to the events which created the myths and religions of our past. Recognizing this you must think of me as a myth-maker" (Herbert 1981 [hereafter cited as *GED*, 247). For Herbert, this myth-making process is more a product of the believers than the god-figures themselves; people believe because they want to believe, not because a messiah-figure is forcing them to. As Leto II puts it, "Myth and reassuring lies are much easier to find and believe [than the truth]. If you find a truth, even a temporary one, it can demand that you make painful changes" (*GED* 128). Myth-believing, for Herbert, unlike Tolkien, takes relatively little effort. What does take an effort is being the bearer of a mythos, the messiah figure behind the fundamentalist (or in Tolkien's case, Catholic) jihad or crusade.[3]

The central religious dilemma of the first four *Dune* novels (*Dune*, *Dune Messiah*, *Children of Dune*, and *God Emperor of Dune*) is how prescience can create godhood, and thereby religious fundamentalism. Leto II, gifted with prescience, eventually finds "the ability to view our futures ... a bore. Even to be thought of as a god, as I certainly was, can become ultimately boring" (*GED* 43). For Leto II and even more for his father Paul, being worshipped is a trap. A god is faced with two equally absurd moral choices. The god can predetermine everything, and therefore hope for a perfect future; or a god can give people free will, and risk them misusing it. Paul tries to limit people's free will, in order to limit the carnage his jihad will inflict and prevent, for as long as possible, the death of his beloved concubine Chani and his consequent responsibility to assume an even more god-like power to prevent future disasters; Leto II works to undo the universe his father created, in order to give humanity a future in which humans "may create their futures from instant to instant" (Herbert 1976 [hereafter cited as *COD*], 349). Yet in order to achieve this ultimate free will for all people, Leto II has to direct human evolution with a nearly predeterministic rigor for some three millennia. Thus, though Leto does not believe in the myth he has created around himself, he is trapped by the consequences of both his own and his father's mythic creations.

In the first *Dune* novel, Paul judges, correctly, that the Fremen have a "simple practical religion." Yet his mother warns him, with prescience equal to his own, "Nothing about religion is simple" (Herbert 1965 [hereafter cited as *Dune*], 383). Paul is left with little choice, however, in encouraging this religion; he needs the support of the Fremen to overthrow the Corrino family from the imperial throne and defeat the Harkonnens. Expediency must take the place of ethics in the formation of religion. Thus, though Paul is far from callous towards his followers, he recognizes that if he is to stay alive, he will, as his mother puts it, "never cease indoctrinating" (383). The roots of Fremen fundamentalism are already there. The Fremen are dependent on a single, harsh environment that rewards quick judgments and cultural fanaticism. Paul's mother Jessica reflects that the Fremen "reacted sometimes like a single organism.... And the thought of coincidence never entered their minds" (393). This adherence to an almost *volkisch* cultural identity, combined with a tendency towards superstition, makes the Fremen ideal targets for religious manipulation, a manipulation that has in fact been going on for millennia even before Paul arrived on Dune.[4] The cultural fanaticism that Paul breeds troubles him; he hopes to avoid the jihad the Fremen will unleash by taking the throne (469).

Yet, Paul realizes that jihad is inevitable, that it is a net result of the need to "mingle" genes, so that "strong new mixtures survive" (*Dune* 482). While Paul's worshippers analyze him in terms of messianic prophecy, Paul analyzes their own culture with the disinterestedness of an evolutionary psychologist. He recognizes that jihads, crusades, and wars are often means of profoundly altering human cultural and biological goals. Fighting against such fanaticism is pointless. Paul feels helpless to change "any smallest bit of this [the jihad]. He had thought to oppose the jihad within himself, but the jihad would be. His legions would rage out from Arrakis even without him. The needed only the legend he had already become." Paul realizes that if he dies for the cause "they'll say I sacrificed myself that my spirit might lead them [the Fremen]. And if I live, they'll say nothing can oppose Muad'Dib" (482). Paul's internal mythology has caught up with him. Even if he martyrs himself to prevent the slaughter, that act will merely serve to whet the appetite of fanatics who seek to spread warfare and chaos throughout the galaxy. Martyrdom, for Paul, as for Christ, carries with it the ultimate negation of the message the martyr brings. Christ preached love and used terror only against the rich and the powerful; yet his message was later used (sometimes, regrettably, by evangelicals) for hate, and to oppress the poor. Paul, a cultured intellectual who wants to prevent as much suffering as he can, is turned into the worst tyrant in human history, totally against his will.

Tolkien had great faith in the Creator, and therefore great faith in both creators' and sub-creator myth-making process; this theo-aesthetic philosophy flowed naturally from Tolkien's Catholic theology, which emphasized both the power of the arts and the power God had to reflect himself through the arts. Herbert's characterization of Paul is a much more negative critique of the power of martyr figures to channel and direct the myths they create. For Tolkien, God's power over his own mythology was total. People could misinterpret or mistranslate the text, but the power of its central myth remained. Thus, Frodo is told: "Bilbo was meant to find the Rings.... In which case you also were meant to have it. And that may be an encouraging thought" (Tolkien 1954 [hereafter cited as *LOTR*], 54–55). Frodo's mission, like all Christian mythopoeic missions, is predestined by his sub-creator; the Creator presciently looks after his creations, as the sub-creator exercises prescience in his work, safely navigating his characters through whatever crises they may face, so that they do not have to encounter any of the ultimate moral dilemmas that their sub-creators must face on a daily basis.

The result, in Tolkien's case, is that many (though certainly not all) of his characters are flat creations, lacking literary power because their sub-creator has decided they should face no situation for which there are moral options open that are other than black and white. Christ's martyrdom's ultimate artistic meaning, in Tolkien, is that the sub-creator's role is imitative, rather than creative, and also totally manipulative, in that the author acts to remove moral choice from his believers (his readers) rather than provide them with issues of moral complexity. The sub-creator reflects nature, reflects God's creation and words, rather than seeking to challenge them. To challenge God's story leads "either to sadness or to wrath" (Tolkien 1994a, 179). In the hands of a genius like Tolkien, this reflection can take on profound meaning, as Tolkien elaborates on Miltonic themes of fall, grace, and redemption. But in the hands of lesser novelists, the prescience the author exercises is utilized solely to make sure there is no possible significant conflict in the heroes' or the Christian martyrs' lives, no illusion that the martyr-God may have felt any emotion that was not divine. In this, modern evangelical novelists (particularly if writing for the Association for Christian Retail market) closely resembles the Docetist heresy, in presenting a totally spiritual, inhuman mythmaker creator figure.

The "gods" of Herbert, by contrast, are clearly aware of their internal limitations and their lack of ability to control the historical forces they've unleashed. Paul realizes, as Tolkien and contemporary evangelicals sometimes do not, that a god can be limited by his believers, even if his power appears omnipotent. As Paul puts it, "I'm a figurehead. When godhead's given, that's the one thing the so-called god no longer controls" (Herbert 1969 [hereafter cited as *DM*], 38). The very act of worshipping a god limits that God's response to his creations. In Christianity, that limitation is supposedly somewhat voluntary. God contractually obligates himself both to ransom human beings from their sins and to forgo his wrath; in return he receives worship, but that worship is implicitly predicated on the assumption that God will bring salvation in return for love. Relatively few evangelicals could agree with theologians such as Samuel Hopkins or the Apostle Paul, who argued that human beings should be willing to be damned for the glory of God (Noll 2002, 132; see also Romans 9:3). Rather, martyrdom, and through it fundamentalism, are created on the implicit assumption that there will be some theological reward for the believer, but not for the god-figure, who being perfect, needs nothing from humanity.

Thus, for Herbert, fundamentalism is the one force that a god-figure cannot control, because that fanaticism is not based on his self-interest, but on his believers'. Paul realizes that a god is trapped by his own "oracle," an oracle that not only tells the future but "makes the future" (*DM* 40). Paul's desire to prevent humanity from succumbing to the forces of jihad, his frantic attempts to avoid the death of Chani and the responsibility of assuming a greater god-like power, trap him in the very prophetic net he wishes to avoid. By knowing the future, Paul ceases to be able to willfully change it. Instead, as he movingly puts it, "I meddled in all the possible futures I could create until, finally, they created me" (270). The necessity of creating his own godhood, of constantly predicting the future, ultimately means that Paul is more created by his creations than his creations (the Quizarate Fremen religion that follows in his wake) are molded by him. Herbert's critique of the Judeo-Christian mythos is extremely subtle here, but profound: the Christian God, in being omnipotent, omnipresent, unchanging, and omniscient, becomes a more limited creature than the human beings who follow him; at least those beings can change their minds. As Paul's prescience limits his options to just one ever-dreamed-for perfect future, so too is God the Father restrained by his inability to violate his own basic nature. A god, after all, can be no more and no less than that.

Paul's critique of the essential problem with fundamentalist belief relates directly to his understanding of prescience. Like Christ, Paul disappears from his world, only to return as a prophet.[5] Paul warns his former believers to "Abandon certainty! That's life's deepest command.... We're [humans are] a probe into the unknown, into the uncertain.... If certainty is knowing absolutely an absolute future, then that's only death disguised" (*COD* 226). The certainty of Fremen fundamentalists, which is supposed to bring them moral and spiritual comfort, instead traps them in the same hopeless quest for a way around the "oracles" that limit god himself. In thinking that they know the future, millenarian and Messianic fundamentalists limit themselves to a very narrow, predetermined future that allows them little flexibility to move beyond larger deterministic forces in society, such as evolution and late-stage capitalism. Societal roles become prescribed by religious leaders who further limit whatever capability either God or one's religion has to act outside predetermined cultural limits. What starts off as fable or legend, what evolved into myth, quickly becomes faith, then fact, then law.

Provocatively, Herbert comes to a conclusion diametrically opposed to Tolkien's. In the Tolkien mythos, men envied the gods; this is most graphically shown in the Numenoreans invasion of the Undying lands (*LOTR*, 1011–1013). That which is artificial — humanity — is always longing for the place of the higher total Reality, which is God. But Herbert reverses this process. Paul longs to "renounce my religion," the religion he has created. The god "never wanted to be a god.... I only wanted to disappear like a jewel of trace dew caught by the morning" (*DM* 38). The god-mythmaker wants intensely to be viewed as a human being, to be appreciated as a fellow sufferer in the universe and not idolatrized (one is tempted to say pathologized) as a deific figure; the last thing on his mind is the self-aggrandizement of gaining more followers.

Herbert hypothesizes that a god's life may ultimately be spiritually empty. Leto II makes this abundantly clear when he reflects, "Gods need take no responsibility for anything except genesis. Gods accept everything and thus accept nothing.... Gods do not need a spirit world" (*GED* 128). Since gods can only worship themselves, they have little motivation to develop a rich spiritual life. And it is precisely that inability to connect with their own internal spirit that makes the worship of them potentially dangerous. In worshiping divine, egotistical gods, one is likely to encourage divine, egotistical followers. Gods without a need for spirituality also have little need for morality. Thus they become divine dictators, shoring up the creeds of bureaucracies such as the Quizarate. And ironically, these creator beings cannot create myths rich enough for themselves to worship: the highest can create nothing higher, more exalted, or more creative than himself. Without imperfection, god becomes stagnant, unmoving, and himself prey to the fundamentalist mentality of his believers. Only in change, in a constant fleeing from certainty and deification, can a god hope to remain himself. For Herbert, true martyrdom is not god-become-man, but man-become-god. No human being deserves that awful fate.

A clear theme throughout the *Dune* books is that while gods may use violence to further their designs, they do not like violence done in their name. Alia, Paul's sister, remarks, "Paul's entire life was a struggle to escape the Jihad and its deification" (*DM* 277). Gods ultimately want to escape the violent definitions imposed on them by promoters of force and killing. And for Herbert, it is the certainty of such fundamentalist believers that differs them from their gods, gods who can comment, like Paul, "There are problems in this universe for which there are no answers.... Nothing" (270). For Paul and Leto, mythmakers of unsurpassed skill, human capability springs from creativity. For Leto, the only rule governing creativity "is the act of creation itself" (*COD* 381). While obviously badly flawed as an aesthetic philosophy, Leto's words hint at the essential difference between fundamentalists and their gods. Fundamentalists, for Herbert, are destroyers, destroyers who destroy in the name of creators. The irony of such a situation is clearly not lost on him.

Forty years after its publication, *Dune* remains the most complex treatment of fundamentalism (both Islamic and Christian) in all of literature; the only novel that even approaches its multi-layered depiction is Toni Morrison's *Paradise*. Herbert's work is strengthened by the slow, methodical way in which he depicts the rise of Fremen fundamentalism. There are occasional asides in the *Dune* series that evoke the more simplistic anti-fundamentalist views of authors such as Jerome Lawrence and Robert E. Lee, such as Leto II's pompous statement, not directly but implicitly targeted at fundamentalist and radical groups, that one should "never attempt to reason with people who know they are right" (*GED* 258). But the overall strength of the series is its union of the messianic and the mythopoeic. By showing how closely novelists both reflect and challenge the messianic ideal, Herbert laid the groundwork for future authors and filmmakers who wanted to tackle Christian evangelicalism and fundamentalism at a mythic level. These authors did so by dealing with some of evangelicalism's most powerful internal mythologies. Some of the works that would result, such as the film *The Rapture* and Brian Caldwell's novel *We All Fall Down*, followed *Dune* in being prescient warnings about the power cultural myth could have within the evangelical tradition. Though evangelical Christians should by no means feel obligated to accept all of Herbert's conclusions about fundamentalist faith, they would be fools not to heed his call to deepen their understanding of God's relationship to the narratives constructed around Him (or told by Him). Otherwise, the best parts of evangelical belief — the craziest parts of evangelical mythology, the wonderful irrationalities, the doubts peculiar to evangelicals and no one else — will cease to matter, and evangelical religion will fade into a desert — a desert every bit as grey and sandy as the dunes of Arrakis.

The Privilege of Being an Evangelical: Peter Watkins Takes the Christian Culture Industry to Task, Without Even Meaning To

Peter Watkins's *Privilege* is one of the most unknown works this study deals with, which is more a reflection on Watkins's politics than on the quality of the film. Watkins pioneered a "you-are-there" documentary style (Watkins 2008, 11) that was later copied, without his ethical vision, by reality television pioneers and filmmakers such as Daniel Minahan in *Series 7* (2001). Contrary to popular belief, smarter sixties filmmakers and writers were keenly aware of the blurring lines between media "life" and "real" life. Thirty years before *The Truman Show* (1998), for instance, Nigel Kneale wrote *The Year of the Sex Olympics* (1968), a dark BBC production about the use of pornographic reality shows being used to lull the masses into apathy.

Privilege represents a wave of radical British filmmaking that critiqued both British and American culture at the end of the sixties and the early seventies: other significant films in this same vein included the aforementioned *The Devils* and *The Wicker Man*, as well as *A Clockwork Orange* and Watkins's own *Punishment Park* (1971). Watkins's films, like Ken Russel's *The Devils*, have been suspiciously hard to find for the last forty years, despite the fact that few people in the cinematic establishment doubt their significance. Watkins's "mockumentary" *The War Game* was judged to be too horrifying for the BBC audience of its time; yet, ironically, when it was shown as a feature film, it won an Oscar (Gomez 1979, 45; *New York Times* 2012).

Watkins was a product of a middle-class education, complete with the typical British floggings, sparse diets, and bullying by other boys (Gomez 18). In 1956, he decided to become a filmmaker and over a ten-year period slowly honed his craft, before producing the television masterpiece *Culloden* (1964). *The War Game, Privilege, Punishment Park, The Gladiators* (1969), and *Edvard Munch* (1974) followed over the next decade. Watkins's films experimented with audience perception of film, as well the audience's perceptual viewpoint (particularly their identification with the camera). Watkins often forced the viewer to first identify with the camera, then question the role of the person behind the camera (Gomez 108–112). He therefore, more than most other filmmakers of the period, was concerned with promoting audience awareness of the media forms they were consuming. In his later work, Watkins stressed the power of the monoform, an overarching narrative or series of narratives that it fits to all forms of mass media consumption. These monoform narratives were an "internal language form (editing, narrative structure, etc.) used by TV and the commercial cinema to present their messages. It is the densely packed and rapidly edited barrage of images and sounds, the 'seamless' yet fragmented modular structure which we all know so well." The monoform is characterized by "techniques of.... montage, parallel action, cutting between long shots/close shots.... It also includes ... voice and sound effects, abrupt cutting for shock effect, emotion-arousing music saturating every scene, rhythmic dialogue patterns, and endlessly moving cameras" (Watkins 2007b). Watkins saw that youth culture was increasingly being commodified by an establishment that sought to use the rhetoric of celebrities, such as rock stars, to promote deeply conservative ends. Though Watkins had not yet developed the idea of the monoform at the time he made *Privilege*, the film's concerns with the manipulation of pop culture for conservative ends remain deeply tied to Watkins's ever-growing distrust of the mass audiovisual media (see Watkins 2007b for his use of that term).

The reason this study includes *Privilege*, despite its origins in Britain, is that it is an indictment of governmental and religious groups co-opting popular culture, and popular artists, for their ends; no other work, American or British, so successfully predicted the rise of the Christian culture industry, with its alternative rock and publishing venues, as did *Privilege*. That the film did so totally accidentally is beside the point; indeed, because Watkins's main concern is less about butchering religion and more about noting government manipulation of pop and youth culture through the use of celebrity, his work has a contemporary relevance about evangelicalism that no American work from this period, save *Dune*, can match.

The protagonist of the film is Steven Shorter, a British rock star whose popularity eclipses that of the Beatles. Played by Paul Jones, himself a British pop star who would later convert to evangelical Christianity (Cummings 2010), Shorter starts out as a symbol of youthful rebellion, a rebellion that the government is carefully manipulating for its own ends. Eventually, the government decides to carefully stage a "conversion" of Shorter so that the youthful rebellion he promoted will be changed into "fruitful" conformity (*Privilege*). Shorter does as he is commanded, but eventually timidly rebels against the mass media image of converted Christian singer that has been forced on him. His rebellion merely provokes the public to turn on him; at the end of the film, he is mobbed by an angry crowd as he tries to make a public statement of apology. The public had known what it had wanted and it no longer wants Steven.

Steven Shorter can be seen as emblematic of an artistic community that finds itself increasingly manipulated by an evangelical union with conservative politicians and economic leaders. At the beginning of the film this is not immediately apparent to the audience. After a brief prologue establishing Steven's popularity, the audience's first introduction to Steven is at an extremely violent (for the time) rock show, in which Steven is locked up, cuffed, and beaten to symbolize his rebel image. Steven then sings to the crowd. His music aligns him with the Nietzschean artist-hero seen in *Inherit the Wind*, while his nearly god-like popularity also gives him the messianic qualities of Paul Atriedes in *Dune*. But Watkins is considerably more skeptical of the Nietzschean ideal than Lawrence and Lee. One should note how carefully the lyrics of his song, "Set Me Free," are constructed to convey a sense of apathy and helplessness to the young. Shorter's soul "is broken," as his corporate, religious, and governmental backers want his young audience to feel; he promises freedom (metaphorically) to his audience, according to the song, yet the path to freedom, we later find, is straight through a union of governmental, corporate, and religious fascists. And even here, through the violence of Steven's show, his lyrics imply that he longs for a salvation that he cannot gain; a salvation without which he has no possibility of "liberty." Steven's lyrics encourage the youth of this near-future Britain to forsake the road of revenge and accept the "helping hand" of ideological state apparatuses, as well as government intervention, for their intellectual sustenance, rather than rely on their own native intelligence (*Privilege*).

Watkins makes it clear that the government, far from hating violent media forms, sees them as allies in their fight against political rebellion. The narrator of the film tells the viewers, as they see Steven's fans mobbing the "cops" who engage in the mock-real beatings of Steven at his concert, "There is now a coalition government in Britain, which has recently asked all entertainment agencies to usefully divert the violence of youth. Keep them happy, off the streets, and out of politics" (*Privilege*). The British government in *Privilege* realizes that youth violence can most directly be diverted not by condemning youth art forms—a then-common practice in the sixties—but by corporatizing them and using them as a means to encourage devotion to British financial, religious and governmental interests. The smashing of guitars, the screaming of *The Who* or *The Beatles*, the faux rebellious lyrics of singers ranging from David Bowie to Eminem are not, in Watkins' estimation, symptomatic of an escape from the corporate, but of succumbing to it. Nor is this really the artists' fault; many of these artists (one thinks here of Bowie or *Rage Against the Machine* in particular) fight to break the corporate hold over their style; ultimately, however, as artists within a capitalist system, such rebellion is futile, even for Watkins himself. By pointing out this media manipulation of the young for religious and corporate ends, Watkins encourages the audience to be suspicious of the narrator (Watkins himself) and what the narrator tells them about the nature of life in Britain. In turn, this creates a suspicion of the camera itself, a crucial move for Watkins as he directs in a "cinema-verite camera style" (Gomez, 1979, 78–79). Watkins's artistic predilection, like that of Herbert, is to distrust "certainties"; but whereas Herbert's analysis of such certainty's relationship to religious belief focused on the similarities between a belief in "prescience" and a subsequent belief in fundamentalism, Watkins's own analysis of "certainties"— religious, political, and corporate — points out the ultimate complicity the artist has in creating the conservative religious and political climate of modernity.

Watkins shows the artist's complicity in supporting the establishment, both through his union of his directorial role with that of government-sponsored narrator, as well as through Shorter's inability to move himself beyond being anything but a figurehead for the fascistic regime ruling Britain. But this complicity in the system is complicated by the limited options open for art figures, particularly celebrities, to protest against the dominant establishment. Alvin Kirsch, one of Shorter's corporate and PR handlers, comments that Shorter is a "gilt edge investment.... He is the most important personality in the ... history of show business.... As I tell him, God has given him something he hasn't given to anyone in the last 500 years. He does not belong to himself. He belongs to the world and therefore he no longer has any right to himself" (*Privilege*). For Alvin, Shorter's artistic popularity makes him a brand and a commodity, rather than a person. In so doing, Alvin dehumanizes Shorter, robbing him of his individuality and reducing him to a commercial good. The artist does not create for his own sake, or for the sake of art, but for the sake of the public. This is bad not so much because it involves communal artistic interaction — Watkins has long supported such "community art" (Watkins 2007a) — but because it makes the artist subservient to larger social processes which the state uses "to divert potential political challenge by young people in particular" (Watkins 2008, 7). Watkins realized that the "British establishment" was "using various facets of the popular culture to divert the attention of the youth from ... becoming too involved in serious political issues" (6). Popular culture, to which filmmakers were subservient, was increasingly enforcing a type of mass conformity onto teenagers and young adults, and Shorter, as a young artist in the sixties, is aware enough to resent that potential limitation, but also powerless to change it.

Alvin rejects any idea of "art for art's sake," yet in a way Watkins does to. For Alvin the rejection of such an artistic philosophy is a result of the need to unite the artist with corporate and religious interests, such as the evangelical wing of the Anglican church. But for Watkins, such an aesthetic philosophy fails to realize the essentially political nature of most art. Whereas corporate art, including the creations of the Christian culture industry, produce artworks that are heavily dependent on market demand, Watkins wants art that speaks to the personal and relational nature of human beings, art that, as Peter Gomez notes, does not reduce human beings to a political slogan, either right or left (Gomez, 1979, 98). Therefore, while most of Watkins's art is political, it is political out of a motivation to escape a world in which such slogans are necessary and in which an artist's mission becomes reduced to a talking head's PR soundbite (e.g., Alvin).

Watkins's "problem" with the Anglican Church (including its evangelical wing, which is clearly a target here), is not the church per se, nor honest expressions of faith (2008, 7). Rather, Watkins wants his viewers to see how the Church, like other ideological state apparatuses, is both subverting sixties youth culture (the direct problem the film addresses) and the artists in whom that youth culture puts their messianic faith in (the indirect subject of the film). A church official explains: "Steven Shorter has the largest following in the history of the entertainment business. We need a larger audience, so we're using Steve's. And we hope that through him, many of these followers will return to the faith" (*Privilege*). For Watkins, the problem with religion's relationship with the arts is not religion's purported anti-intellectualism; it is the cynicism with which religion will exploit the arts for its own agenda, namely the gaining of converts, that Watkins condemns. Religion is not concerned about the quality of the audience, nor its knowledge of the text or artist under discussion (whether it be Steven Shorter or the Bible itself); it is concerned only with endorsing, as one of Shorter's handlers puts it, "a fruitful conformity." Evangelical religion's concern for art also is largely utilitarian; it is concerned, much like the Christian Booksellers Association and other elements of the evangelical "culture" industry, only with the religious effects the arts have on the masses, not the means used to achieve those effects, which often involve crude, brutal indoctrination, as well as the worst elements of theatre. This is most cruelly portrayed when some of Steve's disabled fans are brought forward because his handlers have encouraged the quasi-religious belief that Steve's music has "autosuggestive qualities ... from which the sick may derive some internal benefit" (*Privilege*). Evangelicalism, including its Anglican elements, is not afraid to cast the artist in a messianic role. Its goal, for Watkins, is to maintain its tie to state power: all else is ultimately negotiable.

Steven's final musical performance reflects the ambiguous role the artist plays in evangelical culture — at once both derided and used to advance the church's social agenda. The lyrics of Steven's final composition are only slightly changed from his original act, yet the tone is completely different. Steven's role now is nearly completely the opposite of that in the original version of the song. Instead of the Nietzschean artist-rebel, he is now the messianic Christian convert, bringing the nation "back to Christ." Yet little really has changed. The Nietzschean ideal is not so different from the Christian one; both mythoses envision an *ubermensch* leader whose powers far dwarf those of any mortal person. While the Nietzschean artist is supposed to belong totally to himself, to be an overman, the Christian artist is to belong totally to the community. Yet the Nietzschean's ideals, because they so closely resemble the ideals of the market, ultimately makes it impossible for such artists to move beyond the market system and achieve true and total autonomy. Jack London had bitterly predicted the fall of the individualistic ideal in the arts some sixty years before, in his classic *Martin Eden* (1909); here Watkins provides an equally strong analysis of the overriding power of the market to control what art is and is not produced. The modern artist is now utterly dependent on corporations and corporate sponsorship for the production of his works; he (or she) therefore finds it impossible to not let his music, or poetry, or painting, be molded by the desires of those sponsors. Evangelicals make this process even worse, because they unite the most materialistic elements of spirituality with a corporate model of culture. In the process, any room for a vibrant evangelical arts world of their own, unregulated by corporate gatekeepers like Thomas Nelson or Zondervan, is lost (*Privilege*).

Through Shorter, the artist is identified now with both Jesus and the state. The artist worships "the Sun," e.g., the Son, and therefore the followers of the artist should worship the Son and the state that supports the Son as well. The narrator at Steven's last concert reveals that the coalition government in Britain, with its heavy fascistic overtones, feels, "We need no longer have any disturbing political differences, when we're all of one faith and believe in one God and one flag" (*Privilege*). It thus sponsors the concert and the sermons that the concert promotes because the government wants artistic and cultural conformity. Indeed, "We will conform" is the motto of the minister who conducts the revival session at Shorter's concert. Unity rather than diversity, political cohesion rather than individual artistic expression, are the mottoes of the day. In such a world, the role of the artist himself must be erased, reduced to a signifier for the marketing and spiritual campaigns of his sponsor (*Privilege*).

Watkins suggests that in such a future corporatized world — the world we live in now — there will be little room for true artistic or religious expression. Even the power to create an authentic self will be lost. Steven's own pleading words at the end warn the viewer that even his ability to articulate his angst has been totally stripped from him: "Me ... me ... you ... you worship me as if I were a sort of God. But I'm someone. I'm a person, I'm a person, I'm a person ... I am nothing ... this is me: nothing. And this is you, because you've made me nothing. And I hate you, I hate you, I hate you" (*Privilege*). In making the artist a God and then allying him to the state, Steven's fans have made both their artist and their God a nothing (Gomez, 1979, 80). Spiritual values have come to mean no more than an appreciation of one's favorite rock star, while artistic values have been nullified by trying to force onto the sign of the artist more than what the actual signified (Shorter himself) can bear. Shorter wants to be neither a god, nor a nothing, but a person — yet this is precisely the route not left open to an artistic celebrity, especially a celebrity who is expected to follow the rules of a conservative religious regime.

Steven Shorter's dilemma shares much in common with the situation faced by so-called Christian "crossover" artists, particularly in Christian rock. Whenever such artists appear, they have to navigate a delicate road between producing art that they believe is genuinely good, while not offending those listeners (or viewers, or readers) who might want to peruse their work. As Christian music critics Jay Howard and John Streck sympathetically point out, these artists are caught in a catch-22 where their music is interpreted through an "us and them" dichotomy in which "crossover success" entails "a betrayal of Christian ideals" (1999, 90). In both the music and publishing industry, however, this balancing act becomes problematic, because the artist is also faced by a third force: capitalism. With the Christian publishing and music industries being so dominated by profits, and with no independent evangelical "literary" publishing scene on the horizon, it is unlikely that Christian writers or musicians will be able to develop any art whose production is not ultimately totally a result of preordained market forces (painting may be a very partial exception here).

Privilege is a film that warns evangelical viewers of the limitations of art's relationship to religion. When religion merely seeks to express what it sees as eternal verities through art, there may be some hope for such a union. But when religion unites its spiritual and aesthetic visions with more theocratic and corporatized goals, the result is a hybrid product that is unlikely to appeal to true seekers in either the arts or religion. Art-lovers and religious seekers may not know what the "true" thing is; but they are excellent at authenticating fakes. That *Privilege* could in such minute detail predict the rise of the Christian culture industry — with visuals that could come right out of any D.C. Talk music video or Skillet concert — testifies not only to Watkins's prescient genius but also to the continuing debasement of evangelicalism's original anti-materialistic ideals at the hands of the church growth movement, which has so fueled contemporary Christian music (CCM). What is dangerous in this culture industry is not that the art is kitsch; most of it is sincerely felt, and many of these sincerer pieces are more interesting at an artistic level (Frank Peretti's early spiritual warfare novels, for instance) than the products of the evangelical cultural elite. What is dangerous are the pretensions of those parts of the culture industry that do not think they are being corrupted by the Christian culture industry's marriage to capitalist elites. So long as they are subject to the tight controls of the CBA and Nashville music industry, it is doubtful that any of these artists will construct meaningfully challenging work; but rather than deracinating spiritual and material capitalism out of the Christian culture industry, they marry the church ever closer to it. It remains doubtful whether that marriage can be ended; therefore, a more radical process of deracination, a more fundamental rejection of the basis on which contemporary art forms are founded, is needed. Whether that change can be effected remains to be seen.

Going Apes for Fundamentalists:
Inherit the Wind*'s Unusual Artistic Interrogator*

Of all the novels and films talked about in this study, *The Planet of the Apes* series has the most interesting and complex history; indeed, without an understanding of the players involved, the religious dimensions of the film, particularly its addressing of contemporary concerns over evangelicalism's reaction to racial, scientific, and political Others, fails to make sense.

The original text on which the film series is based is Pierre Boulle's novel of the same name. Boulle, a French author, was primarily interested in issues of communication. His novel, though in its own way as brilliant as the motion pictures, bears little resemblance to them; racial tensions, though present, do not play the part they do in the film versions, and religion is totally absent (as, of course, is evangelicalism) (Greene 1996, 27). The first major attempt to draft a screenplay of the novel was by Rod Serling. Serling introduced the themes of nuclear warfare and Cold War concerns that dominated the original *Apes* movie; though interested in the issue of racial conflict as well, he did not introduce that idea into the scripts; instead this was left to Michal Wilson, who had previously scripted Boulle's *Bridge Over the River Kwai* (1957) and the film *Lawrence of Arabia* (1962). Wilson had been deeply influenced by the anti-communist, anti-leftist campaigns of the fifties, which had blacklisted him (that blacklisting cost him the Oscar for best screenplay in *Bridge Over the River Kwai*) (Greene 1996, 27–28). It was in Wilson's hands that the themes of fundamentalist conflict took shape.[6]

The story of the first *Apes* movie tells of Colonel Taylor, a U.S. astronaut, and his crew, who crash on what they think is an alien world. Taylor's crewmates are quickly killed by the apes who inhabit the planet. Taylor's presence in ape society causes enormous social tension, when the apes learn that Taylor can talk. The only humans the apes know of are the dumb "animal" humans of their own world. Though a few sympathetic chimpanzee intellectuals, notably Cornelius and Zira (the scientist-artist stand-ins), wish to help Taylor, the rest of ape society, particularly the orangutans and gorillas, want to kill him. Taylor is given a show trial and despite the aid of Cornelius and Zira is sentenced to death. With the help of Cornelius, Zira, and Zira's nephew, Lucius, Taylor escapes. He is pursued to one of Cornelius's archaeological digs, where he proves to Dr. Zaius that humanity was the original dominant species on the apes' world. Zaius's men attempt to capture Taylor, but Taylor escapes. Zaius warns Taylor not to seek out the answers to the history of the planet of the apes, but Taylor does not heed his warning. The movie ends with one of the most startling twists in all of film history. As he stares up at a ruined Statue of Liberty, Taylor finds out that he's been on Earth all along; human civilization had finally destroyed itself with the "bomb."

The second movie, *Beneath the Planet of the Apes* (1970), which I will also briefly talk about, depicts a war between mutant telepathic descendants of humanity, who still have the power of speech, and the apes. The movie, besides reflecting some of the racial tensions of the original movie, makes highly cynical comments on the nature of human religion: the mutants worship a nuclear bomb as their god, a god whose name is "Alpha and Omega" (Greene 1996, 67). Apish fundamentalism is little better, as the gorillas, with

Dr. Zaius's connivance, use religion as a cynical ploy to drive the gorilla military into a religiously inspired holy war. The film ends with Earth getting blown up; yet there are three more sequels, as Cornelius and Zira have managed to flee Earth only to find themselves back in time, the progenitors of the very evolved species from which they come.

Planet of the Apes is one of the most successful film franchises ever produced. The original series spanned five movies, a remake in 2001, and a well-regarded reboot in 2011 that looks likely to inspire a whole new *Apes* franchise. An American television series followed the original films, as did a cheap Japanese rip-off that was practically unknown; an animated series also followed the original movies. *Planet of the Apes* inspired a wave of merchandising, serving in many ways as the template for the marketing campaigns of the *Star Wars* (1977–2005) saga (*Behind the Planet of the Apes*). Though not all of the films are well regarded, the original received "generally ... very positive reviews" (Greene 1996, 56). *Beneath the Planet of the Apes* and *Escape from the Planet of the Apes* both are viewed as at least somewhat interesting, and one suspects that the negative critiques of *Conquest of the Planet of the Apes* has more to do with the movie's explosive allegorizing of the Watts riots than with its admitted flaws in scripting. Thus, the *Apes* series can be seen as reflecting, like *Dune*, popular anxieties about race, culture, and religion.

Wilson's narrative of Cornelius and Zira's intellectual conflict with the religious establishment, represented by the orangutan Dr. Zaius, Minister of Science and Chief Defender of the Faith. This conflict is highly reminiscent of *Inherit the Wind*; indeed, it is impossible to imagine that some of the scenes in the film, particularly the trial of Taylor, were not directly based on both Lawrence and Lee's play and the original Scopes Trial. Keeping in mind Wilson's blacklisting experience and the very positive depictions of the ape intellectuals, it is likely that Wilson saw Cornelius and Zira as scientific stand-ins for the artists and intellectuals blacklisted by the McCarthyites. Indeed, the fact that Cornelius and Zira are to be put on trial for heresy at the close of the film makes this supposition practically a certainty.

Yet Wilson's depiction of fundamentalism is much more complex than Lawrence and Lee's. Though apish fundamentalism, like the fundamentalism of Lawrence and Lee, stifles scientific creativity and intellectual freedom, Dr. Zaius does not come off as badly as the ignorant bigots that Brady and Reverend Brown do in *Inherit the Wind*. Indeed, through most of the original *Planet of the Apes* (1968) movie, Zaius possesses more knowledge about the world in which Taylor finds himself than any other character, including Taylor himself. Zaius's fundamentalism is based, not so much on devoutness, as on his knowledge of what humans had done to the Earth when they held possession over it.

Zaius's skepticism about the goodness of humanity walks hand in hand with his religious fundamentalism, creating a kind of odd whiplash effect, in which at moment the audience wishes to condemn him, and at another moment realizes (after first viewing) that Zaius actually is working for understandable and, by his society's standards, noble goals. At the end of the first Apes picture, Zaius tells Taylor:

> ZAIUS: All my life, I've awaited your coming and dreaded it like death itself.
> TAYLOR: Why? I've terrified you from the first ... I still do, you're afraid of me and you hate me. Why?
> ZAIUS: Because you're a man. And you're right, I have always known about man. From the evidence, I believe his wisdom must walk hand in hand with his idiocy. His emotions must rule his brain. He must be a war-like creature who gives battle to everything around him ... even himself [*Planet of the Apes*].

For Zaius, humanity's essential nature is warlike, and therefore hostile to ape interests. Human nature is therefore in fundamental opposition to ape nature, since, as we find out later in the series, "ape does not kill ape" (*Battle for the Planet of the Apes*).[7] In the combination of official science and religion that Zaius and his fellow orangutans represent, he represents a balance between the emotional militarism of the gorillas and the rationalistic intellectualism of the chimpanzees. By promoting a mild form of irrationalism and cautious technological growth (the orangutans allow scientific research, but the chimpanzees' work in this regard is carefully regulated), Zaius minimizes the potential harm that knowledge of the apes' true origins can pose to their society. In this respect, Zaius's role is similar to that of the early fundamentalist critics of evolution, concerned not so much about the veracity of the theory as about its potentially deleterious social effects. Rather than portray Zaius as solely being heartless—a role that Zaius actually in fact played in the original novel—Wilson's depiction allows for the fact that Zaius's concerns are predicated on an overall rational understanding of the intellectual and cultural limitations of his society. Paul Dehn, the scriptwriter for *Beneath the Planet of the Apes*, used Zaius as a mediating, though ultimately cynical, figure between the gorilla military establishment, under General Ursus, and chimpanzee radicals. One particularly memorable scene, for instance, shows Zaius listening with evident boredom to an orangutan preacher; he too, can evidently find religious pomposity frustrating (*Beneath the Planet of the Apes*).

For Zaius, social stability is the prime goal of society. As Zira says, he "has only one motive. To keep things exactly as they have always been" (*Beneath the Planet of the Apes*). Fundamentalism's most important obligation, for Dehn (as it was for Wilson), is to maintain control over the flow and interpretation of both science and history, a role commonly assigned to it by spiritual bourgeoisie writers, but here given a unique twist by these two writers. Since Zaius's control over his society is largely dependent on maintaining the illusion that humanity is an inferior species and that apes did not descend from man, there is a quite explicit commentary here on both the racialized nature of American religion (see Greene 1996, 39) and the ways in which the intellectual arm of the religious establishment limits access to knowledge. Zaius's control over the animal-like human beings of Earth, as well as his own species' privileged place in the ape hierarchy,[8] is dependent on a hierarchalized notion of race. And such a system needs to be religiously justified in order to justify the position of the dominating parties. Much like Presbyterian theologian and eventual Confederate sympathizer Robert Dabney, one of the chief apologists for Southern slavery (Noll 2002, 429–430), Zaius and his fellow orangutans use sacred scriptures as a justification for a dominant slave-system. But whereas few contemporary Americans could have much sympathy for Dabney's racial polemics, both Wilson and Dehn make it easier for viewers to understand Zaius's support for his own culture's hierarchized social system when they realize that human technology twice causes a nuclear holocaust. That the screenwriters, particularly Wilson, could be so understanding of fundamentalist ideas, even at a time when Southern fundamentalists were fighting the civil rights movement on a number of issues (especially interracial marriage) (Leonard 1999, n.p.), speaks to a greater tolerance in their work than is present in Lawrence and Lee. In the turbulent sixties, a desire for a quieting of racial conflict could be felt even among white liberals, let alone among their conservative opponents.

But Zaius also prizes cultural innocence, and it is here that Dehn at least takes Zaius's fundamentalism to task. Zaius proclaims:

> We apes have learned to live in innocence. Let no one, be it man or some other creature, dare to contaminate that innocence.... Is innocence so evil?
> ZIRA: Ignorance is.
> ZAIUS: There is a time for truth.
> ZIRA: And the time is always now.... Are you asking me to surrender my principles?
> ZAIUS: I am asking you to be guardians of the principles of science during my absence. I am asking for a truce with your personal convictions in an hour of public danger [*Beneath the Planet of the Apes*].

For Dehn, Zaius's valuation of cultural innocence ultimately makes him an unwilling pawn of the gorilla military establishment. Rather than supporting Zira and Cornelius, who oppose the gorillas' war with the mutant humans, Zaius's concern for cultural purity ironically turns him into a cynical pragmatist; he is willing to ally with General Ursus's plans for conquest, so long as they go along with his own desire to find out what "other form of life" is in the forbidden zone (the viewer can safely presume that Zaius, knowing the original Earth had only one other sentient species, fears that the form of life is human) (*Beneath the Planet of the Apes*). Thus in the interests of promoting the social stability Zaius values so highly, he unites religion with the power of both the state and the military, ensuring that whatever his fundamentalism is, it is definitely not "innocent." For Dehn, innocence cannot be arrived at through ignorance; still less from pragmatic and cynical manipulations of principle. True innocence comes from the naiveté of looking for the truth and solely for the truth, as Zira does throughout the first three Apes films.

The fundamentalist, therefore, in the *Apes* series, is not a rube out of innocence, nor out of a belief in any Edenic myth; rather it is because the fundamentalist does have knowledge of the world, and powers beyond that of the intelligentsia and the commoners, that he is held guilty. Intellectuals such as Zira and Cornelius, with their childlike wonder at the marvels of talking humans, archaeological digs, and anthropological information, are in a sense more "spiritual" than fundamentalists; they at least continue to see wonder in this post-apocalyptic future, where apish fundamentalists, their mutant counterparts, and the talking humans trapped in between can see none. The defining quality of the scientific intellectual, as it is for the artist whom he represents, is his simple-minded, Edenic desire to portray life as it actually is, rather than as fundamentalists would have one pretend it to be.

In the *Apes* series, the scientist-artist's goal to portray truth means a rigorous examination of the societal values with which one lives. Zira consistently emphasizes throughout the *Apes* series, "We can't live with lies" (*Escape from the Planet of the Apes*). For Zira, truth is the one and abiding value that she lives by. She asks, "How can scientific truth be heresy?" When Cornelius observes that such scientific truth would mean the Sacred Scrolls (the apes' scriptures) are not "worth their parchment," Zira merely observes, "Well, maybe they're not" (*Planet of the Apes*). Zira is willing to overthrow the most sacred books of her culture in order to seek for a greater understanding of the world. But her role as an intellectual truthsayer is not confined simply to science, but extends to politics, archaeology, and theology as well. Once a truthteller in one field, the scientist/artist must endeavor to be a truthteller in all, to not flinch from the cultural or societal implications of what that knowledge may mean for social stability or cultural cohesion. In later films in the series, such truthtelling is contrasted with human scientists such as the villain of *Escape from the Planet of the Apes* (1971), Dr. Hasslein. Hasslein is willing to understand the knowledge Zira and Cornelius bring him from the future (the destruction of the Earth by nuclear weaponry), but in seeking to kill them in order to prevent the apes' evolution, Hasslein, as Zaius did in the two previous movies, emerges as neither truthteller nor social conscience. He, like Zaius, instead embraces the role of the pragmatist, killing today to save tomorrow; and, by so doing, he paves the way for humanity's destruction. Zira, by contrast, is both truthteller and conscience — her ruthless examination of her society's social values leads her to accept the brotherhood of humanity and apes, something neither Hasslein nor Zaius's orangutan allies are capable of doing.

Without the combination of scientific truth and socially evolved conscience, fundamentalists are prone to become suspicious of racial and cultural Others. The fundamentalist prosecutor at Taylor's reverse "Scopes Trial" makes this clear when he argues that the "proper study of apes is apes" (*Planet of the Apes*). The prosecutor's simiocentric view of the universe leads him to proclaim, "Men have no souls"—Wilson's concern here, insofar as it deals with fundamentalism, is that fundamentalism has a tendency to devalue the common humanity of peoples with whom fundamentalists do not share a cultural heritage. By centering on only a simiocentric viewpoint, the prosecutor looks inward, observing only the self. Yet, for apes, as for humans, the talent needed to excel in the arts and science must also inevitably lead to a respect for nature, and for the creatures within it, both sapient and nonsapient. By denying the common biological heritages of humans and apes, the prosecutor is not simply reducing religion to a set of arbitrary clichés; he is also preventing nature from telling his simian civilization new aesthetic and cultural truths about themselves, truths that may enrich his religion as well as enfeeble it. This simiocentrism, like Eurocentric evangelical theology, relies too much on a monocultural, one-sided hermeneutical strategy of scriptural interpretation, one that does not allow for the kind of interpretive flexibility that characterizes, for instance, scriptural high critics or ape intellectuals (Cornelius, as an archaeologist, can be seen as roughly analogous to a supporter of biblical higher criticism).

At its most apocalyptic, fundamentalism can take on a fanaticism that threatens both human and ape existence. The human mutant civilization portrayed in *Beneath the Planet of the Apes*, though more liturgical than the ape society it opposes, is even more fanatically religiously devout. Most of the mutants' fanaticism is expressed through the piety with which they worship the bomb. Their leader, Mendez, proclaims:

> The heavens declare the glory of the bomb and the firmament shows his handiwork.... He descendeth from the outermost part of heaven and there is nothing hid from the heat thereof. There is neither speech nor language, yet his voice is heard among them.... Glory be to the bomb and to the Holy Fallout as it was in the beginning, is now and ever shall be world without end [*Beneath*].

The similarities here between standard Christian confessional responses and liturgies and the mutants' protestations of faith are striking. But whereas Christ is the Word who promotes more words, the bomb negates speech and language; alone is its power heard. The glories of God's heaven are replaced by the terror of atomic destruction, transfigured as a subject of religious awe. Eric Greene has perceptively noted that the worship of the bomb as "'a holy weapon of peace' is perhaps the ultimate extension of the nuclear deterrence theory that envisioned mutually assured destruction as the greatest protector of life" (1996, 68). The mutants' religion creates fundamental paradoxes that mirror the Christianity from which it originally springs; a weapon of war again becomes the emblem of a religion claiming to be peaceful.[9] And the mutants' devotion to pacifism only leads them to find new ways of making their "enemies to kill each other" (*Beneath*). The mutants' liturgical practice, like their telepathic powers, is itself illusory, since the mutants do not really need speech to communally praise their god.

The mutants put faith in the power of their telepathic illusions to protect their society, and much of the portrayal of mutant religion focuses on its illusoriness. The religion itself is an illusion: a bankrupt copy of a religion that was itself a copy of Judaism (which too may have only been an illusion). The supposed ideals of the mutant society — its pacifism and piety — are clearly illusory as well. Even the faces of the mutants, which at first seem normal, are actually illusions. In one of the most chilling scenes of the film, the mutants finally reveal (in unison) their "inmost self(s) unto my God," as they tear off their faces, revealing hideous scarred facial remnants of what they once were. Dehn suggests that in a world threatened with nuclear destruction — as the Earth of the seventies, as well as the apes' world, was — fundamentalist religion only holds power because people must cling to their illusions, whether they be the pietistic bromides Zaius uses to comfort the faithful, or the liturgical utterances of Mendez. Only through the truthtelling and secularly evolved social consciences of apes such as Zira and Cornelius (or in the later movies in the series, humans such as Doctor Lewis Dixon) can prevent the final destruction of ape and man that the last film leaves as an open question (*Behind the Planet of the Apes*). If religion is to survive in this modern, enlightened era, it must do so as a force for cultural enlightenment, a tolerant, liberal force in the mainline tradition. Fundamentalist faith, having seen its day, must disappear.

As the reader can tell, the *Apes* series' rendering of contemporary religious concerns was considerably more sophisticated than Lawrence and Lee's. The scientist as artist-stand-in, oppressed by evangelicalism, remained an occasional motif of science fiction into the Early Postmodern era, seeing particular expression in the conflicts between the Federation's scientific staff and Bajoran fundamentalists in *Star Trek: Deep Space Nine*. But largely, with the gradual marginalizing of McCarthyite views from the American cultural mainstream (even many evangelicals came to look on McCarthyism with distaste), concerns about evangelicalism's purported racial and anti-communist prejudices receded. In the Early Postmodern era, it was primarily feminists who supported the idea of an anti-artistic evangelical tradition, sometimes in a science fiction context, sometimes outside of it.

In continuing this critique, however, feminists inherited the anti-evangelical prejudices of writers such as Lawrence and Lee, Wilson, Watkins, and Frank Herbert. But by the time the first Early Postmodern narratives had started, most writers in the English-language tradition had forgotten the power evangelical ideas had once had over their cultures. Much of the relationship of evangelicalism to American, Canadian, British, and Australian history had also been lost. With particularly skilled writers who had a knowledge of evangelical culture, such as the British novelist Jeanette Winterson, this did not matter. But with most other novelists, the resulting narratives were little better than caricature: *The Poisonwood Bible*'s Nathan Price is only the most infamous example of the general lack of characterizing skill that came to define early Postmodern depictions of evangelicals. For feminists, interests in vocalizing marginalized writers' concerns ironically silenced often understandable evangelical concerns about their own culture's social and religious cohesion.

The Age of Fantasy was the last reprieve for evangelicals—an era in which evangelicalism was usually dealt with through allegory, a literary form that allowed for multiplicities of meaning that the feminist dystopias and missionary narratives of the eighties and nineties simply did not allow. After the last *Apes* movie was released in 1973, evangelical belief was dealt with far more directly and brutally by those who critiqued it. Any sense of realism about evangelicalism's relationship to the arts was lost. Whether it was Offered in *The Handmaid's Tale* or Calvin Becker in the *Portofino* series, artists and aesthetes ultimately had to oppose evangelical religion, often fanatically so, if they wished to evolve into fully developed individuals. "Freedom from" evangelical religion became the motto; the "freedom to" practice evangelical religion, by contrast, though not questioned by these artists, was often portrayed as a liberty that had much more dangerous consequences than evangelicalism actually presented in real life. We are still living with the consequences of this change in artistic portrayals; and that change was birthed in the Age of Fantasy.

6

Feminisms, Fanaticism and Evangelicalism

By the mid-eighties, evangelicalism was a potent political force. Evangelicals, though not absolutely essential to the Reagan coalition of the early eighties, were a very important part of its early victories (W. Martin 2005, 220). Spurred on by concerns over prayer in the schools, abortion, and increasing public acceptance of homosexuality, evangelicals formed a powerful bloc of support for potential political candidates, a bloc that could not easily be ignored. With increased public visibility, however, came a political backlash. Evangelical leaders in the late seventies, inspired by Francis Schaeffer's teachings and the book *The Battle for the Mind* (1980) by prominent evangelical leader Tim LaHaye, had launched an all-out campaign against what they termed secular humanists (Marsden 2006, 245–246), a loose coalition of nefarious atheists that functioned like the evangelical equivalent of the Legion of Doom.

In response, many non-evangelical, primarily secular organizations, began actively campaigning against what they saw as an unnecessary infringement on the First Amendment. People for the American Way, for instance, launched repeated attacks on evangelical censorship campaigns, often considerably overemphasizing the danger these campaigns presented to the wider populace (Diamond 1998, 194).

The eighties and nineties were among the most polarized decades in American religious history. On the right was lined up a coalition of Pentecostals, neo-evangelicals, fundamentalists, Reformed Christians, Holiness supporters, neo-conservatives, some Reagan Democrats, conservative Catholics, and an occasional Orthodox Jew. On the left, mainline Protestants, most secularists, most non–Orthodox Jews, atheists and agnostics, and an overwhelming number of religious and non-religious members of almost all racial minority groups lined up to oppose the right-wing coalition. Because the demographic upswing in black and Latino votes had not peaked, the left found itself evenly matched. Gridlock resulted, preventing either the religious right or the secular left from achieving their political objectives. As a result, this environment was ideal for hyperbolic tales of secular conspiracies and evangelical theocracies (respectively).

The main oppressing force against evangelicals within this period, according to my DDM model, is the feminist movement. However, one should be perfectly honest here: Feminists had quite understandable reasons for opposing evangelical family policy during this period. As Sarah Diamond wrote in the late nineties, "Virtually all of the Christian Right's organizations are preoccupied with the subject of proper relations between men and women" (1998, 126). Politically powerful organizations in this period, such as Concerned Women for America, were, according to Diamond (and any other reasonable observer), "unalterably opposed to feminism as they see it." Diamond argues that the Christian Right's "rhetorical attacks on feminism are directed ... at a caricature of feminism as a movement of man hating, power-mongering ideologues" rather than the feminist movement as a whole (126–127). Diamond is right here, but her subject position as a supporter of the feminist movement makes it difficult for her to realize that in feminist literary depictions of evangelicals during this period such an analysis by evangelicals was hardly unwarranted, particularly when dealing with the outright anti-evangelical misandry of *The Poisonwood Bible* or the more complicated but often still simplistic vision of evangelical men that *The Handmaid's Tale* offers. Both Kingsolver and Atwood fail to note that though patriarchy is a real and very dangerous trait in evangelicalism, it developed within a specific cultural context during the early 1900s, where evangelicals were quite concerned about the absence of men in the church (a concern shared by mainline Protestants) (Bendroth 1994, 16–22) and the triumph of liberal Protestantism (Gallagher 2003, 37–38). Pre-fundamentalist evangelicalism was not an automatically misogynistic faith system. Evangelicals such as Sarah Grimke proved quite capable of attacking male misogyny, often using "both the scriptures and the intuitive truth of their arguments" to "defend women's emerging leadership within the church and society" (35). Because writers such as Kingsolver and Atwood failed to acknowledge the complicated subject position of evangelicals vis-à-vis the feminist movement, their works often resorted to the same classist, spiritually capitalist caricatures of evangelicalism present in works such as *Inherit the Wind*.

In evangelicalism, there were also narrative offenders against polite cultural discourse, particularly *Gideon's Torch* (1995) and *The Lambda Conspiracy* (1993). The latter novel featured gays (which author Spenser Hughes tries to associate with pedophiles) assassinating U.S. senators in order to protect their New Age cabal in a plot that was as ridiculous as it was reprehensible. *Gideon's Torch*, a much more smoothly written novel, still featured people culling fetal baby parts to cure AIDS victims (Hughes, 1993, 30, 186, 207–213; Mason

2002, 110). Evangelical authors during this period eventually came to read secularism in conspiratorial terms sometimes reminiscent of the way early 20th century Germans or late 19th century anti–Dreyfusards had read Jewish culture. Homosexuals, atheists, secularists, and (in the eighties) New Agers all represented a powerful secret bloc of influential leaders who would marginalize evangelical culture.

But if such paranoia characterized evangelicals, it even more characterized the writers of the left, who did not have the excuse of being anti-intellectual or products of a working-class culture. In the eighties and nineties, a slew of novels portrayed the evangelical belief as a system that oppressed women and silenced female and dissident voices. The most famous of these novels, besides Margaret Atwood's *The Handmaid's Tale* and Barbara Kingsolver's *The Poisonwood Bible*, was Octavia Butler's *Parable* series. All of these novels, despite providing some interesting ideas on the nature of religion, proved to be too didactic and formulaic in their presentation of evangelicalism to be truly effective. Meanwhile, Franky Schaeffer's *Portofino* series represented the first narrative of a major ex-evangelical insider, scandalizing the evangelical community while simultaneously attacking the base on which Francis Schaeffer had critiqued the secular world of the arts.

The oppressed artist figure became the dominant theme in this period; artists were always in danger of being killed, stoned, or whipped by evangelical characters. Female writers' voices' are silenced to the point that in *The Handmaid's Tale*, the protagonist Offred can only tape record herself (Atwood 1986, 301–302), rather than risk exposure (and death) by writing. Similarly, Larkin Olamina (better known as Asha Vere) in the novel *Parable of the Talents* loses her name and much of her religious heritage because of the silencing of her mother's religious teachings by a theocratic religious group (her mother is actually enslaved by the Christian Right for a good part of the second novel in the *Parable* series). And in Franky Schaeffer's work there is always the plaintive, if rather unlikely, suggestion that he could have been a great artist had he not grown up in the evangelical church. With the evangelical church then still building its artistic infrastructure, there were few voices capable of responding to these secular stereotypes of evangelical belief; as a result, evangelicals often engaged in even worse cultural name-calling than their non-evangelical opponents. A battle was now on for the artistic soul of America; it was a battle that, whatever the worldview movement's beliefs, was impossible for them to win. And despite Margaret's Atwood's claims of cultural oppression (made rather unlikely by her Ivy League pedigree), it was a combat that she and her feminist allies could not lose; the table had been fixed long before she sat down to play, by a dominant spiritual capitalist narrative that the feminist movement inherited from mainline Protestantism. All Atwood

The Oppressed Female Artist: Margaret Atwood and The Handmaid's Tale

Margaret Atwood's *Handmaid's Tale* (1986), written at the height of the secular panic brought about by Ronald Reagan's election in 1980 (and re-election in 1984), is narrated by Offred, a young handmaid for the Republic of Gilead. The Republic, founded after the fall of the United States, is a theocratic government that is desperately trying to increase its birthrate after a series of environmental and industrial accidents (Atwood 1986 [hereafter cited as *HT*], 304); the handmaidens, representing almost all the fertile women still remaining, are an enslaved breeding class, whose main purpose is simply to reproduce. As a handmaiden of a character known simply as the Commander, Offred finds herself marginalized, incapable of doing anything without the consent or knowledge of an all-knowing fundamentalist patriarchy.

There is a debate about how much Gilead represents the United States of the 1980s and Christianity in particular. Atwood has claimed, rather disingenuously, that evangelical Christianity is not targeted in the novel (Moyers 2006). However, Atwood's "Note to the Reader" comments on how alarmed she was by "statements made frequently by religious leaders in the United States" (*HT* 316); considering the time in which she was writing, it is very likely that she was referring to evangelicals. Atwood also claims inspiration from American Puritanism and the Iranian theocracy that was then becoming prevalent (316); while clearly influences on her writing, neither of these movements seems to have had such a psychological effect on Atwood's writing style as the fear of evangelical hegemony in America. The character of Serena Joy, for instance, the Commander's wife, is clearly patterned after televangelist Tammy Faye Baker, complete to the "mascara blackening her cheeks" (46), a well-known aspect of Tammy Faye's appearance to this day. The execution of abortion providers also mirrors the increasing violence against clinic workers in the eighties and nineties, which eventually escalated into murder (see *HT* 32).

Atwood herself is probably not the best qualified writer to address American evangelicalism. A Canadian, Atwood misses certain American cultural cues that a novelist here would perhaps catch. For instance, the theocracy of Gilead takes control through credit card machines and the manipulation of electronic currency (*HT* 173–178). Since premillennialist evangelicals feel that the Antichrist's regime will try to control the world in part through such manipulations, it is unlikely any evangelical theocracy would attempt to rule the country using this method (Boyer 1992, 267–269, 282–283). Atwood is also a figure of privilege, the daughter of a professor of zoology; she attended Harvard's elite graduate program (Cooke 1998, 21, 92–93). Accordingly, as well meaning as Atwood undoubtedly is, it would hardly be unreasonable to suppose that evangelicalism's foreign and lower-class reputation might not have endeared the movement to Atwood, even were not the more reprehensible parts of its theology painfully in view during the late 1970s and early 1980s.

The Handmaid's Tale is about the silencing of voices. For Atwood, the voices being silenced are women's voices; and as a direct result of that silencing, blacks and Jews also suffer disproportionately as well (*HT* 83, 200–201). But for evangelicals reading *The Handmaid's Tale*, there is also a silencing of their own culture. In Atwood's work, evangelicalism becomes a distinct Other capable only of oppressing; yet, paradoxically, Atwood denies any agency or speck of humanity to the Other, a tactic more often used by the oppressor than the oppressed. Atwood's subject position as a privileged member of the transatlantic social elite, with famous teachers such as Perry Miller and Northrop Frye (Cooke 1998, 62; *HT* 318), movie deals, book contracts, and speaking engagements, puts her in an entirely different sphere from the majority of evangelicals, including evangelical artists, who often, even when now rich, originated from a working-class or lower-middle-class spiritual proletariat and all of whom suffer from being members of an anathemised and marginalized social group.

Offred, the oppressed heroine, wants to be in control of her own story, to be a creator of her own narrative. Offred remarks, "If it's a story I'm telling, then I have control over the ending. Then there will be an ending, to the story, and real life will come after it. I can pick up where I left off" (*HT* 39). Offred's quest for artistic agency here is not unlike Atwood's own or thousands of other female artists and feminist critics during the sixties and seventies who justifiably felt repressed by an overbearing patriarchal system that enforced rigid sexual distinctions and, in the arts (particularly popular arts such as film), objectified women. If Offred gains control over her story, she has the ability also to control her eventual destiny. The person who controls her history has the capability to rewrite it. Thus, it is crucial for Offred's survival that she become the narrative master of her own fate.

Unfortunately, gaining such narrative control is not easy. Offred's situation is complicated by the fact that she has "nothing to write with and writing is in any case forbidden" (*HT* 39). Without the instrument of writing, Offred is forced to resort to memory, and eventually tape recordings, to tell her story. The choice for Offred is between silence and aurality, not silence and retention of literate culture. Offred's narrative, to have any chance of a happy resolution, must seek to navigate the accepted cultural means of communication in Gilead. Rebellion is the muted word.

The repressive evangelical-like regime of Gilead is devoted to muting the handmaidens' voices. Even the lettering of shop signs is painted out, so that only the sign is left (*HT* 25); a literal sign that no longer signifies anything, lest women be tempted into literacy. Evangelicalism may not be the destroyer of worlds, but for Atwood it is the destroyer of words, like all fundamentalisms. Atwood fears that evangelicalism is trying to inscribe its own narrative onto women's lives, its own narrative of women, complete with racist executions, death camps, the enslavement of women's bodies, rape, and undercover religious prostitution. Atwood does not even give the Gileadians the benefit of believing that some members of their theocracy may actually sincerely believe in the rightness of their cause.

The truth of Atwood's narrative of evangelical culture here, stocked as it is with rehashed mainline spiritual bourgeois stereotypes of evangelicalism, is questionable at best. While evangelicals had (partial) control of the church's narrative of women in the eighties and nineties, far more of that narrative in the United States was still being directed either by forces opposed to women for purely sexist or secular reasons (big corporations, for instance) or by feminist writers such as Margaret Atwood herself. And the lack of even one redeeming trait among the evangelical characters Atwood depicts is in itself a kind of reverse designifying, a muffling of counterhegemonic evangelical voices that might disturb both Atwood's and conservative evangelicalism's narrative of female agency. For instance, the first evangelical women's caucus, which promoted a broad vision at once evangelical and feminist, was filled to capacity, and actually had to turn people away — and that was in 1975 (Smith 2008, 141). Even the admittedly sexist complementarian position on gender rights advocated by many evangelical leaders was considerably more nuanced than suggested by the *Handmaid's Tale*. Sociologist Sally Gallagher, while acknowledging that the eighties was a period of social and cultural conservatism, points out that among evangelicals a "pragmatic gender egalitarianism" emerged in that period, as many evangelicals dealt with the reality that their families would need two incomes to support themselves. The range of difference between "biblical" feminists and evangelical gender conservatives was mitigated by the fact that a wider range of "gender experience" was now seen as socially acceptable (Gallagher 2003, 56).

Atwood also suggests that for evangelical theocrats, eroticizing women through control of literacy would be a real possibility. When Offred reads, "the Commander sits and watches me doing it.... This watching is a curiously sexual act, and I feel undressed while he does it. I wish he would turn his back, stroll around the room, read something himself. Then perhaps I could relax more, take my time. As it is, this illicit reading of mine seems a kind of performance" (*HT* 184). The female reader, to an Atwoodian evangelical, is an objectified reader. Her literacy is only allowed in so far as it serves male interests, which are primarily reproductive. Thus female voices are regulated not only through restrictions on writing, but through aurality as well. By restricting information flow to women, evangelical men hope to limit how much evangelical women are able to listen. Discursive communication is restricted to comments on the weather and what food is available; when Offred and a fellow handmaid, Ofglen, go beyond this restriction, Ofglen disappears (and is presumably killed). For males, the aestheticization of women has always been a sexual act; dressing women up in revealing clothes, or engaging in kinky sex play, is merely a means by which the men of Gilead exercise their cultural dominance. By forcing the female subject to become a female object, the Gileadian theocracy engages in the ultimate deprivation of voice. A woman ceases to be a being, ceases even to be, and simply becomes a thing.

Offred's ability to gain agency over this overwhelming patriarchal oppression is ambiguous. Offred comments, "My self is a thing I must now compose, as one composes a speech. What I must present is a made thing, not something born" (*HT* 66). The suggestion of composing oneself would initially suggest a sense of powerful sense of self-actualization; a willing of oneself into the world, and a bending of the world to fit one's will, much in the spirit of Nietzsche. Yet there is nowhere in literature a more un-Nietzschean character than Offred. The only way to compose herself (both in the sense of self-creation and calming) is to make herself into an object, not a being. This, of course, fulfills the very sexual fantasies of aestheticized, objectified women that the Commander and his fellow Gilead patriarchs seek to engage in. Her sense of the self as a product works hand in hand with her realization that her body is a tool ("a made thing"). Thus, even when speaking in language that is deeply tinged with a note of longing for the lost aesthetic life, Offred realizes that ultimately she is part of a system of consumeristic production.

Atwood here, however, puts too much faith in female literacy as an agent of social change. Far from objecting to female literacy, evangelical males from the Puritans on have encouraged it and for purely selfish reasons. A woman that cannot read the Bible cannot find all those "wonderful" verses ordering female submission, female chastity, and male dominance. While the literacy of secular women might present a threat to evangelical men, it is doubtful that any evangelical theocracy would want to dispense with the literacy of its own female population.

More fundamentally, however, Atwood's faith in the artistic process here is naïve. Since the feminist revolution, we have had forty years of feminist novels, both Second Wave and Third Wave, and besides a few relatively minor censorship battles, few of these novels have faced any meaningful attempts at restriction, at least in the United States. Atwood's work is not simply misplaced in its assumptions about evangelicalism and evangelical women; it's also largely irrelevant to how they live their lives. While evangelical female writers such as Lisa Samson and Renee Alston have made strides in recent years, forcing the evangelical male establishment to admit awareness of issues like sexual abuse and mental illness among women, *The Handmaid's Tale* is usually met with a knowing chuckle or rolled eyes by evangelical allies and enemies of feminism alike, when they know about the work at all. If it is meant to be a serious critique of evangelical culture, it simply fails in that attempt among much of the audience it should be seeking to convert: evangelicals themselves, especially the members of the patriarchal class and the victims of that class.

The word brings Atwood strength. It has brought her both power and cultural influence. It is therefore not surprising that Atwood has faith in it. Yet evangelicals should question that perspective, since Atwood herself uses the power of the word to silence words that might operate against her in a counter-hegemonic fashion. Moreover, Atwood silences the voices of evangelical women themselves. Atwood assumes that an evangelical woman such as Serena Joy would be furious if she were actually "taken at her word" about women's rights (*HT* 46). Yet not every reaction in favor of patriarchy need be motivated out of fear or hypocrisy. While fully acknowledging that egalitarianism would be a preferential position, it must be remembered that patriarchy may often be seen as a way, particularly among evangelicals, of making sure that men retain an attachment to the household that their wives and they create. This is especially the case among the true spiritual proletariat— poor, working-class and lower- middle-class evangelicals—who often have to deal with existing in vulnerable parts of the national economy, where the loss of one economic provider can be disastrous. Atwood, coming from a social caste where that is no longer the case, can afford to preach a "gospel" of liberation in a way that evangelical women are simply not yet able to. A more nuanced depiction of Gilead would perhaps more keenly have emphasized how even patriarchy-supporting females manipulate that system to their (occasional) advantage; it would be even better if Atwood could take herself outside of her upper-class subject position for even one moment, to observe the kind of painful questions about gender politics and compromise evangelical women must make every day in negotiating their way through not only patriarchy, but class oppression.

For Atwood, the pen, the instrument of artistic creation, is the ultimate phallic symbol, the tool by which women will reclaim their agency. Offred at one point in the *Handmaid's Tale* is able to use a pen for a brief instant. She relates, "The pen between my fingers is sensuous, alive almost, I can feel its power, the power of the words it contains. Pen Is Envy, Aunt Lydia would say.... Just holding it is envy. I envy the Commander his pen" (*HT* 186). The close physical resemblance of the pen and the penis motivates Offred to see it as the instrument by which she can regain her agency. It is the longed-for Thing, that unavailable but enticing object that is forever outside of one's reach, like the beautiful woman that the awkward virgin can never have sex with.

Yet there is a hidden truth in Offred's words, for the pen is also something violent, something violently alive, every bit as deadly as the phallus used to rape and control women. It was by the pen that many women in the Middle Ages were put to death, courtesy of witch hunt manuals such as *Malleus Maleficarum* (1487). It was courtesy of the pen that Marx wrote his fatal words, that Hitler spewed hatred that was heard around the world, that Joseph McCarthy penned speeches that condemned dozens of Atwood's fellow artists to years of social ostracism and blacklisting. The pen is many things, but it is not innocent. Whether used for good or ill, it is a moral agent in the world, in a sense almost as alive as the person wielding it. Like most dystopian writers (Ray Bradbury in particular comes to mind), Atwood focuses on the promise of the pen; what she does not understand is that there is a peril to it as well, not just to evil patriarchal men, but to everyone. "Pen-Is Envy" is really as immature a concept, and as illogical, as the Freudian misogyny Atwood so rightly laughs at. It is understandable to envy the manipulator of the pen for what he or she gains from the instrument — power, wealth, sexual dominance; to expect the pen, however, to become two crossed phalluses on which to martyr the future feminist saviors of mankind, is perhaps expecting a bit too much of such an object. In other words, we should not envy the pen for the object itself; as an object it does not ennoble or somehow make superior the individuals capable of wielding it.

Thus Atwood merely reenacts the male rape fantasy by engaging in ideological rape of an opponent who is relatively marginalized and helpless compared to spiritually bourgeois feminist academics. The word becomes the tool by which she subjugates and eroticizes the evangelical phallic symbol, the pen that is a penis, the penis that is a pen. By holding up the threat of evangelical male rape, of a horde of Gileadian theocrats hellbent on turning secular academic women into sexual playthings for their every whim, Atwood implies that this is, in fact, what one's next door evangelical neighbor may be contemplating in the darkest recesses of his mind. *The Handmaid's Tale* becomes Atwood's version of *A Birth of a Nation* (1915), with poor, illiterate Northern fundamentalist whites replacing poor, illiterate Southern (presumably fundamentalist) blacks. That the academic left can take such a vision seriously as a threat to their freedoms is perplexing. Indeed that such paranoia is still common today is quite surprising, since similar evangelical fears of "homosexual pedophile rapists" and New Age cabals had largely, if not entirely, dissipated by 2012. But then, of course, evangelicals have begun trying to interact with their gay and New Age neighbors. The same can hardly be said for Margaret Atwood and the cadre of feminist elites who followed in her wake.

Franky Schaeffer's Portofino *Trilogy: The Insider/Outsider Critique of Evangelicalism and the Failure of Worldview Theology*

Most evangelicals do not like talking about Franky (Frank) Schaeffer, son of the famous Francis Schaeffer. His very public split from the evangelical elite scandalized the evangelical community in the early 1990s, when he published the first volume of the *Portofino* trilogy, which is, as Francis Schaeffer's biographer Barry Hankins points out, a rather "thinly disguised expose" of the Schaeffer family (2008, 163). To most evangelicals, the most shocking scenes in the novel are the discovery of Elsa's (stand-in for Edith Schaeffer, Francis Schaeffer's wife) affair with a coworker, and the discovery (in the second novel *Saving Grandma*) of locked-away hardcore pornography that belongs to Ralph Becker (Francis Schaeffer) (Hankins 2008, 163–164). These two scenes, though relatively innocuous in another context, were scandalous to evangelicals who liked to think of their leaders as morally pure and upright. Whether or not they represent actual events is, of course, impossible to know. Certainly, the painfully and overly verbose, almost perverse sex talks that Elsa gives young Calvin Becker (Franky) mirror those that Edith Schaeffer gave her son (Franky Schaeffer 2007 [hereafter cited as *CFG*], 109).

The exact biographical facts of Franky Schaeffer's life are difficult to determine, as Francis Schaeffer's biographer Barry Hankins has a somewhat subtle but very real bias against Franky, and Franky's autobiography is too emotionally laden to be considered fully trustworthy. But it is commonly agreed that Franky was a major force behind his father's motion picture version of *How Should We Then Live?* (1977) (Hankins 2008, 161). Though a major evangelical player in the early eighties, Franky had left the evangelical movement by the late eighties and embraced Eastern Orthodoxy in 1990 (226, 233). He has since spent most of his time writing and commenting on politics, occasionally for MSNBC, where he is considered an expert on evangelicalism (a rather dubious claim).

The *Portofino* trilogy is an uneven series of novels. The first two volumes,

Portofino and *Saving Grandma*, largely read like hack work; there is, however, a considerable improvement by *Zermatt*, which is memorable fiction, if still somewhat constrained by Franky's perceptual limitations. Each novel is mainly concerned with Calvin Becker's escapades as a developing, sexual boy in an evangelical family; the setting is usually the Schaeffer's vacation places in Switzerland and Italy. Ralph Becker, Calvin's father, is a kind-hearted, gruff, working-class man (a description that was commonly applied to Francis Schaeffer), except when he gets in his "moods"; Elsa Becker, Calvin's mother, is a pious, somewhat self-righteous woman who is usually either complaining about Ralph's working-class origins or prying into Calvin's sex life.

Franky's trilogy is a repudiation of his family's legacy as the leading intellectual lights of evangelicalism. Though Franky himself deeply embraces the arts, he faults his evangelical upbringing for the fact that he did not become an important artist. As he puts it in *Crazy for God*: "If I'd had the discipline to concentrate on my art and had found a way of distancing myself from the evangelical community (and the easy money it soon offered), I might have gotten somewhere" (258). But what strikes Franky most about the "tragedy" of his evangelical upbringing is not how much it crippled his own art, but how much it enfeebled his father's own sense of pleasure at the world. Schaeffer laments, for instance, that his father, despite his private preference for Renaissance art, publicly proclaimed Reformational (Northern European, and therefore Protestant) art superior (205).

In the *Portofino* trilogy, the suffering of the elder Schaeffer is most dramatically portrayed in the third and final volume *Zermatt*, where Ralph Becker (the elder Schaeffer) goes through a dramatic breakdown and practically loses his faith. At the beginning of the novel, Calvin reminds the reader of the Schaeffers' elite evangelical heritage:

> Real Christians were mainly found in our denomination. Not even all other Presbyterians were Real Christians. Most were not. In fact, even in our mission Mom and Dad were clearly closer to the Lord than their coworkers.... Real Christians were "Kindred Spirits" as opposed to "just nominal Christians." So many people who seemed at first like Real Christians turned out not to be. In fact, who was and was not a Real Christian was something that had to be closely watched [Franky Schaeffer 2003 (hereafter cited as *Zermatt*), 48].

Schaeffer here points to the inherently divisive nature of the Reformed movement that spawned Christian worldview thinking. A crazy quilt of factional divides, like much of evangelicalism in general, it is a movement prone to a judgmental theology not much in keeping with the artist's need for detachment or disinterestedness from the world around him. Thus, despite the support of some contemporary worldview supporters, Kantian disinterestedness cannot really work in an evangelical context, because the Christian is too concerned with what is "really Christian" or "really art." This desire for the really real Franky sees as profoundly naïve; naturally enough, since the Eastern Orthodox tradition to which he now belongs promotes a more mystical, less rationalistic (in the best sense of those terms) approach to theology.

Also implicit in young Calvin's words is a pointed rejection of the idea that the evangelical elite are one big happy family. The frequent church splits, theological double-crosses and heresy hunting that goes on throughout the *Portofino* trilogy is a painful reminder to evangelical elites that the cosmopolitan class themselves have their own internal quarrels and church battles, battles they often try to hide from the faithful. Ralph Becker's hypocrisy in judging other Christians as less worthy than himself is symptomatic of a wider hypocrisy among the evangelical elite, a feeling that their populist followers are suckers. Franky both condemns and indulges in such exploitation, remarking in *Crazy for God* that he "learned that if you talk 'too fast,' all those huntin,' fishin,' shootin' lifetime-NRA member types, the ones that worry about the United Nations, have their eyes too close together, and have wives caked with about forty pounds of makeup per square inch, start to look at you funny" (*CFG* 325). Clearly for Franky, at least, men like Ralph Becker, men like his father, are engaged in an evangelical sleight of hand, blithely promoting an image of a united front, while secretly looking down their noses at their followers. This vision cannot solely be constrained to the Schaeffers, either. As we saw in chapter 1, evangelicals such as Tim Keller and David Hegeman in part share this elitist view of evangelical culture. Franky's not honest enough to admit he's part of the cultural elite, but he's honest enough to be bothered by it, which is certainly more than can be said for Keller or Hegeman.

Calvin, like Franky, is intensely ashamed of his evangelical heritage. Whenever he tries to tell people what Ralph does,

> people, even children, would get a funny polite stare on their faces and say "Oh, how interesting," then avoid me as much as they could after that, the same way you see people kind of step aside when funny-looking Hasidic Jews in hats, long coats and beards come walking down the street, as if they didn't want to catch something, as if they might wake up in a long coat with weird ringlets of hair ... and all kinds of stuff strapped to their foreheads, if they got too close [Franky 1992 (hereafter cited as *PF*), 54].

Evangelicalism, for Franky, is a disease, a highly contagious disease. Not only does it infect current believers and indoctrinate new believers, but it also culturally separates evangelicals from the "world" as deeply as if they came from a utterly alien people. Evangelicalism is a mark of cultural distinctiveness, but it is a cultural distinctiveness that evangelical elites such as Calvin and Ralph Becker, Francis and Franky Schaeffer, no longer want. Rather, these elites want to blend into the bliss of normality and mutual friendship. The problem is, the NRA-toting, working-class men and mascara-wearing women that Franky derides in *Crazy for God* (2007), the heart and soul of evangelicalism, want nothing to do with this proposition. Far to the contrary; these denizens of the margins of American culture continue to push evangelicalism into increasingly more creative and gaudy expressions of cultural distinctiveness: Jack Chick tracks, purity rings, KJV-only churches, spiritual warfare novels, deliverance ministries, the bizarre (and dangerous) Joel's Army, rapture films, A Beka textbooks, and a thousand other evangelical cultural distinctives that are common knowledge to evangelicals, but unknown outside the evangelical world.

Because Franky is embarrassed and estranged from that evangelical heritage, he reinvents his father, in *Zermatt*, as a modern, nearly secularized individual; again, how much of this image is Franky's and how much reflects reality is difficult to say, but it's certain that the elder Schaeffer never hinted at any repudiation or liberalization of his faith after his brief flirtation with the evangelical left in the sixties and early seventies. Ralph Becker, this reinvented Schaefferian liberal, breaks down in front of his children as he reads a passage he has been writing to his children:

> This is religion. Trust in the experiences of others communicated to us in human words. We have ... a hierarchy of values. The second, lesser reality of knowing is one in which we have invented a whole ritual of life to give it a shape, to feel secure within ourselves. The secular Jew believes most of what he reads in the *New York Times* and the fundamentalist Christian believes most of what he reads in the Bible. Neither one can objectively "know" anything because life is too short to test all hypotheses.... The *Times* is no more the "paper of record" than the Bible is "the truth"—no more and no less, for both describe a reality to readers who are only reading anything to begin with as a religious attempt to reach out and grasp for a sense of meaning.... Life is beautiful and words describe something we all long for. Maybe that means something [*Zermatt* 184].

This new invented Schaeffer focuses, as does both Franky's own Eastern Orthodoxy and certain forms of ethical relativism, on the uncertainty of our own epistemological systems. Ralph's theology here defines God by what he is not, rather than what he is, following the Eastern Orthodox rather than evangelical tradition. Because knowledge is uncertain, the evangelical system must by definition be wrong since it is based on a rationalistic system that presumes there can be epistemological certainty about the universe. In fact, this position is diametrically opposed to the very basis of worldview thinking, which, because it is based on Van Tilian presuppositional apologetics, presumes that there is a fundamental assumption undergirding the entire universe, namely that the Bible is the "ultimate source of truth" by which "all truth claims are judged" (Detwiler 1999, 85). Not only does Franky argue that his father would have accepted his own theological position (to which he was diametrically opposed); no, Franky has the inspiration to put those very words in his father's mouth, creating the ironic, unlikely, but highly entertaining situation of the elder Schaeffer, the century's most fanatical supporter of the ability to know the "really real," in fact knowing nothing.

For Ralph Becker, the elder Schaeffer now speaking in Franky's voice, what comes to matter is communication, and that communication can only be achieved if the epistemological certainties of evangelicalism are abandoned. Words, as in Atwood, are the tie to bind the universe and in Becker's eyes, perhaps find God. Ralph comes to believe, "All faith rests on the faith that we can communicate meaning to ourselves and to others. Everything is, therefore, religious, as we understand religion, because every thought depends on an act of faith in affirming our own sanity and the sanity of others who will understand us" (*Zermatt* 245). For an ex-evangelical, or even a current one, this is one of the most moving passages in the *Portofino* trilogy; to escape beyond fundamentalism and retain some sense of faith, having been birthed in a faith that is both anti-word and full of words, one must trust in the ability of words to communicate. If there is a faith, if there is a God and therefore beauty, it can only come through humanity's sense of the universe as a religious place — a place endowed with aesthetic meaning.

Yet in Schaeffer's work, as in Atwood's, that faith in words may be somewhat misplaced. Schaeffer's realization of the fundamentally religious character of language is the same as the mythopoeics, who were obsessed with its mythic quality. Indeed, it is likely that Schaeffer was inspired by the mythopoeic movement here. But it is one thing to acknowledge the religiosity of language; it is quite another thing to "find hope in beauty and above all, in our response to it" (*Zermatt* 246), as if our aestheticized reactions to the universe are granted to us by God. What if one's response to a beautiful German girl, for instance, is to fight for the right to kill Jewish or African-American girls? What if one's response to the artistry of Kubrick's *Clockwork Orange* is to go out and murder and rape? The fact that people have a sense of beauty, a sense of taste, comforts Schaeffer, as it did Atwood. Yet it should more properly terrify them. From a secular standpoint, that sense enchains virtually everything humans do, from our reactions to human excrement to our embrace of political parties. From a religious standpoint, we simply do not know for whose aesthetic benefit the universe was created. For all humanity knows, God could find the screams of the damned in hell the most moving, entertaining symphony He has ever encountered. In other words, the beauty we find in the universe may not be meant for our particular benefit; indeed, it may be meant for our detriment, even our destruction. And this could be true even if beauty is viewed more secularly. Humans find beauty in reproduction, for instance, and that leads to an overpopulation of the planet. A faith in words and beauty may in the end merely be meaningless vocal sounds about a meaningless concept from an insignificant species. Beauty is a concept humans and other sentient beings impose on the universe; human beings should not be surprised if the universe or its Maker is not impressed by it.

And ultimately, Ralph's realization of the beauty of the words and the world around him is not enough to save him. In the most tragic scene of *Zermatt*, the elder Becker scourges himself rather than let his son be punished for a minor sexual dalliance (218–221). Metaphorically, he is wounded as Franky felt his father was wounded, by the evangelical battles of the twenties and thirties, which entrapped him in a very authoritarian belief system (*CFG*, 114–118). Franky turns his father into a martyr and a fool, the quintessential Christian figure of Christ, and thereby (again) metaphorically crucifies his father to atone for the sins done in his name.

The *Portofino* series ultimately fails as a convincing work of art precisely because it puts too much faith in Francis Schaeffer's ideology, not too little. Though rejecting the specifics of worldview ideology, Franky was powerfully molded by its aestheticization of life. Whether by emphasizing the power of words, having his fictional self taking in the shores of Italy, or concentrating on the beauty of the female body (a frequent preoccupation of the younger Schaeffer), Franky was his father's son. Whether he has created a mythology of himself as long lasting or believable as his father's own self-mythologizing is doubtful. What is certain is the *Portofino* trilogy, by exposing the underbelly of the Schaefferian legacy and the worldview movement, as well as the pain that resulted, condemns the very sense of beauty Franky tries to support.

Octavia Butler: Parables Within Parables

Octavia Butler's *Parable of the Sower* (1993, hereafter cited as *Sower*) and *Parable of the Talents* (1998, hereafter cited as *Talents*) show how easily even well-intentioned feminist writing could stereotype evangelical culture. Octavia Butler, a skilled author who was the winner of a Macarthur Fellowship and a Nebula Award for Best Novel (*Talents* 449), was far from being anti-religious. She realized the value of religion, and speculated that if religion was replaced, something else even worse might take its place. While Butler acknowledged that religion "does a lot of harm" and might be better off not existing, she did not exhibit the kind of phobia of evangelicals that characterizes Franky Schaeffer or Margaret Atwood (Harrison 2010, 9).

Butler's greater sophistication here is not surprising; as a former "Born

6. Feminisms, Fanaticism and Evangelicalism 157

Again Baptist" (Harrison 2010, 9), she had lived in the mainstream of black evangelicalism. As a historical generalization, African-American writers have usually done a better job at depicting evangelical culture, whether its black or white variant, than white novelists, most likely because most of these authors had more than a passing contact with the evangelical mainstream, something not always true of white authors writing about evangelicalism. Among a number of nuanced works on evangelicalism, such African-American classics as Harriet Jacobs's *Incidents in the Life of a Slave Girl* (non-fiction), Richard Wright's *Native Son* (fiction) and *Black Boy* (non-fiction), James Baldwin's *Go Tell It on the Mountain* (fiction) and Toni Morrison's *Paradise* (fiction) all portray variants of black and/or white evangelicalism with considerably more sophistication than is found in works such as *Inherit the Wind* or *The Handmaid's Tale*.

Considering Butler's historical antecedents in African-American fiction, the relative detachment with which she viewed evangelicalism, and her obvious skill as a writer, it is therefore surprising that the *Parable* series engages in some of the same simplistic dichotomies between oppressed female writers (also, in this novel, a messiah-writer) and a theocratic regime seeking to limit the freedom of those writers. The *Parable* series, written at the height of the nineties, reflects completely understandable African-American fears of the Christian Right, with its often implicit, and sometimes explicit, racism. However, the *Parable* series, like *The Handmaid's Tale*, tends to overemphasize both the theocratic and the anti-feminist elements of the Christian Right, while failing to note or even so much as mention evangelicalism's (particularly, in these novels' case, white evangelicalism's) own troubled class position.

The lead character in the *Parable* series is Lauren Olamina, a messiah-figure who slowly builds a peculiar, almost pantheistic religion to take humanity to the stars. Also important in the second book of the series is Lauren's daughter, Larkin (who for most of the novel and most of her life goes under the name Asha Vere), a young woman who has never known her mother and resents her when she does, but uses her own fertile imagination to create "dreammask" virtual-reality scenarios that resemble a combination of novelistic fiction and film. The two women are separated shortly after Larkin's birth by a theocratic government called Christian America led by Texas senator Andrew Steele Jarret, which enslaves Lauren and sends Larkin off to an adoptive home. Lauren goes on to see her religion prosper and reach for the stars. Larkin, however, succumbs to the rhetoric of Christian America for much of her childhood, and though she eventually abandons its tenets, its warped view of life scars her imaginative powers.

Therefore in the *Parable* series we have two figures juxtaposed against each other: the oppressed female messiah-writer, who, in traditional science fiction Nietzschean fashion, overcomes her oppressors and conquers all, versus an oppressed woman who is not so lucky, who has to make long term, rather than short term, compromises with the theocratic system. But in both cases, whether *ubermensch* or *untermensch*, the ultimate consequence is a loss of love and fraternity between mother and daughter. The oppressed messiah is heroic, but is also a partly damaged individual — a master/slave rather than solely a master in the more simplistic Nietszcheanism of science fiction writers such as Robert Heinlein. And this dual identity is a result of an evangelical victimizing culture, which despite its relative weakness in terms of social class and literary reputation is itself solely the negative form of Nietzscheanism.

Lauren's religion is built on one deceptively simple principle: God is change (*Sower*, 242). She means this as a literal truth. God is a liminal being, the thing in between, a process or even a product, as much as he/she is a producer. Nor is there any sense of God being a personal being (195). Instead, God can be whatever change creates in human beings, or however human beings change their universe. Lauren writes, "God is both creative and destructive. Demanding and yielding, Sculptor and clay. God is Infinite Potential. God is Change" (242). Like the self-mythologizing Atriedies family of *Dune*, Lauren's God is as much a creation of its followers as a creator; more so, in fact, since there is no notion of a teleologically significant God forming the universe at the beginning of history or time. Butler's notion here, melding Eastern and transcendentalist views of God, seeks to move beyond the dichotomous notion of a solely good or solely evil being that characterizes so much of evangelical theology.

Furthermore, Lauren's religion focuses on personal agency, but whereas Offred was powerless against her enslavement, Lauren uses tooth, claw, and nails to act on the universe. One has the choice of being either sculptor or clay, of being either a "shaper of God" or a "victim of God" (*Sower* 27). Thus, while Atwood represents evangelical patriarchy as being a hegemonic force of a victimizing God, Butler portrays it more as a dominant force that can still be resisted both passively and actively. Because God is change, God can eventually be sculpted into an artistic and theological creation that the majority of feminists can agree with. As a force both adaptive and maladaptive, it is up to human beings to mold God in their own image, an image worthy not only of themselves, but also of the cultural heritage and children they wish to pass down to posterity. God, in Lauren's theological system, is not static, but is a point of contention, both on the symbolic level of change, and on the literal level, between a static Christian America and Lauren's Earthseed religion, which embraces the change she promotes.

Lauren's main objection to evangelical theology is that its deity is a representation of God, rather than God himself/herself/itself. If God is a process (change), then any attempt to signify It reduces both the adaptive and maladaptive possibilities of that God-process. In this sense, despite the intense creativity the *Parable* series promotes, Lauren's own religion faults evangelicalism for not being iconoclastic enough. It fails to knock down Jehovah Father and Jesus Christ, who themselves can be viewed as icons of something even grander and more magnificent. Lauren warns the followers of Earthseed to "create no images of God. Accept the images that God has provided. They are everywhere, in everything.... The universe is God's self-portrait" (*Sower* 283). God-as-the-universe is an artistic ideal to aspire to in Earthseed; God as beyond or above the universe shows an inadequate representation of who God is. If the universe is God's self-portrait, then creating a portrait in the image of only one tiny portion of that universe — Mid-Eastern and European man, circa 0–300 A.D.— is, by Lauren's estimation, hopelessly limited.

Yet, both Lauren and the evangelicals of Christian America are making God in their own image and are engaged in a form of myth-making. What is happening in the *Parable* series is a battle of rivaling mythologies: a feminist vision of multicultural pantheistic religion, opposed by tyrannical theocrats and an evangelical vision of a "purified" nation state that insists on "being a throwback to some earlier 'simpler' time" (*Talents* 20). This theocracy, led by Jarett, wants to return the country to a "magical time when everyone believed in the same God, worshipped him in the same way, and understood that their safety in the universe depended on completing the same religious rituals and stomping anyone who was different" (20). Yet again, it is unlikely that true theocracy represents evangelical ideals, let alone evangelical interests, for the majority of evangelicals. Butler's representation of evangelicals here therefore takes on many of the classist stereotypes of evangelicals promoted by spiritually bourgeois feminists of the era, where evangelicals are repressive backwoods people engaged in antiquated religious rituals that serve no rational purpose.[1] The evangelical desire for the simple life, a not unreasonable response to the ravages rapid industrialization and sociocultural changes have had on the evangelical community,[2] here takes on the form of a social pathology. More complex explanations for evangelical behavior, which Butler has clearly proven herself capable of providing in both print and televised interviews, are absent in the *Parable* series.

Evangelicalism's desire for sameness Lauren marks off as symbolic of their resistance to change; resistance, in other words, to her God. The evangelicals of Christian America thus can be seen as broadly representative of all the theological forces in America pushing for a slower or nonexistent rate of cultural evolution. Earthseed, a philosophy that thrives on evolution, both biological and cultural, can only see this as maladaptive; one is not showing one's artistry to create the universe. Yet Lauren ultimately puts far more faith in the concept of change than that concept can really hold. After all, social change, as Lauren freely acknowledges, is not always a social good. Evangelicals, like other conservative religious groups, can often make a quite convincing case for maintaining the status quo, particularly considering the fact that evangelicals have reason to fear that their cultural and class position can only go down if they subscribe to the kind of secularized religion that Lauren promotes. This is only natural on their part; as pointed out in chapter one, a class is defined as much by its being perceived as by its being. Even if evangelicals are not lower class, they have been conditioned by secular media from as far back as *Elmer Gantry* to perceive themselves as such. It is not surprising, therefore, that they do not want to fall back into a subservient class position.

Social change, even if it turns out for the good, is often seen as simply too big a risk for most evangelicals to take. Evangelicals do not want to craft their God, to artistically mold their world, but to be molded by it. While feminists long for agency, evangelicals long for the absence of agency. Evangelicals do not mind being God's victims, or God's pawns, which means that in Lauren's analysis their theological system is too geared to being the clay and not enough to being the sculptor. Though the religion of Earthseed stresses adaptability to change, it encourages "believers" to "rig the game" by shaping God — Change — as they will. Indeed, "God exists to be shaped" (*Sower* 22). Focusing on themselves as artistic objects, created *imago dei*, evangelicals risk losing their creative potential because they do not try to overthrow God's authority over that potential.

If Lauren is defined by this fight against evangelicalism's rejection of human creative potential, Larkin is defined by precisely that lack of creative potential. The name she is given after her abduction by Christian America — Asha Vere — is symbolic of that forfeiture of creative potential. Asha Vere is the name of a beautiful black Christian character in some of the Christian America marketed Dreammask programs (*Talents* 241). Even at the level of signification, Larkin is defined by Christian American artistic standards. Those standards, as Larkin relates, enforce a "mindless rigidity" (305). Larkin, a black female whose interests are clearly not being served by Christian America, is enticed to believe in that same state, because her namesake represents all the superficial characteristics to which she aspires to (241). Yet what Larkin never realizes during her lifelong estrangement from her mother is that Asha Vere is in many ways the mirror image of Lauren Olamina, a dark, twisted vision of what her own creative potential could be, unchained from an antifeminist, white-dominated theocratic reading of blackness and femininity.

The reception of Larkin's own creative potential is also minimalized in trials that Lauren never underwent. While Lauren, the product of a proud if poor independent community, eventually is able to escape the residual (and more multicultural and liberal) evangelical training of her own youth, Larkin, marginalized by a much more theocratic, white-dominated evangelicalism, ultimately finds her creativity suppressed by teachers and parental figures. When it is found out that Larkin is creating her own Dreammask scenarios (*Talents* 361), instead of merely viewing the old Christian ones, all her protestations of innocence are in vain: "It didn't matter that I [Larkin] had said from the beginning that the stories were only made up.... And it didn't matter that the Dreammask scenarios we were all allowed to experience were equally imaginary. It was as though my teachers believed that all the possible stories had been created, and it was a sin to make more ... at least it was a sin for me" (358). Theocratic evangelicalism, stuck in staticity, sees a finitude of stories. Larkin, again unknowingly like her mother, longs for an infinitude of narratives—that is the nature of having a God of change. Larkin wants the god of her mother, without knowing it. Instead, she is given the God of Christian America, a God whose narrative has been fixed for some two thousand years, with little variation. But what's even more significant is that Larkin, like Lauren, wants to create her own narratives and therefore have agency over her own creative potential. She does not want to be limited by a nation-state that tries to position her in the passive status of religious object, but like her mother wants to be the sculptor, adapting the illusions of the dreammask to her own fantasies rather than reliving the fantasies of others.

Ultimately, it is as much the boredom of evangelical staticity that repels Larkin as anything else. She finds many of the Dreammask scenarios she is permitted as a teenager to be "tired, dull, boring things. Characters were always being shown the error of their ways, suffering for their sins, and then returning to God" (*Talents* 358). Staticity in culture and theology ultimately leads to formulaic narratives, as old stories are told and retold. A limitation of the number of narratives leads to a sense of ennui, as certain familiar scenarios are played and replayed for the benefit of the evangelical child or teenager. Evangelical narrative in the *Parable* series, at least when implemented by Christian America, ends up being a form of religious indoctrination. Stories are told, not to artistically enrich the indoctrinated individual, but to dominate that individual's sense of their own life-narrative. For Butler, the stories that Christian America tells—its grand religious narratives—are philosophical illusion, dreams of the Dreammask, by which the nation-state maintains its dominance over subject populations.

Yet an unbiased reader would have to fault this depiction in at least two crucial areas. First, in emphasizing the indoctrinatory aspects of evangelicalism, Butler overemphasizes evangelical cultural uniqueness in this regard. For instance, Larkin's adoptive evangelical mother Kayce is more "literal-minded than any human being with normal intelligence" (*Talents* 305). But evangelicalism is hardly alone in restricting imagination. If the bane of theological orthodoxy (theological correctness, if the reader will pardon the neologism) is the indoctrinatory aspect of the religious right, then political correctness has served a similar purpose among many leftists since at least as far back as the bitter crossfire of dialectical Marxists in the 1920s and 1930s. Nor is indoctrination fundamentally a cultural evil, a fact Butler herself perplexingly seems to partly acknowledge in interviews, though refute in her fiction. She has remarked, "Religion kept some of my relatives alive because it was all they had. If they hadn't had some hopes of heaven, some companionship in Jesus, they probably would have committed suicide, their lives were so hellish" (Brown 2010, 186). Clearly, therefore, not every religious narrative, even every evangelical narrative, is a problem, a vision Butler is more clearly able to articulate in interviews than in her fiction.

The second major problem with Butler's critique of evangelicalism's effect on Larkin is that it fails to ask why having a limited number of narratives is a bad thing. What if the old narratives are good? What if they have proven resoundingly culturally adaptive? Self-evidently, if a certain narrative structure has provided a culture with resilience or a sense of self-identity that allowed it to maintain cultural coherence, it is unlikely that that culture will just off-handedly abandon its master narrative(s). And evangelicalism's cultural narrative, by evangelical standards, has proven wildly successful. Evangelicals measure their influence most in the saving of lost souls, and as a relatively fast-growing Christian group (Zein 2007), and in America, one of the few religious groups to retain a fairly steady membership, evangelicalism is resistant to any change that will interfere with that success. Cultural adaptability is not necessarily synonymous with biological adaptability; change too much, or too quickly, and a culture can wilt, as well as flower. By examining only the positive aspects of social change, Butler's narrative of evangelicalism aligns itself with a spiritually bourgeois white feminism that arguably has less in common with Butler's work than the theocratic elements of evangelicalism that Butler opposes.

One could hardly fault any African-American for being suspicious of white evangelicalism. The Christian Right has had a long and sordid history of racism against blacks. But this very real racist effort often masks profound cultural affinities, affinities that unite black Protestants potentially far more with the evangelical community than with white, often upper-class, feminists and humanists. Foremost of these affinities is a shared cultural heritage — among the Holiness, Pentecostal, and evangelical Methodist traditions — with the worship and preaching styles of African-American Protestant churches. Many of these groups, particularly Pentecostals, also have a richer (if not untroubled) multicultural past than the staid mainline Protestant churches or Jewish synagogues. Perhaps these cultural affinities cannot reshape these divided racial-and-religious groupings; but they do point to fruitful alliances on certain issues of common interest.

Art remains one of those issues. If evangelicals should have little love for the arts, African-Americans should have even less. From the very foundation of modern aesthetic theory, the West's standards of beauty and even sense of taste have been profoundly racialized. Both David Hume and Immanuel Kant endorsed the view that blacks were incapable of a "refined taste for the arts" (Shiner 2001, 139). The Romantic cult of the genius may have produced great art, but its inspiration of Nietzsche ended up in turn creating, along with social Darwinism, the Nazi mythology of the *ubermensch*—a mythology clearly not in African-Americans' long-term interest. And despite the overwhelming quantity of quality African-American fiction over the last fifty years, one can still find professors racist or simply ignorant enough to question the value of Richard Wright, Ralph Ellison, and James Baldwin. Meanwhile, popular art and advertising demeans African-Americans by subtly portraying them as intellectually inferior or aesthetically unpleasing. Despite six million deaths and counting, the Aryan man and his blonde cheerleader girlfriend are still the default models for American, indeed Western, standards of beauty, and this seems unlikely to change.

Butler's analysis of evangelicalism is not totally wrong; in its current form it poses a threat to African-American and feminist cultural interests. Nor, as has been pointed out before, would it be advisable for African-Americans to abandon the arts as completely as this work advises white evangelicals to do. Popular stereotypes of African-Americans, playing on America's long racist legacy, have a profounder effect on America's cultural psyche than much more recent, and less inflammatory, depictions of evangelicals. But it would also be wrong to reject a commonly shared heritage because of the difficulty of effecting meaningful social change. By promoting a more respectful attitude towards African-Americans and women in popular media and the arts, evangelicals may be able to change some of their own public image, while helping, if only slightly, a community they have historically wronged. That may not be the kind of radical change Octavia Butler hoped for; but in a bifurcated American political landscape, it may be the best these two communities can do.

Conclusion

By the presidential election of George Bush in 2000, American politics was firmly divided into opposing camps, in large resembling the same camps that had arisen in the early 1980s. While there were signs of liberalization in some parts of evangelicalism — a growing acceptance of rock music, the first meetings of the Emergent Church — by and large the movement was perceived (and perceived itself) as a force of cultural, compassionate conservatism. Yet despite the increasing political division in America, in the arts a strange thing happened in the 2000s; a growing multiplicity of voices commenting on evangelicals led to an opening up of the dialogue about evangelical belief. While most narratives of evangelicalism were still largely hostile to the movement, there were also new voices that articulated an alternative vision of evangelicalism, neither as prosaically rosy as evangelicalism's own narrative of itself nor as hostile as the works of Atwood, Franky Schaeffer, and Butler. Whether these new narratives represented a fully articulated "third way" of viewing evangelicalism or merely another blip of tolerance for evangelical belief, like the Age of Fantasy, is a question that still remains to be answered.

7

More Problems, Added Possibilities

Since the 2000 national election, evangelicals have come increasingly into the national spotlight. There are several reasons for this. The bombing on September 11, 2001, led many Americans to realize that religious fundamentalism was still alive and well in the world. In turn, many American leftists made understandable but rather facile comparisons between evangelicals (the so-called "American Taliban") and Islamic fundamentalists, ignoring the many real differences in strategy and goals that made American evangelicals a somewhat more progressive force in world politics than their Islamic fundamentalist counterparts. Evangelical objections to gay marriage helped sway the 2004 election (W. Martin 2005, 390), leading to a series of movies, reality television series, and documentaries on evangelicalism, ranging from Alexendra Pelosi's excellent *Friends of God* (2007) to the hyperbolic *Jesus Camp* and the expose of the purity ball movement, *Virgin Daughters* (2008). Evangelicalism became a religious movement attracting widespread general attention, as it supported the elimination of abortion, campaigned for abstinence, applauded George Bush's Defense of Marriage Amendment and fought for some rather ridiculous causes, like keeping the phrase "Under God" in the American Pledge of Allegiance (W. Martin 2005, 390).

There is no dominant faction in the DDM model for this period, because the period has not really ended yet. One trend that has emerged, however, has been noted by D. Michael Lindsay: "As more evangelicals have entered the elite strata of society, a significant division has emerged within the movement between ... 'cosmopolitan' and 'populist' evangelicalism" (2007, 218–219). For Lindsay, this emergence of an evangelical elite has been developing for far longer than has often been credited; he, for instance, expresses understandable consternation at media reporters' inability to understand that there are not more evangelicals today; they are just a lot better organized (xi). Obviously such organization takes long-term effort and also political skill, intellectual traits that the left does not often associate with evangelicals.

Certainly, however, there have been cosmopolitan organizations, often but not always Reformed, which have felt emboldened by the increased prominence and visibility of evangelicals within the wider American culture. The marginal evangelical group Christian Exodus, for instance, sincerely believed that it could get South Carolina to secede from the Union — again (Charalambous 2007). Reformed guru Doug Wilson tried to create his own tiny religious empire in Moscow, Idaho, tying his newly founded university New St. Andrews with the worst kind of theocratic and pro-slavery, neo-Confederate rhetoric imaginable (Worthen 2007; Quinlan and Ramsey [2012]). Other thinkers such as William Lane Craig have delighted in highly gymnastic feats of debating skill, often emerging victorious in debates not because they answer opponents' objections, but precisely because they do not. Learning a lesson from Schaeffer, they "take the roof off" their opponents' beliefs while never bothering to examine their own.

There are two reasons why this kind of debate is culturally toxic. First it encourages in Reformed evangelicals an unwarranted sense of their cultural superiority over both their fellow evangelicals and non-evangelicals as well. As a result, the Reformed movement's penchant for being the think-tank behind evangelical political action is likely in the future to take on an increasingly dictatorial stance, if not averted by concerted non-Reformed efforts. Secondly, this Reformed dictatorialness, when combined with other evangelicals' unfortunate cultural predilection for hostile rhetoric, may embolden secular novelists to continue to use the tired clichés of the eighties and nineties as their defining paradigms for judging evangelical culture.

Much of the recent focus on evangelicalism has indeed been negative, and this has extended to the arts as well as documentaries. The major fictional film on evangelicalism in the 2000s was the teen comedy *Saved!*, a satire that tended to be singularly lacking in any deep analysis of what made evangelicals tick. Instead its characters reeked of type casting: cool tolerant liberal Christian, sympathetic single mother, intolerant homophobe, clueless pastor, persecuted gay believer, and hip secular Jewish girl. Television series including *Battlestar Galactica* (2004–2009), *Firefly* (2002), and *Law and Order* (1990–2010) showed an ambivalence to fundamentalist movements, but an ambivalence that often masked real fear of religious belief. In mainstream literature, evangelicals received a largely hostile response: Tom Perotta's novels *The Abstinence Teacher* (2007) and *The Leftovers* (2011) were perhaps the most emblematic anti-evangelical novels of the 2000s. Though Perotta superficially claimed the former was well-researched, allowing for him to have a "submerged" feeling about evangelicalism (Perotta Reading Guide), in reality his works, especially *The Abstinence Teacher*, promoted the old, rehashed, religion-as-opiate metaphor of Karl Marx. Brian Caldwell's *We All Fall Down* was considerably superior in cultural analysis to Perotta's works and was also somewhat more ambivalent about evangelical belief, but it did see reason for concern in evangelicals' easy embrace of premillennialist dispensationalism. Meanwhile, *The Devil and Daniel Silverman* continued to express the nearly phobic reaction to evangelicals that had characterized eighties and nineties writers; only now, the victims of evangelicalism were LGBT individuals, not feminists.

But at the same time, the expanding search for new, uncovered fields of literary fiction and the increasing entry of evangelicals and recently deconverted ex-evangelicals into the literary world allowed for a greater deal of complexity than had been seen since the mid-sixties. One particularly moving example of this was the graphic novel *Blankets*, an elegant eulogy to an artist's loss of faith in his search for artistic creativity. Sigrid Nunez's *Salvation City* also showed real narrative fairness in its complicated, multifaceted rendering of an evangelical youth's maturation into adulthood. But the most unique work of the 2000s on evangelicals was Leif Enger's *Peace Like a River*— it was the first major novel on evangelicals by an evangelical since the racist works of Thomas Dixon almost a century before. Enger's work spelled a partial end to evangelicalism's exodus from the arts. Whether that end represent a blessing or a calamity is one of the major themes of this chapter.

The Devil Made Him Do It: Theodore Roszak and the Continued Stereotyping of Evangelicals

Theodore Roszak's *The Devil and Daniel Silverman* was a moderately successful satire published in the early 2000s. Roszak was a professor of history at California State University and a prominent social commentator on the sixties and that decade's social meaning (Roszak 2003 [hereafter cited as Devil], Author Note). While Roszak is individually more famous than Thompson or Leif Enger, *The Devil and Daniel Silverman* seems not to be particularly well known, largely disappearing from view after its release (to moderate acclaim) in 2003.

The Devil and Daniel Silverman, much like the film *Saved!*, is something of a farce, and deliberately so. It tells the story of a sarcastic left-wing Jewish homosexual author from San Francisco who goes to Minnesota to speak at a fundamentalist evangelical college and gets trapped there when a snowstorm ensues. This allows Roszak to put the author, Daniel Silverman, in a number of awkward and dangerous situations where he is confronted by the nemesis of evangelical intolerance.

Even this basic summation of the plotline partly conveys the lack of creativity that went into this production, as the setup of the novel could hardly be considered very original; Jewish–evangelical conflict has been the subject of many secular novels, even leading to such charged (and extremely unlikely) accusations as that an evangelical theocracy would dump Jews in the ocean if given a chance (*HT* 307); and of course, evangelical condemnation of homosexuality had understandably provoked outrage among many non-evangelicals. Yet *The Devil and Daniel Silverman* made no effort to contextualize these phenomena within the broader spectrum of evangelical culture. Instead, Roszak said that he designed the novel from a

> composite of any number of evangelical, and fundamentalist congregations I have come across.... I made a collage of their beliefs. Every moral position and theological doctrine mentioned in *The Devil and Daniel Silverman* is represented by a conservative Christian congregation somewhere.... Remember: we live in a country where Planned Parenthood Clinics have been fire-bombed and doctors have been killed for performing abortions. There are churches that resort to aversion therapy to deal with homosexuality and others that would like to take over the entire curriculum in our schools. There are many evangelical congregations that pray for the conversion of the Jews because they think God doesn't listen to anything but their prayers and many that believe AIDS is God's judgment on homosexuals (Archer Books [2012]).

Roszak's lack of understanding of evangelicalism is painfully obvious. One could create a collage of Catholicism that would make the Church into a group of Naziistic pedophile priests who conduct war against Muslims; or one could describe a secularist collage of atheist Marxist Randian Objectivists who are responsible for the deaths of millions. But these collages would make no sense, because they are generalizing from vastly differing subgroups of these ideologies, and different historical periods as well. Creating such collaged belief systems makes about as much literary — not to mention ethical — sense as calling all Muslims terrorists or all blacks good athletes. What Roszak is creating, in other words, is a thinly veiled cultural stereotype, one apparently countenanced by a number of spiritual bourgeois literary reviewers, if the novel's blurbs are to be believed. The truth is evangelicalism is a vastly Byzantine theological system with any number of theological viewpoints. Evangelicalism's position on both Judaism and AIDS are far more complex than Roszak acknowledges: As mentioned before, on the former issue, evangelicals have both a deep love of Jewish religious belief and a theological system that does promote anti–Semitism, but in a way that most evangelicals can themselves not really see. From an evangelical standpoint, they are a fanatically pro-Semitic group, and not just because of the Jews' place in pre-millennialist theology, as some secular critics maintain. As David A. Rausch points out in his *Communities in Conflict*, the most dangerous evangelical stereotypes of Jews are their "constant denigration of Pharisees and misunderstanding of Judaism." On the other hand, Jewish "stereotypes and caricatures abound in the belief that evangelicals are (or tend to be) anti–Semitic

7. More Problems, Added Possibilities 169

... and that evangelicals are lurking around every corner to convert Jews" (1991, 4). This kind of complexity, particularly in noting that the prejudices between these communities are mutual, acknowledged by Rausch, is nowhere present in Roszak's works. Roszak's point on AIDS is even more inexcusable. By the early 2000s, evangelicals were pushing for more AIDS funding, particularly in Africa (Lindsay 2007, 47–48); although that funding has often had negative and even homophobic consequences, the motivation behind it was sincere enough.

Thus from the start of *The Devil and Daniel Silverman*, Roszak operates from the assumption that many, and probably most, evangelicals are going to be anti–Semitic, anti–AIDS research, and anti-gay. These are essential elements of the novel and are problematic from the start, because the movement is, as pointed out before, not necessarily anti–Semitic, and is increasingly supportive of AIDS research (Lindsay 2007, 47–48); while considerable anti-gay sentiment does remain, the theological reasons for this phenomenon are often dramatically deemphasized, while the aspect of deliberate bigotry is often overemphasized, leading many people to falsely assume that evangelicals simply "hate" gays unilaterally, with no variance in degree of emotion or motivating impulse. Again, secular research does not bear this out. As critic Tanya Erzen has pointed out, after the eighties evangelical rhetoric about gays changed from a hate-filled rhetoric to a more-therapeutic approach, claiming "change is possible" for gays and lesbians (Erzen 2006, 145–149, 201–202). True evangelical discourse on homosexuality now tends to focus on gay individuals' need for love and redemption, if only out of the necessity to sell anti-gay politics to a modern audience (Apostolidis 2001, 81). This is important because that public shift in rhetoric has led to a greater complexity of responses to homosexuality to emerge from the evangelical mainstream. Even in the early 2000s, evangelical voices such as Jim Wallis and Brian McLaren were arguing for more nuanced vision of homosexuality (McLaren posits a rather interesting view of homosexuality in his book *The Last Word and the Word After That* [2005, 20–22] by imagining an evangelical family's reaction to an intersexual individual). By the time the film *Save Me*, a pro-gay, nuanced depiction of negative evangelical responses to homosexuality, came out in 2007, even a moderate press organ such as *Christianity Today* was willing to even give this pro-gay movie some (qualified) positive praise (Chattaway 2008). If Roszak had been creating a collage of voices, should not he have tried to listen to some of these voices, as well as agents of intolerance such as Fred Phelps and Jerry Falwelll?

In its narrative of the arts, *The Devil and Daniel Silverman* deviates little from other negative secular and mainline portrayals of evangelicalism's hatred of the artist. The novel begins with an inscription by Max Born: "The belief that there is only one truth and that oneself is in possession of it seems to me the deepest root of all evil that is in the world." Though Daniel Silverman is in some ways a flawed character, he is not someone who believes in such a monistic vision of morality. Evangelicals in the novel, however, clearly do. From an artistic standpoint, this is a problem for the modern secularist author because it prevents the kind of culturally pluralistic attitude that is considered desirable in modern fiction. After all, people who still are capable of utilizing terms like "faggots" and "yids," as Daniel thinks the inhabitants of North Fork (the setting of the novel) are, are obviously more likely to burn books than read them. While Silverman acknowledges that evangelicals possess a kind of cultural literacy, it is a dangerous literacy, because it is based on one book, rather than a plurality of texts (*Devil* 230–233).

Indeed, if Silverman deviates from other characters in secular novels it is only in that his analysis of the role of the arts in culture as a whole is somewhat sharper than, say, Franky Schaeffer's. Indeed, Silverman, much like Lauren Olamina, is in many ways a kind of iconoclastic iconophile, both book-loving and book-fearing. Silverman starts the novel as a total believer in the value and worth of literature. After meeting the people at North Fork, however, he reflects:

> Scripture was their cosmic security blanket; they looked to it for certainty guaranteed on the highest authority. Instead of opening the heart to free experience, their one book had slammed shut all the doors and windows.... That was where they found the confidence to revile and condemn and reject. Words in a book, words written by men. This, too, literature could do. It could devour the mind and chew it into mush, harden the heart and make murder legitimate. Worse than any physical threat he felt, this dim-witted idolatry of the book made him wonder if the written word, however dear it might be to him, was worth all the misery that had come of it [*Devil* 233].

Silverman therefore sees, as no other secular character had before him, that evangelicalism threatens the arts at a fundamental level. However, for Silverman, the threat of evangelicalism lies not in its being iconoclastic, as in *The Handmaid's Tale*, but in its being selectively iconophilic. Evangelicals do love to read, Silverman suggests, but only one book. And because evangelicals are devoted to one book and no other, it causes them to devalue works of art not made in their own cultural image. True art is supposed to, in Silverman's estimation, open the reader (or the viewer) to new experiences and new points of view; instead, the people of North Fork become devoted to one text and end up being incapable of opening their minds to any other way of reading. The book, for evangelicals, is to be a device by which they comfort themselves. However, in order to find that comfort, they must suppress any other emotion that books bring to readers, both to secular and evangelical readers. Thus, the secular reader presents a deadly threat to the evangelical reader, and vice-versa. The evangelical threatens the secular reader with the possibility that there may only be one way of reading; moreover, even if there is more than one way of reading, the whole methodology of selective iconophilism leading into iconoclasm calls into question the whole basis on which secular intellectuals construct their defense of the written word: the power of freedom of speech and ideas to create greater liberty and humanity throughout the world. Instead, Silverman thinks that the evangelical reader strikes at the very core of art because his selective iconophilism is more dangerous than any iconoclasm — the word is the most dangerous thing of all. The evangelical reader, in turn, is threatened by the fact that the secular reader promotes a diversity of experience that he is often incapable of appreciating or morally accepting.

Silverman also quite accurately critiques the kind of comprehensive view of the world that philosophies such as Christian worldview theology promote. The people of North Fork believe that in their book, there "was nothing that wasn't known, nothing strange, nothing new, nothing startling. Their book was all science, all history, all law, all politics enshrined in the quaint, often inscrutable English of seventeenth century divines" (*Devil* 232). Because philosophies such as worldview thinking use the Bible to try to encompass all forms of reading and thought, they end up devaluing any form of knowledge derived from non-biblical experience. As a result, worldview thinking and similar evangelical theologies risk simplifying a very complex book, while also placing more literary and theological weight on the book than it could possibly bear, *even if one assumes the book represents a form of factual truth.*

Given the thesis of this book, it should not surprise the reader to find that this work concurs with Silverman's dim view of the written word. What this work disputes is that devotion to one book, or to no books at all, "shuts all the doors and windows" to our experience of the world. It matters a great deal what books are being accepted and which rejected, and here I would take issue with Silverman's description of the Bible as being created by "a small band of underfed, know-it all schnorers dragging themselves around the deserts of Palestine five thousand years ago" only to be translated into the "inscrutable English of seventeenth century divines, most of whom still thought the world was shaped like a pancake and that women were the vessels of Satan" (*Devil* 232). That the Bible is a literary creation is, of course, a perfectly valid opinion. But one need not be a believing Christian or Jew to find literary merit in its pages, or to prefer it to all other books. In the wisdom of Ecclesiastes, the subtle musings of the book of Job are some of our profoundest philosophy. In the Torah and the Four Gospels are the cultural narratives of two of the world's greatest religions, and the foundational impetus for their sister religion, Islam. The Book of Revelation has both terrified and excited artistic imaginations for 2,000 years. In 1 Corinthians 13 is perhaps the definitive exploration of love in all of Western literature. Given that kind of literary pedigree, and the Bible's influence on writers ranging from Dante to Shakespeare to Hemingway, it is not surprising that evangelicals love this book, their narrative.

The Bible does not shut the door to all areas of worldly experience. What the Bible does perhaps shut the door to, and what threatens Silverman (and Roszak), is that the Bible challenges the production of fiction at its most fundamental level. This does not just mean the Old Testament, whose prohibitions against lying and idolatry long held up the development of fictional formats such as the novel and epic poem. What offends Roszak's sensibilities is that after 2,000 years, the great religious narratives of history — the various holy books of Buddhism, the Torah, the Four Gospels, Greco-Roman mythology, the hadith literature — continue to have a power that more secular texts lack. They tell stories of universal human significance, translatable across vastly differing cultures and nationalities. By contrast, *The Devil and Daniel Silverman* is chiefly to be appreciated by a small coterie of West Coast intellectuals and East Coast college professors. It is the Bible, the Dhammaparada, the Koran, the Torah that promote diversity of experience, that impel people to travel to far-off lands, to adventure into China or brave the oceans to settle a "new world" for God — all because of not the power of many works, but the power of one particular work of art over a widely divergent audience. And this means that evangelicals, in their ever-active iconoclasm, threaten to reduce art to its most foundational level — the respect for one work, for an overarching unity that creates oneness out of diversity. That work, which for evangelicals is the Bible, has within it the seed of all reality both within and without the universe. Art, for evangelicals, as for Lauren Olamina, is ultimately the universe, but made manifest in one text, rather than in the universe's physical structure. Thus, when evangelicals oppose the "arts," they do so because they see the arts as being but a pale imitation of the power of the evangelical master narrative. And considering how long that master narrative has survived, as well as the Christian ancestral beliefs that preceded it, who can blame them?

In the very things Silverman loves about the arts, evangelicals would find their greatest concern. Silverman

> loved being a writer, loved every vibrant, self-absorbed minute of it. He liked being inside his own head, working out angles and variations on stories. Fine-tuning a plot had for him the sensual reward of craftsmanship.... It was his love of writing that made him so vulnerably desperate. Because he knew in the mar-

row of his bone that he couldn't give up this addictive pleasure — even if he had to go begging in the streets to support his habit [*Devil* 34].

Silverman's experience of the arts is a hedonistic one. It is centered on his own personal experience, without any reference to community or communal standards. The arts are for him a place of solitude and aloneness, unconnected to a wider world. This should not come as any surprise. Most artists, even if they no longer openly subscribe to the Nietzschean cult of the genius, tend to promote themselves (or have their works promoted) as original, non-conformist, daring, exciting, etc.

What makes Silverman — and his creator — ultimately more honest is that they fundamentally admit the egocentric, self-oriented nature of the arts. The arts, in fact, so unhinge the individual that they are comparable to a narcotic in their effect. And although Silverman is a junkie, he does not care whose lives he will interfere with by panhandling on the artistic "streets" for more "dope." He enjoys the fact that whatever he works on is "*his* story, a piece of his life" (*Devil* 34). The fact that other communities might have stories to tell, stories that are different from a secular, left-wing Jewish homosexual from San Francisco, are immaterial to Silverman. Though he claims to support diversity in the novel, in reality Silverman never attempts to understand the people he's dealing with in North Fork, instead labeling them with the kind of stereotypes his own artistic creator, Theodore Roszak, apparently believes in. And ultimately, the threat that evangelicalism tells a story that does not buy into a secular vision of what pluralism is threatens Silverman at a level that goes beneath the mere ideological. Evangelicalism offers spirituality in place of sensuality, and communal story-making in place of the continuation of the Romantic cult of genius. And because its story is so radically different from Silverman's (and Roszak's), any attempt to give that narrative even the tiniest legitimacy is denied.

The Devil and Daniel Silverman and Franky Schaeffer's conclusion to the *Portofino* trilogy (*Zermatt*) represent the last major secular narratives of the oppression of the arts by evangelicals. While Craig Thompson's *Blankets* did in some ways share this narrative construction as well, it was ultimately a more complex work. With the entry of more evangelicals into contemporary high culture, it is perhaps harder to publish stereotypes as extreme as Roszak's; on the other hand, considering the success of Tom Perotta's works (which stereotype evangelicals without reference to the arts), maybe writers are just growing tired of examining the artist figure's relationship to evangelicalism. What is clear is that if *The Devil and Daniel Silverman* is any indication, secular writers have a long way to go before they truly develop a culturally sophisticated vision of evangelical belief.

Blanketed with Extreme Care: Craig Thompson's Tragic Vision of the Evangelical Artist

Craig Thompson's *Blankets* (2003; cited as *Blankets*) is one of the most phenomenally successful graphic novels of the last 10 years. Widely considered a classic of the genre, Thompson's work won praise from such major figures as major contemporary novelist Neil Gaiman (*Blankets* blurbs) and was the first high-quality work of fiction by an ex-evangelical since the publication of British Pentecostal Jeanette Winterson's *Oranges Are Not the Only Fruit* in 1985. America had not seen such a nuanced depiction of evangelicalism by a non-evangelical since *Go Tell It on the Mountain*, written some fifty years before. Critics loved *Blankets*, as the work won three Harvey Awards and two Eisner Awards, the highest marks of achievement in the graphic novel world (*Blankets* back cover).

Blankets is a semi-autobiographical tale of Thompson's youth, focusing mainly on his brief, failed romance with Raina, a fellow evangelical, during his teenage years. Interspersed with his description of Raina is a narrative of his troubled relationship with his family and the evangelical community, which in turn affects how he perceives the arts. In many ways quite similar to James Baldwin's *Go Tell It on the Mountain*, Thompson more directly addresses the issue of artistic censorship, both communal and self-inflicted, in evangelicalism than does Baldwin. Whereas Baldwin is more ambivalent about the effect of evangelicalism on John's young life, the narrator Craig (who seems fairly similar to the real Thompson) sees evangelicalism as having largely negatively affected himself, most graphically through the guilt he suffered as a child for being unable to prevent his brother Phil's sexual abuse — or his own abuse.[1]

For the young Thompson, the arts are a desperate attempt to avoid the pain his evangelical upbringing has caused him. With painful, self-effacing honesty, he tells the reader:

> My other get-away car [from life] was drawing, where my brother accompanied me at the wheel. He didn't share my escapist approach it seemed, but drew as a means of spending time with me, of connecting with me. And indeed, when we drew together, often collaborating on the same page, I felt connected to Phil. An entire day would be consumed by drawing.... These were the only wakeful moments of my childhood that I can recall feeling life was sacred or worthwhile [*Blankets* 44].

For Craig, the arts become a form of escapism, escapism from the pain that is evangelical belief. Being a good young evangelical, his approach to the arts is communal, even in its purely relaxed form. He wishes to use art as a means of communication, a way of creating a bond between Phil and himself.

7. More Problems, Added Possibilities   175

Because evangelicalism, as a belief system, tends to subsume other narrative systems in its own master narrative, Craig is desperate for a means of connecting to the wider world that does not necessarily involve evangelical thinking. The arts, for Craig, become something "sacred," a higher calling as the Bible is a higher calling to him. But for much of the novel, Craig has to suppress his artistic instincts in favor of the church's.

The evangelical churches and schools that Craig attends explicitly set themselves against his artistic identity. Craig's vision of heaven is drawing for all eternity (*Blankets*, 136). But when he brings this vision of heavenly bliss up to his teacher, she replies, "Our new lives in heaven will be devoted to praising and worshiping God ... bowing to Him, singing his songs, and exclaiming His name for all eternity.... And we'll love every second of it.... I mean 'Come On, Craig.' How can you praise God with drawings?" (137). For Craig, as for many evangelicals who have heard this particular vision of heaven (including the author of this book), his teacher's heaven sounds like something out of Dante's *Inferno*. One form of heavenly art is prescribed by God the Father, who forces every being in the universe to conform to it at the threat of artistic damnation. As pointed out before, this kind of iconoclasm is a form of aesthetic absolutism, a dictating of artistic standards by a heavenly elite that is every bit as reprehensible as the glorification of art as a narcotic by the secular cultural elite.

Indeed, in many ways there is little difference between this teacher's vision of God and Hitler's vision of himself. Just as Hitler appointed himself art dictator of Germany and often made important decisions concerning Nazi artistic policy (Spotts 2002, 30–33, 36), so does God, in this twisted vision, serve as an artistic dictator, defining certain forms of art as acceptable while excluding others. Craig's understandable objection to his teacher, "Creation — like trees and stuff" is art (138), merely leads his teacher to argue that God has already drawn everything in existence. Since God has created everything, there's no way of coming up with new artistic pieces. This is, of course, a rather confusing argument, considering the fact that one would expect God has been able to imagine every song in existence as well. Presumably, therefore, God only enjoys art so long as it glorifies Himself, a completely egocentric vision of Godliness very much at odds with the Christian value of humility, though unfortunately not very much at odds with the Christian vision of who God is (a vision that has always had more than a tad of the Oriental despot in it).

Craig briefly considers doing Christian cartoons as a means of reconciling faith and art, but realizes that art done solely for faith is compromised art by definition. He also, at an earlier point in the novel, considers iconoclasm as a possible response to his artistic gift. He reflects:

> I realized I'd only been half-committed to my faith and that something had been distracting me from my Bible studies.... I wanted to burn everything I'd ever drawn.... I've wasted my God-given time on Escapism. Dreaming and Drawing—the most secular and selfish of worldly pursuits. I acted as if I was sacrificing a burnt offering before God—a new spiritual pact. But really I wanted to burn these childhood artifacts.... I wanted to burn my memories [*Blankets* 58–59].

Craig's burning of the artifacts—in a makeshift incinerator doubling as a trash can, no less—shows how deeply his vision of his artistic self-identity is shaped by his cultural constraints. Art, in evangelical culture, because it has the sensuality, the "selfishness" of "worldly pursuits," is diametrically opposed to Thompson's evangelical faith. Craig initially cows himself into thinking that he is engaging in iconoclasm for God's glory. In reality, however, he ultimately feels that this act of iconoclasm is as much a form of escape as the art he produced in the first place. In both cases, he is trying to find a relief from the power of art to invoke memory. And for Thompson, like many other religious individuals, memory is a mental phenomenon deeply tied to both faith and art. In the evangelical church, for instance, many art forms are opposed because of the effect evangelicals fear this art will have on their keeping "pure minds." Bans on R-rated movies, or books with sexual content, or roleplaying games with magic in them, are often predicated on this basis. In Judaism, memory is an even more complex phenomenon, leading to the artistic veneration of Holocaust survivors (a presumably good thing) and at the same time an exploitation of those survivors in art for political or aesthetic gain, which seems like a travesty of their memory. Like the Jewish artistic community, Thompson is torn between his duty to protect his faith community and his duty to protect his art. Thompson is unambiguous in his analysis of the relationship between art and faith: Art destroys faith, and faith destroys art. There is no possibility of these two mental systems reconciling themselves, at least not within an evangelical context.

The reason for this irreconcilability is dramatically demonstrated by a discussion Craig has with a few church members while he is deciding on whether to go to art school:

> MALE CHURCH MEMBER: Craig, I'd highly advise.... That is, I warn you ... not to go to art school. My brother went to art school and ... you know, he had to draw people, but they, uh ... didn't have any clothes on. It was like running into the arms of temptation. Soon he couldn't get enough naked people, so he got addicted to pornography—And then, that wasn't enough either ... which led ... uh ... I'm sorry—which led to the next logical step
> CHURCH WOMAN: K-k-killing people?
> MALE CHURCH MEMBER: HOMOSEXUALITY.

CHURCH WOMAN: Oh, how tragic.
YOUNG CHURCH WOMAN: The same thing happens at regular college.... Your only choice, Craig, is to attend CHRISTIAN college. The entire curriculum there is centered around Christ. In fact, they reject any text that strays from Biblical Truth [*Blankets* 514–518].

Art, for evangelicals, is a sensuous trap. Evangelicals, for Thompson, engage in a kind of "slippery slope" argument, in which painting nudes leads to gay prostitution and the so-called "homosexual agenda." The position of visual artists—filmmakers and painters, in particular—is made doubly hard by the fact that their art is so connected to evangelical concerns about bodily and mental purity. In Craig's case, this leads to his community's expectation that he will devote whatever aesthetic skills he has to God, or even bury them completely by sacrificing those skills for "Biblical truth." The choice between a Christian college and art school, or even a Christian college and a regular college, is not just a choice between competing philosophies—it is a choice between competing artistic identities. While there are an increasing number of evangelical colleges that pride themselves on their connection to the arts—Grove City College, Wheaton, Gordon, New St. Andrews, even Bob Jones University—what these schools lack is a diversity of texts, artistic pieces, and aesthetic ideologies to choose from. In addition, as Craig is no doubt aware, most evangelical schools with good art programs lack the racial and cultural diversity that is necessary to create an intellectually vibrant artistic community. By contrast those evangelical schools that are racially and culturally diverse—primarily among Pentecostals and certain Holiness groups—lack the artistically richer traditions of a school like Wheaton or Gordon. Choosing to go to an evangelical college for your artistic formation is not just unproductive; it is a kamikaze run on any chance you have of developing a distinct independent identity as an artist, apart from the whims of your community.

Craig eventually leaves the evangelical community, but he does not tell his parents that he has left. Craig tells his brother, "I still believe in God; the teachings of Jesus even, but the rest of Christianity ... its Bible, its churches, its dogma—only sets up boundaries between people and cultures. It denies the beauty of being human and it ignores all these gaps that need to be filled in by the individual" (*Blankets* 533). Craig's ultimate conclusion is that if he is to have faith in anything, it must be in the "beauty of being human." Evangelicalism, by denying the beauty of the physical body, by rejecting the splendor of visual representations of those bodies and of other objects within nature, is rejecting what it means to be human, and by so doing, ceases to be humane. As a religious system, Craig sees Christianity as a means of division, rather than a community-enhancing organic entity. It creates community by destroying other communities—nations, cultures, and families—and leaves nothing in these communities' place. Evangelicalism becomes a world-destroying system, at every level from the national to the individual.

But it is at the level of the individual that Craig feels most affected. One of the saddest scenes in *Blankets* is a set of two panels on page 560. The first panel shows Craig's fanatically religious parents telling him how proud they are of him as they hug him. Here they make no reference to religion. In that panel, Craig is shown as a normal human being. In the second panel, Craig's parents talk about his religious life — the panel shows them holding an empty cipher version of a human being. The nullity created by that vision is deeply haunting, nearly ghost-like in its effect. Religion does not simply interfere in Craig's relationship with his parents. It prevents them from ever envisioning Craig as he actually is. What they see is a ghost, a figural representation of what Craig used to be, or more likely, an idealized vision of who they expect him to be. Religion does not just destroy art; it destroys the most intimate community with which an artist wishes to bond — his own family.

Blankets is a heartbreaking depiction of the costs of aesthetic absolutism. But Thompson's warning is also largely accurate. Evangelicalism and art do not mix well — they never have, and perhaps never will. However, this does not make the average anti-art fundamentalist or evangelical any more inhumane than being a skilled artistic craftsman makes Thompson humane (or inhumane). The basic idea behind evangelical iconoclasm — that evangelical culture needs to be separate from a materialistic, consumeristic culture — remains as sound as when this justification was used against the novel form some two hundred years ago. What is inhumane is that evangelicals enforce such artistic standards by coercion, including on children, rather than by persuasion, directed only at able-minded adults.

If there should be one basic guideline for a principled iconoclast — or for that matter, a principled iconophile — it should be that no one has the right to dictate what aesthetic standards anyone else has to believe in. Persuasion is fine, yes. And certainly, a government may need to regulate what art is actually produced; obviously we cannot have real snuff films being made. But in actually trying to coerce a change in belief, rather than a change in action, one steps over the line from being an iconoclast to being a simple censor, an aesthetic absolutist as dictatorial as Hitler or Schaeffer ever were. This is a path no one should want evangelicals to go. And this basic respect for differing artistic beliefs, if not artistic actions, will ultimately affect how we view faith as well, as we will see in chapter 8.

Secularism's Olive Branch: Sigrid Nunez's Salvation City

Sigrid Nunez's *Salvation City* (2010, hereafter cited as *SC*) represents a possible secular olive branch to the evangelical community. Though the secular artist (here an aspiring young cartoonist, Cole Vining) is oppressed by evangelicals in *Salvation City*, just as Craig Thompson was in *Blankets*, the depiction of evangelicals is largely reasonable in the text, without the resort to demagoguery present in most works by non-evangelicals present in the eighties and nineties. Nunez makes it clear she is not interested in satire (Nunez [2012]b), and this lack of a satirical bent enhances her work, preventing Nunez from falling into the didactic traps that parallelized other talented writers, such as Franky Schaeffer, Octavia Butler, and Margaret Atwood.

A winner of numerous writer's awards (Nunez [2012]a), Nunez has published six novels. She has been included in several literary anthologies as well, including anthologies on Asian-American fiction and the prestigious Puschcart Prize volumes. As of 2012 she taught at Boston University (Nunez [2012]a). The daughter of a Chinese Panamanian father and a German mother, Nunez's deftness at portraying vastly differing cultures is quite evident in *Salvation City* (*Birnbaum* 2007). Whether depicting Cole's adoptive evangelical parents or his part Jewish, part-atheist family, Nunez is observant of minor cultural details. For instance, Pastor Wyatt, Cole's adoptive father, is very sensitive about rapture predictions because he does not believe in "second guessing" God. This is a common position among premillennialist believers, due to the frequent failed rapture predictions throughout evangelical history, but it is a point few secular writers have picked up on, even in otherwise excellent depictions of evangelical culture, such as Michael Tolkin's *The Rapture* (*SC* 113).

Salvation City tells the story of Cole Vining, a young thirteen-year-old who is taken from an orphanage to Salvation City by a Christian family, after a massive flu epidemic. Cole's adoptive parents, Pastor Wyatt and Tracy, are for the most part kind individuals, though there is some reason to believe they took Cole from the orphanage even though they knew one of his relatives was probably alive (*SC* 205–207, 253). Cole is interesting in that, though he aspires to artistry, in the form of comics and graphic novels, he has never read a whole book in his life (60–61).

Cole represents a post-literary artist, the product of a cybernetic age. Sympathetically, Nunez engages Cole's generation's dislike for the written word. Rather than being based on stupidity, Cole's lack of infatuation with the arts is due to the low value placed on literature in contemporary society. He feels:

> The kind of reading they [his parents] did was something almost no one did anymore. Lots of successful people didn't read books and the smartest kids at school weren't necessarily the biggest readers, either. Things had changed, and Cole knew you didn't have to feel bad anymore for not reading novels or poetry. Even

his parents didn't read poetry. And no, he didn't feel proud that his parents had tried writing novels themselves ... he felt embarrassed [*SC* 60].

Nunez here portrays an understandable anxiety of the postmodern author — that her words will no longer find an audience, because words are no longer read. But though Cole eventually does accept the power of words (266–267), Nunez is sensitive to the fact that his generation, facing a media-saturated culture, is often unable to articulate its artistic needs effectively. The desire for art is there — Cole's love of comics is real and present throughout the novel — but it is in a form that to a modern novelist can only seem somewhat debased. Worse, the artistry of the past — novels, poetry, and the like — only embarrass a younger generation, for whom the arts are both socially irrelevant and culturally passé. Cole's opinion, as conveyed by Nunez, is quite rational. For Cole the Internet and other electronic sources are his main source of information (60–61) and throughout the novel Cole's trust in that information source is justified, allowing him to adapt to changing cultural conditions quicker than the adults in the novel. Indeed, Cole's eventual, sincere aspiration to join the educated classes is, ironically, prompted by a TV program (265–267).

There is a certain latent undercurrent in *Salvation City*, never openly expressed, that the children of the Internet age will be especially prone to the cultural influence of evangelicals, a theme earlier expressed about the cinematic age in Peter Watkins's masterpiece *Privilege*. Cole's Jewish aunt Addy for instance, worries that in his short time with Pastor Wyatt, Cole has been "brainwashed" (*SC* 213), which she lays at the feet of Cole's Christian homeschooling: "There are Christians everywhere, but it's only here [in America] that you have this craze for keeping kids out of school and trying to ban whatever's not in the Bible. I know you're too smart to believe there were dinosaurs on Noah's ark, but what kind of education can you be getting from people who do believe that" (214). Addy's fears (despite her European origins) are emblematic of the educated, artistic caste of America — the professors at secular universities, novelists, painters, etc.— who feel that evangelicalism endangers the educational achievement and artistic evolution of contemporary young adults. Nunez portrays this fear as rational, and indeed from a secular perspective it can hardly seem otherwise, since creationism and Noah's ark clearly belong to a mythic story structure, regardless of whatever spiritual truths they impart. Addy's fears about literary "bans" hearken back to fears of censorship expressed as far back as Sinclair Lewis's *Elmer Gantry*. So in a superficial sense, Nunez can be interpreted as indulging in a typical secular analysis of evangelicalism.

But only if one reads the text superficially. For within this same passage there is a deep understanding, expressed for the first time since *Elmer Gantry*, of evangelicalism's troubled class position vis-à-vis other religious and secular movements. Nunez's conveying of class differences is extremely subtle. For instance, Addy comments on "how insane Europeans think the whole American gun culture is" (*SC* 204), reflecting urban and European biases against evangelicalism's presumably agrarian and rural, "hick" heritage. Similarly, Addy comments on Tracy, who's the person homeschooling Cole, that she "could never pass herself off as a teacher in any other civilized country" (213). While this comment reflects literal truth, Nunez clearly sees Addy's hysterics at Cole's educational level as reflecting a partial class bias. Addy's snobbery at the lower-class, spiritual proletarian roots of Tracy and Pastor Wyatt is of course an old story for evangelicals — such snobbery has been openly expressed in works such as *Inherit the Wind*, the film *Elmer Gantry*, *The Poisonwood Bible*, and even the works of ex-evangelicals such as Franky Schaeffer. What Nunez does so successfully is question the basis of that snobbery. Cole himself could easily have succumbed to an evangelical education, just as Tracy and Pastor Wyatt had fallen "victim" to evangelicalism, were it not for the influence of his aunt and the television program he just happens to fall upon. Nunez points out how almost accidental religious belief is, and yet how ingrained it can be, once instilled through vigorous indoctrination and subcultural influence. *Salvation City*'s location in Indiana, near the South, powerfully influences the cultural options open to all three of these major characters; in a sense, therefore, Nunez partially absolves Tracy and Pastor Wyatt of their sins of omission against Cole. They are a product of a culture that allows for few other options: Pastor Wyatt comes from a long line of (presumably working class) miners, and considering Tracy's education, she likely comes from a similar social outlook. Nunez ultimately allows Cole to escape from this social background, as most evangelical artist-intellectuals must do if they want to produce truly meaningful art. But she does evangelical culture the courtesy of pointing out that the desire to escape such a cultural background is based on class concerns. Evangelicals could ask for little more than that from any secular writer today.

Moreover, the reason for Cole's rejection of evangelical beliefs is convincingly offered by Nunez. Cole feels trapped by his evangelical surroundings, and feels that because of those surroundings, the art he has produced is immature. Cole reflects bitterly:

> Then the thought of drawing — the thought of all the drawings he had done and the pleasure they had given him and the pride he'd felt at being praised for them — suddenly all this struck him as embarrassing, cause for shame. He thought of the comics he'd lavished so much of himself on and he cringed. He'd made a fool of himself, he thought.... It would be a relief to destroy them, to burn every one of them. Then he could start all over again [*SC* 259].

Evangelicalism, as a belief system, suppresses Cole's artistic skills. Though Pastor Wyatt and Rachel do not discourage Cole's artistic gifts (indeed they encourage him), the cultural environment they place him in offers him little real ability to enhance his abilities. Evangelicalism's unique capability to turn artistic pleasure into a source of moral guilt undoubtedly plays a part in causing Cole "shame." So too does the realization that Cole's subject position as an evangelical will prevent him from reaching the cultural heights of his richer peers. Indeed, Cole, like many an ex-evangelical, is something of a class climber in the final analysis. He reflects that nowhere in the TV program about prestigious students was there "any mention of God or church or any kind of religious instruction" (267). The price for admission into the upper classes, as Nunez makes pointedly but honestly clear, is a rejection of the religious mythological systems that give evangelical culture its self-identity. For American culture, the simultaneous embrace of education and evangelical identity, the arts and high culture, is a fundamental impossibility. As chapter 1 points out, this is in one sense a silly assertion given the number of evangelicals now working in the arts and offering up arguments for an aestheticized evangelicalism. Yet, a century of cultural stereotyping, justified or not, along with the self-limitations evangelicalism has placed on its own artistic traditions, perhaps suggests that there is more to Nunez's arguments than most evangelical artistic elites would like to admit. Nunez has the courage to say to evangelical elites what Atwood and Barbara Kingsolver can only say in private: Sorry, you guys have to ride on the back of the artistic bus.

Nunez emphasizes how damaging evangelicalism is to Cole's memory, which is already damaged by the plague; yet, in a very real sense, secularism is equally toxic to evangelical cultural memory. Secular education tends to emphasize solely evangelicalism's negative cultural distinctives, to the exclusion of other points of view. For instance, according to a study published by the Jewish Research Council, evangelicals are by far the most disliked population in academia. Of faculty surveyed, 71 percent believe the country would be better off if evangelicals kept out of politics, while 53 percent of faculty said they had cool feelings towards evangelicals. By contrast, atheists had only an 18 percent disapproval rating, and Jews only 3 percent. Mormons, the next most unpopular group after evangelicals, trailed evangelicals by 20 percent (Tobin and Weinberg 2007, 3, 12, 81). Regardless of whether these negative feelings are merited — and in some case, they are — the plain fact of the matter is that evangelical students, intellectuals, and artists frequently feel discriminated against by a hostile secular culture. Secular educators and artists will give evangelical students negative information about their culture, information they normally do not receive from their pastors and parents; but these same elites will also tend to gloss over more favorable or complicated analyses of evangelical cultural identity. Memory of evangelical culture is constructed by the dominant social group, and in the university and arts world, that is clearly not evangelicals. The arts, for evangelicals, may create dreams; but they usually do so by destroying the cultural identity that evangelicals cherish.

Salvation City perhaps represents a détente in evangelical and secular relations. But it also points out artists' continued inability to imagine an artistic evangelicalism. This study, by contrast, can imagine an artistic evangelicalism, with poetry readings, literary soirees, and Festschrifts for evangelical literary critics. But the question remains: Why is that a heritage evangelicals should aspire to?

Peace with One's Heritage: Leif Enger and the Reemergence of Evangelical Literary Culture

Leif Enger's *Peace Like a River* (2001, hereafter cited as *PLR*) received massive critical acclaim upon its release, gaining positive reviews from the *Los Angeles Times*, the *Boston Globe*, the *Seattle Times*, *Entertainment Weekly*, the *San Francisco Chronicle*, the *Christian Science Monitor*, and numerous other major press organizations (*PLR* blurbs). *Time Magazine* named it one of its five books of the year, and was named Best Book of the Year by the *Christian Science Monitor*, the *Denver Post*, and the *Los Angeles Times*. A *New York Times* bestseller (Grove/Atlantic, Inc. [2012]), *Peace Like a River* is the one indisputably major novel by an evangelical novelist since the early 1900s.

Enger is a Christian writer commonly associated with the evangelical tradition (Tischler 2009b, 112). A graduate of Minnesota State University, Moorhead, Enger wrote a few mysteries before publishing *Peace Like a River*, a novel he toiled on for some five years (113). Enger's narrative tells the story of the Land family, composed of young Reuben (the narrator), his aspiring writer-sister, Swede, his vengeful brother Davy, and his father, Jeremiah. The family is a prototypical evangelical family, united by the children's love for their father and the protectiveness of Davy and Jeremiah for the two younger children of the family. When two teenagers molest Swede and then, after words, break into the Lands' house, Davy shoots them. Tried and convicted, Davy escapes, and the Lands set out on a trek throughout the Northwest, searching for him.

Though this section will dwell primarily on the significance of evangelicals again having a major novelist in their ranks, Enger's novel also addresses the place of the artist in evangelical culture in significant ways. Two figures in the novel play the role of the artist. Reuben is the artist as witness (*PLR* 3, 311); he is a testifier to the truth of his father's miraculous talent for healing, and to the deeper eternal significance behind that healing. Swede is the artist-poet, a creator of thrilling epic sagas, in verse form, of the West. These two figures represent two aspects of the evangelical artist. Reuben sees his job as "someone to declare, Here's what I saw. Here's how it went. Make of it what you will" (3). The art of writing, therefore, for Reuben is an art of evangelization, of testimony for the faith. What distinguishes Reuben from a host of similar narrators in evangelical fiction is that Reuben does not coerce the non-believer into obedience, either through overly rosy portraits of evangelical belief or through a glorification of the rest of his family members. While he and his sister come off as fairly innocent children, his father can occasionally lack ambition and his brother Davy is a vengeful individual, somewhere on the cusp between belief and non-belief. Indeed, the witnessing talk in *Peace Like a River* is so self-effacing, so invisible, that it would be fairly easy for an unobservant secular reader to miss it entirely. Much like the autobiographical narrator of *Blankets* or Esther Summerson in Dickens's *Bleak House* (1852–1853), Reuben's very self-condemnations endear him totally to the reader, because they show the reader how deeply and naturally humble the narrator is.

Reuben testifies to the truth of evangelical experience and evangelical faith in a trustful yet non-confrontational manner. He does not seek to antagonize the secular reader, as Charles Colson would do in *Gideon's Torch* or Jerry Jenkins and Tim LaHaye would so regrettably do in the *Left Behind* series (1995–2007). Nor does Reuben oversimplify the ease of belief. Though Reuben has gone through a visionary religious experience in which he sees heaven — or a place just like — he realizes that his "telling [of this experience] falls pitifully short of what the place is. What mortal creations are language and memory!" (*PLR* 310–311). Reuben realizes that some will doubt his words (311). This is not because his experience did not happen, but because he realizes that language is ultimately a fragile medium by which to convey religious truth. This should, after all, not be surprising to an evangelical. It is a truism of evangelical belief that Jesus is the Word. Any human attempt to describe that word must by definition fall short. Reuben's realization here in many ways mirrors, for instance, Eastern Orthodox theology, with its vision of Christ as being-beyond-being, a deity who by definition cannot be constrained by the limitations of language.

Reuben's words thus serve as a warning, both to evangelicals and to non-evangelicals, about relying on the act of writing as proof (or disproof) of religious belief. The atheist can no more define God out of existence than the religious believer can define Him (or It) into existence. If God is a real entity, He will likely transcend any human qualities of being or non-being. If He is not a "real" entity, there seems little chance of proving that supposition, considering the almost limitless number of ways there are of defining God.

Reuben, ultimately realizes that there is not a "single person on whom I can press belief.... All I can do is say, Here's how it went. Here's what I saw. I've been there [heaven] and am going back. Make of it what you will" (*PLR* 311). Ultimately, all any of us can testify to with (relative) certainty is our subjective feeling about what we experienced. And that is all Reuben testifies to. He believes with all his heart that it is true, but he allows the reader the freedom to doubt, the one freedom that evangelical authors—and when applicable, their narrators—have never given their secular audiences.

Swede's vision of art comes largely through interaction with the Western fiction she so loves, particularly Zane Grey and his *Riders of the Purple Sage* (1912) (*PLR* 241). Throughout the novel, Swede is constantly constructing the epic poem of the law man Sunny Sundown. The depiction of Sunny is straightforwardly Western, yet Swede and Reuben do not realize how Swede's recreation of Western mythology in many ways mirrors Christianity's own great mythological system. In one section, for instance, the innocent Sundown is about to be hanged along with two criminals in a scene faintly reminiscent of Christ's crucifixion. It causes Reuben to reflect: "There was something about the poem—I almost felt I had read it before" (100). Enger, without preaching to his reader, shows the power of the Christian myth, that of the dying innocent, the martyred God, to transcend cultural and genre boundaries so that it is universally acceptable to all peoples, at all times. This, he suggests, is a great story, the Greater story behind the great story. Swede, in mythologizing the West, is teaching herself the Christian values her father wants her to have, but attaching her own artistic significance to them.

The narrative of the West is the narrative of Christianity writ large, in both its greatness and its weakness. The United States' expansion in the West is the expansion of Christianity. The slaughter of Native Americans resembles Christianity's slaughter of other indigenous peoples throughout the world (which is not to say Christianity did not play a part in killing Native Americans as well). The division between farmers and ranchers, lawmen and outlaws, often takes on the aspect of the dichotomous divide between good and evil, heaven and hell, that Christianity promotes. And the posses that wrongly hunt Sunny down (*PLR* 258–259), and who engaged in frontier justice in real life, are very much akin to how human beings themselves purportedly martyred Christ in the first place. Yet that frontier, blooded and wounded, is redeemed by the promise that something good, something holy will come out of the men who did not compromise: the upright lawman, the soldier who would not kill the Indians. It is a very American myth—but an American myth of redemption that is molded seamlessly onto the greater Christian myth.

Swede, though a child, realizes the connection between these myths.

When Reuben observes that her poem bears more than a passing resemblance to *Riders of the Purple Sage*, particularly in its promise of a "snakeless Eden," a "hidden valley of meadows and rippled green" (*PLR* 241) that recalls Lassiter's situation in that novel, Swede concurs. But she points out that

> other writers had told this story also and that not even Zane Grey was the first. She said it was such a true story it needed recurrent tellings so as not to fall out of circulation completely.... Well, secret valleys with sealable entrances were just the same, Swede said: places and things that were so real in the world they were often disbelieved [241].

Swede here echoes the mythopoeic movement. Behind every Zane Grey novel there is a far deeper myth. There are only so many myths in the world, and the Christian one is a central one, though not necessarily unique. The problem for the Christian myth is that it has been told so many times that it is often disbelieved. Yet the myth must be told and retold, generation to generation. It's an important story, and for evangelicals is the means by which their cultural tradition is preserved. If it is not told, it is in danger of being lost, and with it all the accrued cultural significance evangelicals have attached to the myth will be lost with it. That's why evangelicals keep telling the same story over and over. It's not because they are fanatics, though they sometimes are; nor is it because they are anti-intellectual or anti-rational. No, it is because evangelicals are so moved by this one story that they feel they can play an infinity of variations on it, a symphony of their varied lives, and never risk gutting the story of its literary and spiritual meaning.

How many authors can succeed in replicating Enger's unique contribution to this symphony? Probably very few. Of the major contemporary evangelical novelists writing today there are maybe a handful who write worthwhile prose: Larry Woiwode, a Presbyterian writer of some skill (Woiwode [2012]); Stephen Lawhead, whose Arthurian fantasy is excellent, but who also is likely to remain unacknowledged because of bias against his religious beliefs among fantasy critics; and perhaps Lisa Samson, who achieved some success in writing compelling inspirational fiction, such as her novel *Songbird*. Woiwode and Lawhead are likely too old now to be constructing major masterpieces. Samson, though talented, is more of a skilled second-line novelist than a top-line artist in the tradition of Enger or Harriet Beecher Stowe. Though there have been very creative art pieces produced by populist evangelicals—such as the spiritual warfare novels of Frank Peretti, and perhaps Jack Chick's extremist but often interesting religious graphic tracts—overall, populist evangelical art is likely to get little respect, even if it is good. If Christians are going to succeed in the arts, they are going to have to do so outside of their own cultural ghetto, which means that evangelical novelists will have to venture beyond the confines of the CBA market and the Christian culture industry it supports.

And there is a very good reason not to do this: historical precedent. Once before, evangelicals tried to leave the evangelical ghetto. This was during the 1970s, when Francis Schaeffer and his son encouraged evangelicals to forsake political separatism (Marsden 2006, 245–247; W. Martin 2005, 201–202). As William Martin points out, evangelicals rather self-servingly condemned political activism during the civil rights marches of the sixties, only to engage in it themselves in the eighties under the rubric of the Moral Majority (2005, 201–202). Whether Christianity as a whole should involve itself in politics is a complex issue; some religious movements have consistently promoted policies that most Americans, indeed most people everywhere, approve of. One could cite the Quakers or the majority of black Baptists as examples of this. But when talking about white evangelicalism, the movement has done nothing but harm to itself and the United States as a whole (not to mention the rest of the world) by its forty-year sojourn into the field of political activism. True, some allies have been gained and most evangelicals now do not scream whenever they hear the word Catholic or Eucharist. But Schaeffer's method of cultural confrontation and persistent attack of political and theological rivals has led to an adversarial relationship between evangelicals and non-evangelicals that has sapped evangelical political strength. Worse, the promotion of engaging "with the world" has led many evangelicals to believe they can interact with secular culture, particularly the secular arts, without being affected by that culture. Yet from Christian sex toys to t-shirts supporting Bloodweiser (Jesus's blood, get it?), the more culturally compromising elements of evangelical culture have proven themselves singularly incapable of thoughtful interaction and critique of material culture. And leaving evangelical culture in the hands of Schaeffer's current generation of Reformed descendants, firmly rooted in cosmopolitan spiritual capitalism, seems only likely to perpetuate this kind of interaction, not because the Reformed movement compromises theologically or is unsophisticated aesthetically — it almost never comprises and its view of the arts is rapidly complexifying — but because it is so hell-bent on "cultural stewardship" and victory over opposing worldviews that it has not stopped to count the cost of continuing the culture wars. An evangelical culture dependent on merely thinly transposed secular art forms (whether classicist or pop) and PR campaigns is an evangelicalism that will not last through the twenty-first century.

And that is a future no evangelical should want.

8

You Picks Your Worldview, You Takes Your Chances

This book is, to a certain extent, an exercise in futility. No matter how much one might wish for the destruction of the art world as a dominant cultural institution, that destruction is unlikely to take place. Likewise, so long as evangelicals perceive themselves as being threatened by secular artists, they are likely to try to create a rival Christian art world of their own. Neither the secular art world nor the Christian art world seem very concerned with questioning the economic basis on which the arts, whether popular art or high art, are founded. Still less do either of these movements want to examine how aesthetic standards of taste may dictate class politics. As the secular art world is already in the elite, and the evangelical cosmopolitan class is trying to create its own cultural elite to rival the secular art world, it is in neither group's interests to admit that they *both* perpetuate stereotypes of non-cosmopolitan (usually non-Reformed) evangelicals. It is likely, therefore, that the spiritual proletariat will continue to await the "Rapture of the Arts" for the foreseeable future, so long as neither art world is interested in meaningful change to the economic system under which the art world—particularly the "high art" world—operates.

Evangelicalism, as a religious movement, has a potential to reject the more materialistic elements of the arts as few other religious movements in the world do. Only perhaps Mormonism, the Amish, the Jehovah's Witness movement (all three are movements that share a distant common heritage with evangelicalism), and in some cases fundamentalist Islam can match evangelicalism in this regard. Eastern Orthodoxy and Catholicism, though beautiful faiths, are so fully tied to the aesthetic project that it is difficult to see either system rejecting the contemporary art world unless it becomes far more materially corrupted than it already is. Catholicism, in particular, is so tied to its art treasures that even its protests against art movements many Catholics abhor, such as Modernism, are somewhat muted. Liberal Protestants and atheists, as two of the most prominent ideological groups in the arts, are likely to cry censorship whenever anyone objects to the high place given art in contemporary culture, while non-fundamentalist Muslims are not ideologically unified enough on the arts to pick one position or another. Considering the use of state censorship in many Muslim countries, it is doubtful iconoclasm is in the Islamic world's current interests, as it is for evangelicals. Eastern religious believers, particularly in the states, seem equally ill-enthused to engage in iconoclasm, an understandable reaction to censoriousness and violence by Christian, Muslim, and sometimes Hindu fundamentalists.

Evangelical anti-artistic views, by contrast, though not borrowing from as intellectually a rich tradition as Dada or modern anti-art provocateurs such as John Carey, have the advantage of having a longer tradition of activism to draw on. Nor does an anti-art evangelicalism have to be against all pieces of art; rather, it should oppose the institution of art as a dividing mechanism in human society. No one, including evangelicals, should have the right to dictate another person's aesthetic beliefs. We do not have to all agree the emperor of the art world has clothes, if some of us believe that world is spiritually and morally naked.

Many a critic, particularly among Christian worldview supporters, would argue that the arts make individuals into better people, usually by helping us understand how others think. Carey is scathing in his debunking of that idea: "To believe that, from reading books, you know what it really feels like to starve, to be in continual pain, to watch your children die — in short, to subsist in the Third World — is not a refinement of sensibility but a trivialization of others' suffering" (2006, 108–109). No matter how many times one sees *Schindler's List* (1993), one does not understand what it is like to be gassed; nor is it likely that watching *Dances with Wolves* (1990) or *Avatar* (2009) really saves indigenous peoples or the rain forests. As an alternative to the philosophical teachings of Jesus or the Buddha, the arts run a poor second in motivating moral accountability. *Survivor: Ethopia* or Holocaust simulations for a genocide awareness campaign may entertain people for a day, but it also gives them the mistaken impression that they could handle what others around the world have suffered. Westerners, and particularly Americans, thus become victims-by-proxy, trying to establish their own honorary claims to suffering and fortitude, even as they bask in unprecedented wealth and resources. Evangelical stoicism, which has served the movement well in the past (both when it was a victimizer and when it was a victimized social group), should lead evangelicals to question the ease with which we turn art into vicarious suffering. Being moved to tears by a Strauss concert did not prevent Nazis from executing Jewish violinists; in the case of Hitler himself, art, as we have seen, may have at least partially contributed to mass murder, rather than preventing it.

This desperate push to see the arts as morally enriching is, of course, actually a push to see the art that the singular individual supports as enriching. Daniel Silverman's love of Kafka and Camus does not extend to the hellish items of art he finds in the North Fork congregation (Roszak 2003, 232), nor does Drummond's taste go beyond *The Origin of Species*; Robert Ingersoll is, on rather dubious grounds, an enriching source in *Elmer Gantry*. One gets the distinct impression that Lewis would not say the same of the collected writings of Billy Sunday, whom he lampoons in the novel. In almost every work studied in this book, one form of taste is put down for another taste that is seen as superior, with the reason for the put-down often being explicitly class-based. Now that the evangelical art world is finally producing a few capable artists, it is likely that this art world will snipe at its non-evangelical opponents with righteous abandon, merely copying the condemnations it has for so long received and directing them back at its attackers.

If the evangelical church should ask itself anything, it is a question I routinely put to my classes: Is there any art work worth even one human life? If there is, how do we justify that kind of devaluation of the human, in a faith which prides itself on its connection to the idea of *imago dei*? In evangelical belief, we human beings, not our creations, are what is truly wonderful to God. That is the opposite side of saying that no art is sacred. To God, all art he creates, that is the sentient beings that form His universe, are sacred, both because they are created in his image and because they are his children. By contrast, our own creations are but pitiful sub-creations when compared to the simplest mentally disabled child or even the most deformed demonic dictator. There is more of the god-stuff in the twisted soul of Hitler than there would be in 10,000 paintings by Rembrandt. No matter how much we might humanize them, those paintings were not alive — but that mentally disabled child and that dictator were.

Paraphrasing from John Carey, no matter how hard you try, you cannot gain a surrogate soul from buying a Klimt or a Klee (2006, 135). You can easily lose one, though, if you ignore real human suffering in the pursuit of such treasures. The path of the worldview movement has been to increasingly identify with the high culture aspirations of such connoisseurs. Though most dramatically presented in the works of David Hegeman and Franky Schaeffer's early evangelical writings, this elitism is broadly characteristic of the movement as a whole, where elite evangelical artists such as Edward Knippers can snidely remark, "Egalitarians don't like designations such as good and bad, high and low, better and best, but I find such distinctions helpful. And such distinctions are more than a matter of personal opinion. They really exist" (2006, 70). One wonders how Knippers was heaven-sent this revelation. Why would an immaterial deity, for instance, care about the relative material qualities of Manzoni's excrement versus the most skilled works of Goya or William

8. You Picks Your Worldview, You Takes Your Chances   191

Holman Hunt? Does a God who does not even need to sit on a toilet really have a profound aesthetic dislike for Duchamp's Urinal compared to the hallowed works of Leonardo? Such claims are on their face absurd. Human beings have no way of knowing God's aesthetic values. Indeed, most likely, if God created the universe, he finds everything in it beautiful, even (perhaps disturbingly) our suffering. Knippers' profoundly anthropomorphized vision of what constitutes divine beauty works hand in hand with the general tepidness of contemporary evangelical visual artists, who, if their art books are any indication, seem to find beauty mainly in pictures of flowers, idealized Romantic paintings, and Reformation prints. Somehow a God who writes a human narrative in which He sacrifices His own son to Himself while committing suicide simultaneously does not seem like the kind of deity that would be dictating His art views through a small coterie of primarily Northern European–descended Presbyterians who have at one time worked in Pennsylvania or attended Westminster Seminary. It might be just possible that God's vision is just a tad bigger than that.

Of course, perhaps the worldview movement wants to lose its soul to the arts. As John Carey points out, the arts engender "disparaging estimates of other people," often based on class assumptions (2006, 150); it seems therefore perfectly natural that Knippers, contradicting two thousand years of Christian teaching, warns that his art "is not for everyone" and therefore it does not matter whether he offends his weaker brothers by painting nudes (2006, 78). That viewpoint is by any sane reading of the New Testament, evangelical, non-evangelical, or secular, a complete inversion of scriptural teaching; it is, however, perfectly consistent with secular art's desire to offend gratuitously, and with the worldview movement's continuous disregard for more traditional, less elitist views of evangelical art. It does not seem to this critic, however, any better to replace a secular elitist hierarchy, which at least understood the history of art and the basic limits of aesthetic theory, with an evangelical elite that merely enforces a tired classicism with no understanding of the artistic traditions that came after the Reformation and Enlightenment. Daniel Siedell, therefore, is absolutely right to call the worldview movement on its questionable use of Marcel Duchamp and Andres Serrano as whipping boys for the sins of modern art (2008, 163). Considering the fact that Schaeffer's and Rookmaaker's objections to modern art (that it was fragmented and disunified) differed little from Hitler's, either in intellectual heft or sophistication of analysis, it would behoove evangelical critics to be a little more cautious in their analysis of modernism.[1]

So, if one cannot replace religion with the arts, and if the arts themselves are, as we have seen, indestructible under the current definition of art, how does one resolve this impasse? Perhaps here one should trust to the forgotten (and some theorists argue discredited) words of Ludwig Wittgenstein: "It is clear that ethics cannot be expressed. Ethics is transcendental (Ethics and aesthetics are one)" (Wittgenstein 1994, 29). Religious concepts, for Wittgenstein, cannot be meaningfully expressed in language. For instance, two people may claim they believe in God, but how does one know they mean the same thing by the word God? The same could be said for the Trinity or any other religious concept (Clack 1999, 57). While Wittgenstein's thought modified somewhat over the years, he came to closely associate the religious with the aesthetic, because religion and aesthetics were not in disagreement over facts, but over transcendental values that could not be meaningfully expressed in linguistic terms. As Brian Clack points out, "The clash between belief and unbelief [for Wittgenstein] is not a disagreement over the *facts* of the world: it is more akin to a disagreement over *aesthetic taste*" (38). What motivates us to build cathedrals and destroy them, to start charities and start wars, to protect children from starvation and priests from child-abuse accusations all reduces down to a few simple questions: What is heaven wearing this time of year? Is your God a Da Vinci or a Damien Hirst? And based on our particular aesthetic taste for deities that year, you either write *Reading Lolita in Tehran* (2003) or fly a jet into the Two Towers, come out with a masterpiece like *Peace Like a River* or shoot a clinic worker in cold blood. It is my hope that evangelicalism will eventually embrace a theology of tastelessness, one that does not decree Jesus a prettier painting than Buddha, nor Leif Enger a more moving novelist than Sinclair Lewis. But until evangelicalism can embrace that kind of radical aesthetic, though not moral, relativism, I hope that it will at least remember that in art, unlike religion, two tastes are fine, three tastes are better, but one taste can kill. And there's plenty of poison to go around.

Take your pick.

Glossary

Aesthetic absolutism—The belief that there are absolute, knowable aesthetic standards. This view is often accompanied by a dictatorial leader who enforces such standards. Examples in this study include Adolf Hitler and (used somewhat against his will) Francis Schaeffer.

Aesthetic relativism—The lack of any absolute standard of artistic excellence or barometer by which to distinguish between art and non-art.

Amillennialism—A theory of prophecy that holds "that the prophecies concerning both the struggles with anti–Christ and the reign of Christ are being partially fulfilled already in the present church age so that the 'millennium' does not represent a separate historical period" (Marsden 2006, 270).

Arminianism—This book largely uses Mark Noll's definition of Arminianism, which emphasizes that Arminian belief is the idea that "God gave prevenient grace (a grace coming before full salvation) to all people so that original sin could be overcome and all could make a free choice for God" (Noll 2002, 563). Noll's work covers a period when Arminian belief was largely confined to Methodism and Anglicanism within the United States; today it is theologically dominant among most non–Reformed Protestants and is seen as the bipolar opposite of Calvinism. Originally, Arminians also believed that it was possible for Christians to be "liberated from all known sin" (563). While this belief persists in some more dogmatically Wesleyan churches, most Arminians today would not go that far.

Church Growth movement—See seeker-sensitive church.

Cosmopolitan evangelicals—A term used by D. Michael Lindsay in his work *Faith in the Halls of Power* to denote those new urbanized, more educated evangelicals now entering the social elite. Lindsay characterizes them as being preoccupied with "status concerns" (2007, 219), though I am not sure he would appreciate my critique of the cosmopolitan class.

Dispensational Marxism—The basic format of DDM is simple. Each dispensation of the church reflects a dispensation of art, in which particular artistic modes of expression (not necessarily artistic schools) dominate. Each age has a central conflict, which evangelicals almost always eventually lose. But there's always the promise of "The Rapture of the Arts," when traditional anti-art evangelical views will be accepted.

Emergent Church—A group that self-consciously seeks to elide definition. Nevertheless it is characterized by a general postmodernist critique of evangelical culture, asserting, "America's youngest generations doubt the human ability to know absolute truth" (Bielo 2011, 8). The Emergent Church eclectically borrows from a number of theological traditions, though its origins are clearly evangelical in the main. It is widely seen by many evangelicals as the greatest heresy within the contemporary evangelical church. This work emphatically does not take that position, while disagreeing just as emphatically with the Emergent Church's combination of evangelical theology and deconstructionist theory.

Fundamentalism—Fundamentalism was a conservative Protestant movement that, during its period of national prominence in the 1920s, opposed theological modernism and evolutionary theory (Marsden 2006, 3–4). Detwiler lists "insistence on the Virgin Birth, the miracles of the Bible, the bodily resurrection of Jesus, and the power of Jesus' sacrificial death to remove the stain of sin from us," along with personal conversion, as the main markers of fundamentalism (Detwiler 1999, 151). Fundamentalists are chiefly distinguishable today by their whole-hearted support for biblical inerrancy (in the original texts), creationism, and traditional as opposed to higher critical hermeneutical strategies.

Higher criticism—Term commonly used for the advanced methods of biblical criticism pioneered in the late 18th and 19th century, primarily by German theologians. These methods were widely seen as calling traditional interpretations of scripture into disrepute.

Holiness tradition—Holiness Christians "emphasize religious behavior and the moral life as the marks of a true Christian" (Detwiler 1999, 152). Holiness Christians tends to emphasize pietism over political activism.

Kantian disinterestedness—For Kant, true aesthetic taste is "a pure, disinterested pleasure in which we only contemplate an object," apart from its "sensual pleasure or utility" (Shiner 2001, 146). In other words, ideally from a Kantian standpoint, one does not approach a painting, a book, or any other artwork from a solely "material" or pragmatic standpoint.

Mythopoeic criticism—Not exactly a defined school of criticism; rather, it is a means of reading that focuses on the qualities of scripture as "true myth" and the power of authors as "sub-creators," who, as servants of God, imitate God's creative process when they are working in harmony with Him. The Inklings are commonly called mythopoeic writers.

Neo-evangelical—The term is used here approximately as the term born-again evangelical is deployed in Fritz Detwiler's *Standing on the Premises of God*: Neo–evangelicals would be characterized by a "conversion experience" similar to other evangelicals, but would not (necessarily) have the hard-line position on inerrancy and creationism that fundamentalists would have, nor the emphasis on spiritual gifts that is a part of Charismatic and sometimes Holiness practice (Detwiler 1999, 153). The term is a nebulous one in many ways, and the rule of thumb that an evangelical "was [once defined as] anyone who identified with Billy Graham" (Marsden 2006, 234) still holds some validity even today.

Nietzschean or Romantic cult of genius—According to Frederic Spotts, Romantics "worshipped the artist and his achievement as the embodiment of the highest social aspirations of an age" (2002, 11). It is from this term that the idea of the cult of the genius, in which the genius is worshipped, is derived. Nietzschean thinkers, particularly Ayn Rand in *The Fountainhead* and Jack London (in London's case satirically, as a Nietzschean anti–Nietzschean) in *Martin Eden* and *The Sea Wolf*, frequently invoked these Romantic or Nietzschean tropes, as do some contemporary evangelical aestheticians.

Glossary

Pentecostal or Charismatic Christianity—Distinguished by belief in the gifts of the spirit (Detwiler 1999, 154), such as speaking in tongues, prophecy, and the casting out of demons. This is the fastest growing segment of evangelicalism, tending to a more emotive, less rationalistic theology than Reformed Christianity (for which it is often criticized).

Pietism—"The tendency to emphasize individual devotion and ethical behavior rather than the authority and corporate life of a church" (*OED*). Used here particularly to refer to Holiness and fundamentalist churches that forsake political activism for the inner spiritual life.

Populist evangelicals—Mass movement evangelicals, usually from less affluent, less art-involved lifestyles than cosmopolitan evangelicals.

Postmillennialism—The idea that "the prophecies in the book of Revelation concerning the defeat of the anti-Christ ... were being fulfilled in the present era, and were clearing the way for a golden age.... Christ would return after this millennial age (hence 'post-millennialism') and would bring history to an end.... Postmillennialists typically were optimistic about the spiritual progress of the culture" (Marsden 2006, 49). Postmillennialists tend to be more optimistic about social change than premillennialists and therefore are more willing to alter society to bring about positive social change.

Premillennialism—Premillennialists "believe in Jesus Christ's bodily return before His Thousand-year earthly reign" (Boyer 1992, 2). Please note that not all premillennialists are dispensational premillennialists. Dispensational premillennialists believe that the history of the world is divided into a number of divinely decreed historical eras (dispensations), and that we are currently in the Church Age, stuck between one crucial event—the Crucifixion—and another, the Rapture (where Christians will be taken bodily up in the air to be with God). The Rapture will be followed by the Tribulation, a 7-year period of great suffering. This will gave way to the Battle of Armageddon, in which Jesus and his saints will return to earth and defeat the Antichrist. Following this is the Millennium, in which Christ reigns a thousand years. A brief final revolt will then be conducted by Satan, the dead will be resurrected, and history's final event, the Last Judgment, will occur (88). Please note however, that this is merely the most popular narrative of the "End Times." "Post-trib" premillennial dispensationalists believe that the Rapture will occur only after the Tribulation, even for Christians. "Mid-Tribbers" believe the Rapture will occur halfway through the Tribulation.

Preterist—"A person who believes that the prophecies of the book of Revelation have already been fulfilled" (*OED*).

Prosperity Gospel—"Name It and Claim It" or "Health and Wealth" gospel. Emphasizes the power of a motivated spiritual life to gain the adherent wealth and influence. Often this is done through donating to the ministry that promotes the prosperity gospel, leading to justifiable charges that prosperity ministries exploit their members.

Rapture of the Arts—The era when traditional anti-art evangelical views will be accepted.

Reformed Christianity—This tradition "draws its defining characteristics from the theological teachings of John Calvin" (Detwiler 1999, 154). It is noted mostly among other evangelicals for its emphasis on God's power to predestine individual salvation. Reformed Christianity, though the smallest part of the "Christian Right," is also the most theologically influential on the movement as a whole (154). This work followers Detwiler in arguing that Reformed Christianity, at least in the field of aesthetic theorizing, has influence disproportionate to its size.

Seeker-sensitive church—Evangelical churches devoted to gaining new followers and maintaining current membership. There is no set denominational affiliation for such churches, though many do seem to straddle a middle ground between neo-evangelicalism and a "charismatic-lite" gospel. Seeker-sensitive churches are often associated with the church growth movement and sometimes with the prosperity gospel.

Spiritual bourgeoisie—Generally synonymous with spiritual capitalists, the bourgeoisie is an exploiting force within each dispensational age of the arts, usually the dominant spiritual class.

Spiritual capitalists—individuals and groups seeking to aggrandize money and/or power to dominant theological bodies of the time.

Spiritual proletariat—those populist evangelicals whom this works hopes to convince not to subscribe to Christian worldview, Emergent, or other more elitist evangelical artistic ideologies. The spiritually and economically disadvantaged evangelical "folk" peoples.

Typology—"The study of classes with common characteristics; classification, esp. of human products, behavior, characteristics, etc., according to type; the comparative analysis of structural or other characteristics; a classification or analysis of this kind" (*OED*). Or to put it more bluntly, in this work *typology* is an analysis of a certain set of character types, all revolving around the arts that secular or non-evangelical texts set up when dealing with evangelicalism. It is emphatically not an attempt to draw biblical parallels to characters in modern fiction.

Übermensch—For the purpose of this book, the Nietzschean superman, characterized by a "romantic rebellion against realism" (Langa 1). The Nietzschean hero has no concern for traditional "herd" morals (*EB*, "superman") and promotes a cult of his own genius.

Untermensch—The slave class.

Weltanschauung—German term used largely interchangeably for worldview. They are roughly linguistically equivalent.

Worldview (or Christian worldview) theory—Broad theory of culture. When extended to the realm of art, however, worldview theology tends to emphasize the thought content of art pieces. For worldview aestheticians, the worldview that is shown through a body of art pieces must be seen ultimately in terms of Scripture (Francis Schaeffer 1973, 64). This does not mean that an artwork has to be explicitly Christian in content, but that it should in some way reflect Christian values.

Chapter Notes

Introduction

1. For instance, *Inherit the Wind* and *Planet of the Apes* support dominant mainline paradigms of evangelicalism, while Octavia Butler's *Parable* series and Margaret Atwood's *Handmaid's Tale* support a dominant feminist viewpoint of evangelicalism that tends to portray evangelicalism in a very one-handed way.

2. See Marty 1996, 119, for Marty's assessment of Reinhold Niebuhr's questionable late career anti–Communism for instance; see Burns 2009, 124–125, for Burns's assessment of Rand's anti–Communist HUAC testimony.

3. Reformed evangelicals, in modern evangelical parlance, usually are evangelicals who support 5-point Calvinism. See Noll 2002, 265–268, for a good description of Reformed theology. The term *Reformed* has had a variety of different meanings. However, today, most evangelicals imply some sort of practicing Calvinism by the use of this term.

Chapter 1

1. Goldsmiths is a prestigious art institution in Britain.

2. They also tend to miss out on the subtleties of Foucault entirely, whose concept of episteme, for instance, seems particularly suited to evangelical thinking (due to its superficial similarities to the worldview concept in worldview theory).

3. Lack of space prevents me from covering two critics who I believe do a better job of representing evangelical aestheticians, but have more limited appeal. Nicolas Wolterstorff's *Art in Action* (1980) crucially points out that artworks are not simply objects, but "instruments of action." Wolterstorff's philosophy therefore leaves open the possibility that art can be used for evil as well as good. Daniel Siedell's *God in the Gallery: A Christian Embrace of Modern Art* (2008) is the first major evangelical work on the arts that critiques the evangelical art world itself; though one could wish for a fuller treatment of that subject (it receives only a chapter of full coverage), Siedell correctly points out the overall dominance of Rookmaaker and Schaeffer over evangelical views of the arts, and addresses some of the limitations that weakened their approach to aesthetics, and to contemporary and modern art in particular. Siedell's work is the analysis par excellence among evangelical art critics, and in literature only James Herrick's *Scientific Mythologies* (2008), with its splendid critique of the problematic nature of science fiction's origins, can match it. Interested readers should also seek out, while it's still available, Calvin Seerveld's *Rainbows for the Fallen World* (1980), which, like the other two works on the arts mentioned here, deviates from the three main schools of contemporary evangelical aesthetics.

4. Not that cosmopolitan evangelicals are any better. Here, the racism is veiled by a concern over the infusion of rock music into popular culture and the church, which needs to be replaced by more refined classical music that does not feature that "jungle" beat (a complaint sometimes unfortunately made by working-class fundamentalists as well).

Chapter 2

1. For information on Methodist populism, see Sweeney 2005, 62–65, and Hatch 1989, 91–93.
2. See Bielo 2011, 10, on the Emergent Church. Bielo acknowledges the Emergent critique of modernism, though he might not classify the Emergent Church as always explicitly postmodern.
3. I use the term myth here without making a judgment on whether the myth is true or false.

Chapter 3

1. Witness how few evangelicals have acknowledged the theologically radical implications of mythopoeic criticism, when taken to its logical conclusion. Even more noticeable is how evangelicals try to explain away the universalist yearnings in Lewis's works, though those yearnings were clearly inspired by the well-documented spiritual influence of Scottish novelist George Macdonald over his life.

Chapter 4

1. Koop's position was motivated out of a logically worked-out pro-life position; but to evangelicals who equated AIDS with homosexuality, Koop's efforts were a betrayal.
2. Indeed, the rapid growth of Pentecostalism has roughly temporally coincided with the growing influence of deconstructionism and other radically postmodern philosophies.
3. Please note this kind of blatant racism is different from the non-racist arguments used about the differences in art definitions across cultures that Larry Shiner, for instance, invokes. The former position is by definition racist; the latter position almost never intentionally is, but seeks merely to try to show a cultural sensitivity to overarching Western conceptualizations of non–Western cultures.
4. See for instance Alan Perott's (2002) "Jedi Order lures 53,000 disciples" in the *New Zealand Herald*, which describes the recent Jedi census phenomenon.

Chapter 5

1. The implications of this idea are pointed out by Herbert himself on page 75 of *God Emperor of Dune*.
2. *Locus* is one of the preeminent science fiction magazines.
3. It should be noted here that Herbert's work can be seen equally as Islamic or Christian in orientation, as Herbert borrows from a number of religious traditions in constructing the *Dune* universe, allowing him a generalized critique of more than one form of fundamentalism.
4. Dune is also variously referred to as Arrakis or Rakis in the series.
5. However, he, unlike Christ, did not "die" in his martyrdom but was instead blinded; his re-appearance leads to a conclusive final death.
6. This is documented by a careful perusal of Serling's and Wilson's scripts. See Greg Plinowski's excellent work at the following link, which has versions of each script: "Ape Movie Scripts," http://pota.goatley.com/scripts.html.
7. We find out in *Battle for the Planet of the Apes* (1973), however, that apes eventually break this most sacred of ape laws.
8. The orangutans seem to be at the top of ape society in the film version, with the important military gorillas being only slightly beneath them; this role was ostensibly shared

by all apes in the novel, but with the more intelligent gorillas in Boulle's novel having slightly more power than the outnumbered orangutans (Boulle 1963, 138–139).

9. Greene points out that the bomb's shape is even that of an upside-down cross (1996, 68).

Chapter 6

1. Butler herself hardly qualifies as a bourgeois anything, as her mother was a domestic and her father a shoeshine man (McCaffery and McMenamin 2010, 15).

2. The high divorce rate among evangelicals may be one of these "ravaging" factors motivating evangelicals to a simple life. Another may be a sense of futility at maintaining evangelical tradition in the light of cultural marginalization in contemporary media forms.

Chapter 7

1. See Morton 2011 for Craig Thompson's description of being abused. I have been unable to document whether the abuse Phil suffered in the novel was similarly suffered by Thompson's real-life brother.

Chapter 8

1. This does not, however, mean that Siedell's vision of the arts is without holes either. In his otherwise excellent work, he exhibits a tone-deafness to the market aspects of art, as well as towards sociological theories like Bourdieu's, which delineate strict taste hierarchies between classes.

Bibliography

Adams, Jay E. 1970. *Competent to Counsel*. Grand Rapids: Zondervan.
Aesop. [2012]. "The Donkey and the Lapdog." *Aesop-fable.com*. http://www.aesop-fable.com/donkey/the-donkey-and-the-lapdog. September 5, 2012.
Amazon.com. [2012]. "The Damnation of Theron Ware." *Amazon.com*. http://www.amazon.com/The-Damnation-Theron-Ware-Illumination/dp/0140390251/ref=cm_cr_pr_product_top. April 11, 2012.
Anonymous. 2008. *The Cinema of Peter Watkins: Privilege*. In *Privilege* DVD. Project X Distribution Limited.
Apistolidis, Paul. 2001. "Homosexuality and Compassionate Conservatism in the Discourse of the Post-Reaganite Right." *Constellations: An International Journal of Critical & Democratic Theory* 8.1 (March): 78–105. *Wiley Online Library*. http://onlinelibrary.wiley.com/. September 3, 2010.
Archer Books. [2012]. "Theodore Roszak Answers Some Question [sic]." http://www.archer-books.com/trquest.html. January 31, 2012.
Artdaily.org. [2012]. "Christie's 2010 Global Art Sales Total $5.0 Billion, Highest Sales Total in History." http://www.artdaily.org/index.asp?int_sec=2&int_new=44514#.UFpla5U2uI. September 5, 2012.
Atwood, Margaret. 1986. *The Handmaid's Tale*. Boston: Houghton Mifflin.
Baldwin, James. 1953. *Go Tell It on the Mountain*. New York: Delta Trade Paperbacks.
Bebbington, D.W. 1989. *Evangelicalism in Modern Britain: A History from the 1730s to the 1980s*. London: Unwin Hyman.
Becknell, Thomas. 1991. "Implication Through Reading 'The Damnation of Theron Ware.'" *American Literary Realism, 1870–1910* 24.1 (Fall): 63–71. *JSTOR*. http://www.jstor.org/. May 5, 2012.
Bendroth, Margaret Lamberts. 1994. *Fundamentalism and Gender: 1875 to the Present*. New Haven, CT: Yale University Press.
Bennett, Bridget. 1997. *The Damnation of Harold Frederic: His Lives and Works*. Syracuse, New York: Syracuse University Press.
Biblica. 1984. *New International Version Bible*. East Brunswick, NJ: International Bible Society.
Bielo, James A. 2011. *Emerging Evangelicals: Faith, Modernity, and the Desire for Authenticity*. New York: New York University Press.
Birnbaum, Robert. 2007. "Sigrid Nunez." *The Morning News*. March 29. http://www.themorningnews.org/article/sigrid-nunez. October 5, 2012.
Blodgett, Jan. 1997. *Protestant Evangelical Literary Culture and Contemporary Society*. Westport, CT: Greenwood.
Bloom, Harold, ed. 2005. *Bloom's Modern Critical Interpretations: Nathanael West's Miss Lonelyhearts*. Philadelphia: Chelsea House.
_____. 2005. Introduction. In *Bloom's Modern Critical Interpretations: Nathanael West's Miss Lonelyhearts,* ed. Harold Bloom, 1–10. Philadelphia: Chelsea House.

Boulle, Pierre. 1963. *Planet of the Apes*. Trans. Xan Fielding. New York: Vanguard.
Bourdieu, Pierre. 1984. *Distinction: A Social Critique of the Judgment of Taste*. Trans. Richard Nice. Cambridge, MA: Harvard University Press.
Bowden, Sandra. 2006. Foreword. In *It Was Good: Making Art to the Glory of God*, ed. Ned Bustard, 1–2. 2nd ed. Baltimore, MD: Square Halo.
Bowler, Peter J. 2003. *Evolution: The History of an Idea*. 3rd ed. Berkeley: University of California Press.
Boyd, Herb. 2008. *Baldwin's Harlem: A Biography of James Baldwin*. New York: Atria.
Boyer, Paul. 1992. *When Time Shall Be No More: Prophecy Belief in Modern American Culture*. Cambridge, MA: Harvard University Press.
Britt, David. 1989. Modern Art: *Impressionism to Post-Modernism*. New York: Thames and Hudson.
Brown, Candy Gunther. 2004. *The Word in the World: Evangelical Writing Publishing and Reading in America: 1779–1880*. Chapel Hill, NC: University of North Carolina Press.
Brown, Charles. 2010. "Octavia E. Butler: Persistence." In *Conversations with Octavia Butler*, ed. Conseula Francis, 181–188. Jackson: University Press of Mississippi.
Burns, Jennifer. 2009. *Goddess of the Market: Ayn Rand and the American Right*. Oxford: Oxford University Press.
Bustard, Ned, ed. 2006. *It Was Good: Making Art to the Glory of God*. Baltimore, MD: Square Halo.
Butler, Octavia. 1993. *Parable of the Sower*. New York: Warner.
_____. 1998. *Parable of the Talents*. New York: Aspect.
Butor, Michael. 1967. "Science Fiction: The Crisis of Its Growth." *Partisan Review*, Fall, 595–602.
Carey, John. 2006. *What Good Are the Arts?* New York: Oxford University Press.
Carpenter, Humphrey. 1979. *The Inklings: C.S. Lewis, J.R.R. Tolkien, Charles Williams, and Their Friends*. Boston, MA: Houghton Mifflin.
Carpenter, Joel. 1997. *Revive Us Again*. New York: Oxford University Press.
Charalambous, Nick. 2007. "Christian Exodous [sic]: An anti-government religion." *IndependentMail.com*. February 23. http://www.independentmail.com/news/2007/feb/23-/christian-exodous-anti-government-religion/. October 12, 2012.
Chattaway, Peter T. 2008. "*Save Me*." Review of *Save Me*. Dir. Robert Cary. *Christianity Today*. September 5. http://www.christianitytoday.com/ct/2008/septemberweb-only/saveme.html. October 17, 2012.
Clack, Brian. 1999. *An Introduction to Wittgenstein's Philosophy of Religion*. Edinburgh: Edinburgh University Press.
Clute, John, and John Grant. 1997. *The Encyclopedia of Fantasy*. New York: St. Martin's Griffin.
Cooke, Nathalie. 1998. *Margaret Atwood: A Biography*. Toronto, Ontario: ECW.
Cox, Harvey. 1995. *Fire from Heaven: The Rise of Pentecostal Spirituality and the Reshaping of Religion in the Twenty-First Century*. Reading, MA: Addison-Wesley.
Cummings, Tony. 2010. "Paul Jones: The Broadcaster's Journey from Militant Atheist to Christian Convert." *Crossrhythms*. May 28. http://www.crossrhythms.co.uk/articles/music/Paul_Jones_The_broadcasters_journey_from_militant_atheist_to_Christian_convert/39679/p1/. September 5, 2012.
Dawkins, Richard. 2006. *The God Delusion*. Boston, MA: Houghton Mifflin.
Dennis, Lane T. 1976. Publisher's foreword. In *How Should We Then Live?* by Francis Schaeffer, 9–11. Wheaton, IL: Crossway.
Detwiler, Fritz. 1999. *Standing on the Premises of God: The Christian Right's Fight to Redefine America's Public Schools*. New York: New York University Press.
Diamond, Sara. 1998. *Not by Politics Alone: The Enduring Influence of the Christian Right*. New York: Guilford.

Donaldson, Scott. 1986. Introduction. In *The Damnation of Theron Ware*, by Harold Frederic, viii–xxx. New York: Penguin.
Dondero, George. 2003. "From *The Congressional Record.*" In *Art in Theory: 1900–2000, An Anthology of Changing Ideas*, ed. Charles Harrison and Paul Wood, 665–668. 2nd ed. Malden, MA: Blackwell.
Donovan, Barna William. 2011. *Conspiracy Films: A Tour of Dark Places in the American Conscious.* Jefferson, NC: McFarland.
Dooley, Patrick. 1982. "Fakes and Good Frauds: Pragmatic Religion in the Damnation of Theron Ware." *American Literary Realism, 1870–1910* 15.1: 74–85.
Dorrien, Gary. 2001. *The Making of American Liberal Theology: Imagining Progressive Religion.* Vol. 1. Louisville, KY: Westminster Knox.
Dutton, Denis. 2009. *The Art Instinct: Beauty, Pleasure and Human Evolution.* New York: Bloomsbury.
Ellwood, Robert. 1994. *The Sixties Spiritual Awakening: American Religion from Modern to Postmodern.* New Brunswick, NJ: Rutgers University Press.
_____. 1997. *The Fifties Spiritual Marketplace: American Religion in a Decade of Conflict.* New Brunswick, NJ: Rutgers University Press.
Emerson, Michael, and Christian Smith. 2000. *Divided by Faith: Evangelical Religion and the Problem of Race in America.* New York: Oxford University Press.
Enger, Leif. 2001. *Peace Like a River.* New York: Atlantic Monthly.
Erzen, Tanya. 2006. *Straight to Jesus: Sexual and Christian Conversions in the Ex-gay Movement.* Berkeley: University of California Press.
Flixter, Inc. [2012]. "Elmer Gantry: 1960." *Rotten Tomatoes.* http://www.rottentomatoes.com/m/elmer_gantry/. September 22, 2012.
Francis, Conseula, ed. 2010. *Conversations with Octavia Butler.* Jackson: University Press of Mississippi.
Francis, Philip. 2011. "We Dive and Reappear in New Places: Aesthetic Experience and Fundamentalism Undone." Dissertation. Harvard Divinity School. Cambridge, MA: Proquest. Retrieved from Proquest Digital Dissertations. http://proquest.umi.com/.
Franklin, H. Bruce. 1980. *Robert A. Heinlein: America as Science Fiction.* New York: Oxford University Press.
Frederic, Harold. 1895. *The Damnation of Theron Ware.* Cambridge, MA: Belknap.
Frykholm, Amy Johnson. 2004. *Rapture Culture: Left Behind in Evangelical America.* Oxford: Oxford University Press.
Gallagher, Sally. 2003. *Evangelical Identity and Gendered Family Life.* New Brunswick, NJ: Rutgers University Press.
Garfield, Bob. 2007. "Hear Their Roar: Transcript" (interview with Jeff Sharlet). *On the Media.* April 6. http://www.onthemedia.org/2007/apr/06/hear-their-roar/transcript/. September 29, 2010.
Gasque, Laurel. 2005. *Art and the Christian Mind: The Life and Work of H.R. Rookmaaker.* Wheaton, IL: Crossway.
Gomez, Joseph. 1967. "Privilege." In *Cinema of Peter Watkins* (booklet accompanying *Privilege* DVD).
_____. 1979. *Peter Watkins.* Boston: Twayne.
Goodstein, Laurie. 2005. "Murder and Suicide Reviving Claims of Child Abuse in Cult." *New York Times.* January 15. http://www.nytimes.com/2005/01/15/national/15cult.html?_r=1. September 28, 2012.
Grant, John. 1997. "Wicker Man." In *Encyclopedia of Fantasy*, ed. John Clute and John Grant, 1012–1013. New York: St. Martin's Griffin.
Greene, Eric. 1996. *Planet of the Apes as American Myth: Race and Politics in the Films and Television Series.* Jefferson, NC: McFarland.
Grossman, Lev. 2005. "All Time 100 Novels: Go Tell It on the Mountain." *Time Entertain-*

ment. October 16. http://entertainment.time.com/2005/10/16/all-time-100-novels/#go-tell-it-on-the-mountain-1953-by-james-baldwin. September 18, 2012.

Grove/Atlantic, Inc. [2012]. "Peace Like a River by Leif Enger." *Grove/Atlantic, Inc.* http://www.groveatlantic.com/grove/bin/wc.dll?groveproc~enger~peace%29. November 2, 2012.

Guterman, Gad. 2008. "Field Tripping: The Power of *Inherit the Wind*." *Theatre Journal* 60: 563–583. *Project Muse.* http://muse.jhu.edu/. October 7, 2012.

Hankins, Barry. 2008. *Francis Schaeffer and the Shaping of Evangelical America*. Grand Rapids, MI: William B. Eerdmans.

Hansen, Collin. 2008. *Young, Restless, Reformed: A Journalist's Journey with the New Calvinists*. Wheaton, IL: Crossway.

Hardy, Clarence, III. 2003. *James Baldwin's God: Sex, Hope, and Crisis in Black Holiness Culture*. Knoxville: University of Tennessee Press.

Harrison, Rosalie G. 2010 . "Sci-Fi Visions: An Interview with Octavia Butler." In *Conversations with Octavia Butler,* ed. Conseula Francis, 3–9. Jackson: University Press of Mississippi.

Hatch, Nathan. 1989. *The Democratization of American Christianity*. New Haven, CT: Yale University Press.

Hegeman, David Bruce. 1999. *Plowing in Hope: Toward a Biblical Theology of Culture*. Moscow, ID: Canon.

Heinlein, Robert A. 1961. *Stranger in a Strange Land*. New York: Ace.

Hendershot, Heather. 2004. *Shaking the World for Jesus: Media and Conservative Evangelical Culture*. Chicago: University of Chicago Press.

Henry, Carl. 1947. *The Uneasy Conscience of a Modern Fundamentalist*. Grand Rapids, MI: Eerdmans.

Herbert, Frank. 1965. *Dune*. New York: Berkley.

———. 1969. *Dune Messiah*. New York: Berkley.

———. 1976. *Children of Dune*. New York: Ace.

———. 1981. *God Emperor of Dune*. New York: Berkley.

Home, Stewart. [2012]. "Art Is Like Cancer: Interview with Roger Taylor." *Stewart Home.* http://www.stewarthomesociety.org/pol/taylor.htm. September 5, 2012.

Howard, Jay R., and John M. Streck. 1999. *Apostles of Rock: The Splintered World of Contemporary Christian Music*. Lexington: University Press of Kentucky.

Huelsenbeck, Richard. 2003. "From *En Avant Dada*." Trans. Ralph Mannheim. In *Art in Theory 1900–2000: An Anthology of Changing Ideas,* ed. Charles Harrison and Paul Wood, 260–263. 2nd ed. Malden, MA: Blackwell.

Hughes, Robert. 2004. "A Bastion Against Cultural Obscenity." *The Guardian,* June 2. http://www.guardian.co.uk/artanddesign/2004/jun/03/art. September 5, 2012.

Hughes, Spenser. 1993. *The Lambda Conspiracy*. Chicago: Moody.

Hunter, James Davison. 1982. *American Evangelicalism: Conservative Religion and the Quandry of Modernity*. New Brunswick, NJ: Rutgers University Press.

Jeansonne, Glen. 1997. *Women of the Far Right: The Mother's Movement and World War II*. Chicago: University of Chicago Press.

Johnson, Thomas H. 1935. "Introduction: Section III, Edwards as a Man of Letters." In *Jonathan Edwards: Representative Selections,* by Jonathan Edwards, ed. Clarence H. Faust and Thomas H. Johnson, xcviii–cxv. New York: Hill and Wang.

Jones, Beverly. 2005. "Shrike as the Modernist Anti-Hero in Nathanael West's *Miss Lonelyhearts*." In *Bloom's Modern Critical Interpretations: Nathanael West's Miss Lonelyhearts,* ed. Harold Bloom, 113–121. Philadelphia, PA: Chelsea House.

Kaye, Randi. 2007. "Young Man's Suicide Blamed on Mother's Cult." *CNN.* December 4. http://www.cnn.com/2007/US/12/04/kaye.murdersuicide/index.html. September 25, 2012.

Keller, Tim. 2006. "Why We Need Artists." In *It Was Good: Making Art to the Glory of God*, ed. Ned Bustard, 117–124. 2nd ed. Baltimore, MD: Square Halo.
Kleiner, Fred. 2009. *Gardner's Art Through the Ages: A Concise Global History*. 2nd ed. Boston, MA: Wadsworth Cenage.
Klopfenstein, Glen D. 1997. "The Flying Dutchman of American Literature." *American Literary Realism, 1870–1910* 30.1 (Fall): 34–46. *JSTOR*. http://www.jstor.org/. September 7, 2012.
Knippers, Edward. 2006. "The Old, Old Story." In *It Was Good: Making Art to the Glory of God*, ed. Ned Bustard, 67–86. 2nd ed. Baltimore, MD: Square Halo.
Landa, Ishay. 2007. *The Overman in the Marketplace: Nietzschean Heroism in Popular Culture*. Lanham, MD: Lexington.
Larson, Edward. 1997. *Summer for the Gods: The Scopes Trial and America's Continuing Debate over Science and Religion*. Cambridge, MA: Harvard University Press.
Lawrence, Jerome, and Robert E. Lee. 1955. *Inherit the Wind*. New York: Random House.
Leitch, Vincent, ed. 2001. *Norton Anthology of Theory and Criticism*. New York: Norton.
Leonard, Bill J. 1999. "A Theology for Racism: Southern Fundamentalists and the Civil Rights Movement." *Baptist History and Heritage* 34.1 (Winter): n.p. *Academic Onefile*. September 15, 2012.
Lewis, Sinclair. 1927. *Elmer Gantry*. New York: Signet.
_____. 1935. *It Can't Happen Here*. New York: New American Library.
Lieberman, David. [2011]. "DVD Disaster? Study Says Sales Plummeted in 2010, Contrary to Industry Report." *Deadline New York*. http://www.deadline.com/2011/05/dvd-disaster-study-says-sales-plummeted-in-2010-contrary-to-industry-report/. May 12, 2011.
Lincoln, C. Eric, and Lawrence H. Mamiya. 1990. *The Black Church in the African American Experience*. Durham, NC: Duke University Press.
Lindlof, Thomas. 2008. *Hollywood Under Siege: Martin Scorsese, the Religious Right, and the Culture Wars*. Lexington: University Press of Kentucky.
Lindsay, D. Michael. 2007. *Faith in the Halls of Power: How Evangelicals Joined the American Elite*. Oxford: Oxford University Press.
Lingeman, Richard. 2002. *Sinclair Lewis: Rebel from Main Street*. New York: Random House.
London, Jack. 1909. *Martin Eden*. Charleston, SC: BiblioBazaar.
Lorch, Thomas. 1967. "Religion and Art in Miss Lonelyhearts." *Renascence* 20: 11–17.
Los Angeles Times. 2009. "Today in Oscars History: 'Elmer Gantry' Opened in Theaters." Review of *Elmer Gantry*, screenplay by Richard Brooks. September 1. http://goldderby.latimes.com/awards_goldderby/2009/09/oscars-movie-entertainment-news-291573648-story-article.html. October 10, 2012.
Lumsden, Michael. 2005. "God's Politics: An Interview with Jim Wallis." *Mother Jones*. March 10. http://www.motherjones.com/politics/2005/03/gods-politics-interview-jim-wallis. October 12, 2012.
MacCulloch, Diarmaid. 2003. *Reformation: Europe's House Divided, 1490–1700*. London: Allen Lane.
_____. 2009. *Christianity: The First Three Thousand Years*. New York: Viking.
Macey, David. 2000. *The Penguin Dictionary of Critical Theory*. London: Penguin.
Marsden, George. 2006. *Fundamentalism and American Culture*. New York: Oxford University Press.
Martin, Jay. 1970. *Nathanael West: The Art of His Life*. New York: Farrar, Straus and Giroux.
Martin, William. 2005. *With God on Our Side: The Rise of the Religious Right in America*. Revised ed. New York: Broadway.
Marty, Martin E. 1986. *Modern American Religion: The Irony of It All, 1893–1919*. Vol. 1. Chicago: University of Chicago Press.

———. 1991. *Modern American Religion: The Noise of Conflict, 1919–1941.* Vol. 2. Chicago: University of Chicago Press.
———. 1996. *Modern American Religion: Under God, Indivisible, 1941–1960.* Vol. 3. Chicago: University of Chicago Press.
Mason, Carol. 2002. *Killing for Life: The Apocalyptic Narrative of Pro-life Politics.* Ithaca, NY: Cornell University Press.
McCaffery, Larry, and Jim McMenamin. 2010. "An Interview with Octavia Butler." In *Conversations with Octavia Butler,* ed. Conseula Francis, 10–26. Jackson: University Press of Mississippi.
McLaren, Brian. 2004. *A Generous Orthodoxy: WHY I AM a missional + evangelical + post/protestant + liberal/conservative + mystical/poetic + biblical + charismatic/contemplative + fundamentalist/Calvinist + Anabaptist/Anglican + Methodist + catholic + green + incarnational + depressed-yet-hopeful + emergent + unfinished CHRISTIAN.* Grand Rapids, MI: Zondervan.
———. 2005. *The Last Word and the Word After That.* San Francisco: Jossey-Bass.
Miner, Earl. 1977. *Literary Uses of Typology from the Late Middle Ages to the Present.* Princeton, NJ: Princeton University Press.
Monroe, Chris. 2003. "Gods and Generals." Review of *Gods and Generals,* dir. Ron Maxwell. *Christian Spotlight on Entertainment.* http://www.christiananswers.net/spotlight/movies/2003/godsandgenerals.html. November 15, 2012.
Morton, Paul. 2011. "'Horrible Things Happen Everywhere': The Millions Interview with Craig Thompson." *The Millions.* October 4. http://www.themillions.com/2011/10/horrible-things-happen-everywhere%E2%80%9D-the-millions-interview-with-craig-thompson.html. October 1, 2012.
Moyers, Bill. 2006. "Bill Moyers on Faith and Reason: Bill Moyers and Martin Amis and Margaret Atwood." Transcript of televised interview. July 28. http://www.pbs.org/moyers/faithandreason/print/faithandreason106_print.html. November 15, 2008.
Mulder, Karen. 2006. "An Architecture of Living Stones." In *It Was Good: Making Art to the Glory of God,* ed. Ned Bustard, 3–16. 2nd ed. Baltimore, MD: Square Halo.
Myers, Robert. 1994. "AntiModern Protest in the 'Damnation of Theron Ware.'" *American Literary Realism, 1870–1910* 26.3 (Spring): 52–64. JSTOR. http://www.jstor.org/. May 15, 2012.
NARAL Pro-Choice America Foundation. 2010. "Anti-Choice Violence and Intimidation." *NARAL Pro-Choice America.* January 1. http://www.prochoiceamerica.org/assets/files/-abortion-access-to-abortion-violence.pdf. September 5, 2012.
Nash, J.M. 1989. "Cubism, Futurism, and Constructivism." In *Modern Art: Impressionism to Post-Modernism,* ed. David Britt, 159–201. New York: Thames and Hudson.
New York Times. 2012. "The War Game (1965)." Overview of *The War Game,* dir. Peter Watkins. *New York Times.* http://movies.nytimes.com/movie/53327/The-War-Game/overview. September 12, 2012.
Niebuhr, Gustav. 1993. "'The Family' and Final Harvest." *Washington Post,* June 2, A01. http://www.washingtonpost.com/wp-srv/national/longterm/cult/children_of_god/child1.htm. November 3, 2012.
Noll, Mark. 1994. *Scandal of the Evangelical Mind.* Grand Rapids, MI: Eerdmans.
———. 2002. *America's God: From Jonathan Edwards to Abraham Lincoln.* Oxford: Oxford University Press.
Numbers, Ronald. L. 1992. *The Creationists.* New York: Alfred A. Knopf.
Nunez, Sigrid. 2010. *Salvation City.* New York: Riverhead.
———. [2012]a. "About the Author." *Sigrid Nunez.* http://www.sigridnunez.com. November 7, 2012.
———. [2012]b. "A Conversation with Sigrid Nunez, author of Salvation City." *Sigrid Nunez.* http://www.sigridnunez.com/qanda_salvation.htm. November 7, 2012.

Owens, Craig. 2003. "From 'The Allegorical Impulse: Towards a Theory of Postmodernism.'" In *Art in Theory 1900–2000: An Anthology of Changing Ideas,* ed. Charles Harrison and Paul Wood, 1025–1032. 2nd ed. Malden, MA: Blackwell.
Patterson, William, Jr. 2010. *Robert A. Heinlein: In Dialogue with His Century.* Vol. 1, *1907–1948: Learning Curve.* New York: Tom Doherty.
Perott, Alan. 2002. "Jedi Order Lures 53,000 Disciples." *New Zealand Herald.* August 31. http://www.nzherald.co.nz/nz/news/article.cfm?c_id=1&objectid=2352142. September 17, 2012.
Perotta, Tom. 2007. *The Abstinence Teacher.* New York: St. Martin's Griffin.
Pew Research Center. 2007. "Income Level by Protestant Denomination." *Pew Forum on Religion and Public Life.* http://religions.pewforum.org/pdf/table-income-by-denomination.pdf. September 19, 2012.
Phillips, Doug. 2003. "Review for Parents Evaluating Gods and Generals." Review of *Gods and Generals,* dir. Ron Maxwell. *Vision Forum.* February 20. http://www.visionforum.com/news/articles/2003-02-20_003.aspx. October 8, 2012.
"Pierre Bourdieu." *Norton Anthology of Theory and Criticism.* Ed. Vincent B. Leitch. New York: Norton, 2001.
Quinlan, Sean, and William L. Ramsey. [2012]. "Southern Slavery as It Wasn't: Coming to Grips with Neo-Confederate Historical Misinformation." Unpublished paper. University of Idaho. http://www.tomandrodna.com/notonthepalouse/ November 5, 2012.
Radosh, Daniel. 2008. *Rapture Ready! Adventures in the Parallel Universe of Christian Pop Culture.* New York: Scribner.
Rausch, David A. 1991. *Communities in Conflict: Evangelicals and Jews.* Philadelphia, PA: Trinity.
_____. 1993. *Fundamentalist-Evangelicals and Anti-Semitism.* Valley Forge, PA: Trinity.
Reesman, Jeanne Campbell. 2009. *Jack London's Racial Lives: A Critical Biography.* Athens, GA: University of Georgia Press.
Romaine, James. 2006. "Creator, Creation, and Creativity." In *It Was Good: Making Art to the Glory of God,* ed. Ned Bustard, 87–116. 2nd Ed. Baltimore, MD: Square Halo.
Rookmaaker, H.R. 1970. *Modern Art and the Death of Culture.* Wheaton, IL: Crossway.
_____. 1981. *The Creative Gift: Essays on Art and the Christian Life.* Westchester, IL: Cornerstone.
Roszak, Theodore. 2003. *The Devil and Daniel Silverman.* Wellfleet, MA: Leapfrog.
Ruse, Michael. 2000. *The Evolution Wars.* Santa Barbara, CA: ABC-CLIO.
Sanchez, Casey. 2008. "Todd Bentley's Militant Joel's Army Gains Followers in Florida: Militant Joel's Army Followers Seek Theocracy." *Intelligence Report* 131 (Fall). Southern Poverty Law Center. http://www.splcenter.org/get-informed/intelligence-report/browse-all-issues/2008/fall/arming-for-armageddon. October 6, 2012.
Schaeffer, Francis. 1973. *Art and The Bible: Two Essays.* Downers Grove, IL: Intervarsity.
_____. 1976. *How Should We Then Live?* Wheaton, IL: Crossway.
_____. 1990a. *Escape from Reason.* In *Francis A. Schaeffer Trilogy.* Wheaton, IL: Crossway.
_____. 1990b. *Francis A. Schaeffer Trilogy.* Wheaton, IL: Crossway.
_____. 1990c. *The God Who Is There.* In *Francis A. Schaeffer Trilogy.* Wheaton, IL: Crossway.
_____. 1990d. *He Is There and He Is Not Silent.* In *Francis A. Schaeffer Trilogy.* Wheaton, IL: Crossway.
Schaeffer, Frank[y]. 1981. *Addicted to Mediocrity.* Wheaton, IL: Crossway.
_____. 1992. *Portofino.* New York: Berkley.
_____. 1997. *Saving Grandma.* New York: Da Capo.
_____. 2003. *Zermatt.* New York: Carol and Graff.
_____. 2007. *Crazy for God: How I Grew Up as One of the Elect, Helped Found the Religious Right and Lived to Take All (or Almost All) of It Back.* Cambridge, MA: De Capo.
Schultze-Naumberg. 1993. "From *Art and Race.*" In *German Expressionism: Documents*

from the End of the Wilhelmine Empire to the Rise of National Socialism, ed. Rose-Carol Washton Long, 298–301. Berkeley: University of California Press.

Seerveld, Calvin. 1980. *Rainbows for the Fallen World.* Toronto: Toronto Tuppence.

Shiner, Larry. 2001. *The Invention of Art.* Chicago: University of Chicago Press.

Shuck, Glenn. 2005. *Marks of the Beast: The Left Behind Novels and the Struggle for Evangelical Identity.* New York: New York University Press.

Siedell, Daniel A. 2008. *God in the Gallery: A Christian Embrace of Modern Art.* Grand Rapids, MI: Baker Academic.

Simon, Stephanie. 2005. "Calling Dr. Dobson…" October 16. *Seattle Times.* http://community.seattletimes.nwsource.com/archive/?date=20051016&slug=dobson16. November 8, 2012.

Singh, J.P. 2011. *Globalized Arts: The Entertainment Economy and Cultural Identity.* New York: Columbia University Press.

Smith, Andrea. 2008. *Native Americans and the Christian Right: The Gendered Politics of Unlikely Alliances.* Durham, NC: Duke University Press.

Soper, J. Christopher. 1994. *Evangelical Christianity in the United States and Great Britain.* New York: New York University Press.

Spence, H.T. 2011. *Confronting Contemporary Christian Music: A Plain Account of Its History, Philosophy, and Future.* Dunn, NC: Forwarding the Faith.

Spotts, Frederic. 2002. *Hitler and the Power of Aesthetics.* Woodstock, NY: Overlook.

Sweeney, Douglas. 2005. *The American Evangelical Story: A History of the Movement.* Grand Rapids, MI: Baker Academic.

Thompson, Craig. 2003. *Blankets.* Marietta, GA: Top Shelf.

Thompson, Don. 2008. *The $12 Million Stuffed Shark: The Curious Economics of Contemporary Art.* New York: Palgrave.

Tischler, Nancy. 2009a. *Encyclopedia of Contemporary Christian Fiction from C.S. Lewis to Left Behind.* Santa Barbara, CA: Greenwood.

———. 2009b. "Enger, Leif." In *Encyclopedia of Contemporary Christian Fiction from C.S. Lewis to Left Behind.* Santa Barbara, CA: Greenwood.

Tobin, Gary, and Aryeh Weinberg. 2007. "Profiles of the American University, Volume II: Religious Beliefs Behavior of College Faculty." *Institute for Jewish and Community Research.* http://jewishresearch.org/PDFs2/FacultyReligion07.pdf. September 11, 2010.

Tolkien, J.R.R. 1954. *The Lord of the Rings.* Boston, MA: Houghton Mifflin.

———. 1994a. "On Fairy Stories." In *Poems and Stories,* 113–188. Boston, MA: Houghton Mifflin.

———. 1994b. *Poems and Stories.* Boston, MA: Houghton Mifflin.

Tomkins, Calvin. 1996. *Duchamp: A Biography.* New York: Henry Holt.

Tommasini, Anthony. 2001. "The Devil Made Him Do It." *New York Times.* September 30. http://www.nytimes.com/2001/09/30/arts/music-the-devil-made-him-do-it.html.

Touponce, William. 1988. *Frank Herbert.* Boston, MA: Twayne.

Tricomi, Albert. 2011. *Missionary Positions: Evangelicalism and Empire in American Fiction.* Gainesville: University Press of Florida.

Turner, Chris. [2012]. "'Gods and Generals' Portrays Strong Faith on Both Sides." *Baptist Press. The Fish.* http://www.thefish.com/movies/features/1185447/%27Gods-and-Generals%27-Portrays-Strong-Faith-on-Both-Sides/. September 5, 2012.

Tzara, Tristan. 2003. "Dada Manifesto 1918." Trans. Ralph Mannheim. In *Art in Theory 1900–2000: An Anthology of Changing Ideas,* ed. Charles Harrison and Paul Wood, 252–257. 2nd ed. Malden, MA: Blackwell.

Urbanczyk, Aaron. 2006. "A 'Study of Church in America': Catholicism as Exotic Other in the Damnation of Theron Ware." *Religion and the Arts* 10.1: 39–58. *Academic Search Premier.* September 8, 2012.

Veith, Gene Edward, Jr. 1991. *State of the Arts: From Bezalel to Mapplethorpe.* Wheaton, IL: Crossway.

Vergine, Lea. 2003. "From 'The Body as Language.'" Trans. Henry Martin. In *Art in Theory 1900–2000: An Anthology of Changing Ideas*, ed. Charles Harrison and Paul Wood, 906–910. 2nd ed. Malden, MA: Blackwell.
Wade, Wyn Craig. 1987. *The Fiery Cross*. New York: Simon and Schuster.
Waliszewski, Bob. 2003. "Gods and Generals." Review of *Gods and Generals*, Dir. Ron Maxwell. *Focus on the Family's Plugged In*. http://www.pluggedin.com/videos/2003/Q1/GodsandGenerals.aspx. November 7, 2012.
Washton Long, Rose-Carol. 1993. *German Expressionism: Documents from the End of the Wilhelmine Empire to the Rise of National Socialism*. Berkeley: University of California Press.
Watkins, Peter. 2007a. "Peter Watkins Media Statement: Public Alternative Processes and Practices." http://pwatkins.mnsi.net/public.htm. October 11, 2010.
———. 2007b. "Peter Watkins Media Statement: Role of American MAVM, Hollywood and the Monoform." http://pwatkins.mnsi.net/hollywood.htm. October 11, 2010.
———. 2008. "Privilege: A Self-Interview by Peter Watkins." In *Cinema of Peter Watkins*, booklet in *Privilege* DVD. Project X Distribution Limited.
Weaver, John. 2010. "Jesus Freaks, Freaking Jesus: Evangelicalism and American Literature." Dissertation. State University of New York at Binghamton, 2010. Binghamton, NY: Proquest.
Wells, H.G. 1933. *The Shape of Things to Come*. New York: Macmillan.
West, Nathanael. 1933. *Miss Lonelyhearts and Day of the Locust*. New York: New Direction.
Wilkins, Stephen, and Douglas Wilson. 2010. "Southern Slavery as It Was." http://www.tomandrodna.com/notonthepalouse/SSAIW.htm. November 1.
Wilson, A.N. 1999. *God's Funeral*. New York: W.W. Norton.
Wittgenstein, Ludwig. 1994. *The Wittgenstein Reader*, ed. Anthony Kenny. Cambridge, MA: Blackwell.
Woiwode, Larry. [2012]. "Larry Woiwode: Biography." *Larry Woiwode: The Official Website*." http://www.larrywoiwode.com/WoiwodeBio.html. October 5, 2012.
Wolterstorff, Nicholas. 1980. *Art in Action*. Grand Rapids, MI: William Eerdmans.
Worthen, Molly. 2007. "Onward Christian Soldiers." *New York Times*. September 30. http://www.nytimes.com/2007/09/30/magazine/30Christian-t.html?pagewanted=1&_r=1;. October 15, 2012.
Wu, Chin-tao. 2002. *Privatising Culture: Corporate Art Intervention Since the 1980s*. London: Verso.
Zein, Qassem. 2007. "The List: The World's Fastest Growing Religions." *Foreign Policy*. May 14. http://www.foreignpolicy.com/articles/2007/05/13/the_list_the_worlds_fastest_growing_religions. October 5, 2012.

Films, Television Shows, and DVDs

Architecture of Doom. 1989. Dir. Peter Cohen. Rolf Arsenius, Bruno Ganz, Sam Gray, Josef Goebbels, P.L. Troost, Sweden: First Run Features. 119 minutes.
Behind the Planet of the Apes. 1998. Dir. David Comtois, Kevin Burns. Perf. Roddy McDowall. USA: 20th Century–Fox.
The Believer. 2001. Dir. Henry Bean. Perf. Ryan Gosling, Billy Zane, Theresa Russell, Summer Phoenix. USA: Palm Pictures. DVD.
Beneath the Planet of the Apes. 1970. Dir. Ted Post. Perf. James Franciscus, Kim Hunter, Maurice Evans, Linda Harrison. USA: 20th Century–Fox.
Elmer Gantry. 1960. Dir. Richard Brooks. Perf. Burt Lancaster, Jean Simmons, Arthur Kennedy, Dean Jagger, Shirley Jones. USA: MGM. DVD.
Escape from the Planet of the Apes. 1971. Dir. Don Taylor. Perf. Kim Hunter, Roddy McDowall, Bradford Dillman, Natalie Trundy, Eric Braeden. USA: 20th Century–Fox. DVD.

Go Tell It on the Mountain. 1985. Dir. Stan Lathan. Perf. Paul Winfield, James Bond III. USA: Monterey Video. http://www.imdb.com/.
Goldsmiths: But Is It Art? 2010. Dir. Victoria Silver. Perf. Blue Curry, Roisin Byrne Ian Gonczarow, David Mabb. UK: BBC4.
Jesus Camp. 2006. Dir. Heidi Ewing, Rachel Grady. Perf. Becky Fischer, Ted Haggard, Lou Engle. USA: Magnolia. DVD.
Max. 2002. Dir. Menno Meyjes. Perf. John Cusack, Noah Taylor, Leelee Sobieski, Molly Parker. British/Hungarian/Canadian. Lionsgate. DVD.
Missionary Positions. 2006. Dir. Mike Day. Perf. Tyler Cash, Jeff Colon. Smiling Zebra Productions. DVD.
Planet of the Apes. 1968. Dir. Franklin J. Schaffner. Perf. Charlton Heston, Roddy McDowall, Kim Hunter. USA: MGM. DVD.
Privilege. 1967. Dir. Peter Watkins. Perf Paul Jones, Jean Shrimpton. UK: Universal. DVD: New Yorker Video, 2008.
Pussycat Preacher. 2008. Dir. Bill Day. Perf. Heather Veitch, Matt Brown, Lori Albee. U.S.A: Smiling Zebra Pictures.
Year of the Sex Olympics. Theatre 625. Perf. Leonard Rossiter, Tony Vogel, Brian Cox. BBC/BBC2, 1968. DVD: British Film Institute, 2003.

Index

abortion 53, 112, 143–144
Adams, Jay 112, 201
aesthetic absolutism 16–17, 62–63, 72, 77, 175, 178, 193
aesthetic relativism 4, 16–17, 62–63, 73, 193
Aesthetics 1, 3–6, 8, 15–18, 20–27, 35, 41–51, 54, 62–63, 69–70, 72, 83, 90, 92, 94–95, 115–116, 125, 155–156, 196, 197ch1n3; *see also* aesthetic absolutism; aesthetic relativism; modernism; worldview theory
AIDS 53, 86, 112, 143–144
African-Americans 33, 42, 86–97, 135, 137, 139, 156–164
Amillenialism 8, 195
Anglicanism/Episcopalian church 11, 22, 24, 30, 43–44, 50, 55–58, 130–131, 206; in *Damnation of Theron Ware* 43–44; in *Elmer Gantry* 55–58; in *Privilege* 130–131; in relationship to C.S. Lewis, the arts 22, 24, 43, 50, 55–58;
Arminianism 8, 10, 12, 193
Atwood, Margaret 18, 33–34, 53–54, 63, 112, 143–151, 155–156, 158, 164, 179, 182, 197*Intro n*1, 201, 202, 206; *Handmaid's Tale* 3, 8, 24, 27, 31–32, 52, 141–151, 157, 170, 197*Intro n*1, 201
avant-garde 67

Bacon, Francis *see* Common Sense rationalism
Baldwin, James 86–97, 157, 163, 201–204; *Go Tell It on the Mountain* 7, 50, 86–97, 157, 174
Barton, Bruce 79
Battlestar Galactica 33, 166
Boulle, Pierre 134, 199*ch5n*8, 202
Bourdieu, Pierre 199*ch8n*1, 202; on class and aesthetic taste 23, 31–34, 78

Bowden, Sandra 18, 24, 50, 202
Bright, Bill 62, 111
Brooks, Richard: *Elmer Gantry* (film) 108, 109, 205, 209
Bryan, William Jennings 74, 76; parallels to Dr. Zaius in *Apes* movies 135–139; portrayal as Brady in *Inherit the Wind* 97–105
Bush, George W. 27, 34, 163–165
Butler, Octavia 85, 87–88, 93, 144, 156–164, 179, 197*Intro n*1, 199*ch6n*1, 202–204, 206; *Parable* series 8–9, 32, 93, 102, 144, 197, 202

Caldwell, Brian: *We All Fall Down* 50, 126, 166–167
Carey, John 2, 15–19, 26, 189–191, 202
Carrie 110, 113
Catholic Church 21–22, 32, 55–56, 58, 60, 77, 80, 106, 109, 111, 113, 121–122, 142, 168, 188, 20; *Damnation of Theron Ware* 40, 41–50; mythopoeic tradition 27–29, 119–126
Charismatic movement *see* Pentecostal/Charismatic movement
Chick, Jack *see* Jack Chick tracts
Christian rock/Christian Contemporary Music (CCM) 89; parallels in *Privilege* 126–133
Christianity Today 84, 169, 202
Christians in the Visual Arts (CIVA) 18, 24, 50, 72
church growth movement *see* seeker sensitive/church growth movement
A Clockwork Orange 113, 127, 155
Cohen, Peter 1, 16–17, 63, 209; *Architecture of Doom* 1, 16, 63, 209
Common Sense Rationalism 42, 103
cosmopolitan evangelicalism 23, 24, 27,

211

29–30, 34, 36, 49, 153, 165, 187–188, 193, 195, 197ch1n4; *see also* Lindsay, D. Michael; populist evangelicalism
Craig, William Lane 92, 166
creationism/creation science 11–12, 52, 97–105, 133–141, 180, 194, 206
Cubism 48, 94, 206

Dada 19–20, 47–49, 69–72, 189, 204, 208
Danto, Arthur 15–16, 49
Darwin, Charles 71, 97–105, 163; *Origin of Species* 98, 104, 190; Social Darwinism 39, 100, 163
Dawkins, Richard 99–100, 202
Deconstructionism 9, 29–31, 194–196, 197ch1n2, 198ch2n2; *see also* Emergent Church; McLaren, Brian
Dehn, Paul 136–138, 140
Derrida, Jacques 9, 20, 29–31; *see also* Emergent Church; McLaren, Brian
The Devils 106, 113, 127
Dialectical Dispensational Marxism (DDM) 5–10, 72–73, 78, 85, 93, 97, 143, 149, 165, 193
Dilling, Elizabeth 80
Dobson, James 9, 12, 86, 208
Duchamp, Marcel 15–20, 36, 48–49, 63, 71–73, 117, 191, 208; Dispensational Marxism and Duchamp 15, 20, 36, 71–73; *The Fountain* 15, 19; worldview analysis of Duchamp 117, 191

Eastern Orthodox 21, 151–154, 184, 188; and Franky Schaeffer 21, 151–154
Eisenhower, Dwight 85, 87
Ellison, Ralph 88, 163
Elmer Gantry (novel) *see* Lewis, Sinclair
Emergent Church 9, 20, 29–31–85, 164, 193–194, 196, 197ch1n2, 198ch2n2, 206; *Damnation of Theron Ware* 42–51; definition 9–11, 13, 193–194; *see also* McLaren, Brian
End Times 5–10, 31, 48, 50, 72–73, 78, 85, 93, 97, 100, 111, 126, 143, 145, 149, 154, 165, 167–168, 179, 188, 193, 195, 203
Enger, Leif 9, 50, 167–168, 183–187, 192, 203, 204, 208; *Peace Like a River* 9, 67–68, 183–187, 192, 203, 204
Eugenics 39, 100; *see also* Darwin, Charles

evangelicalism, definition 10–13, 193–196
The Exorcist 110, 113
Expressionism 18, 69, 72, 207, 209

Falwell, Jerry 31, 85–86, 112, 169
fascism 1, 6, 62–63, 77–83, 128–129; *see also* Holocaust/anti-Semitism; Nazism
feminism and sexism 8–9, 53–54, 143–151, 156–164
Fischer, Becky 3–4, 18, 20, 210; *see also Jesus Camp*
Frederic, Harold 6, 37–51, 201, 203; *Damnation of Theron Ware* 3, 6, 37–51, 59, 101–102, 107, 201, 203, 206, 208
Fujimura, Makoto 9, 18, 63, 92
fundamentalism 2–3, 6–12, 18–20, 25–26, 32–34, 37–39, 45, 49–51, 54, 57, 60–62, 65–66, 76, 80–86, 93, 98, 100–103, 105, 112, 134, 142, 145, 151, 155, 165–168, 178, 188, 194–195, 197ch1n4, 201, 203–207; in *Dune* 121–122, 124–125, 126, 129; in *Inherit the Wind* 97–105; in *Planet of the Apes* 134–140

genius, cult of 26–27, 29, 61, 101; *see also* Nietzsche, Friedrich
Gideon's Torch 143–144, 184
Graham, Billy 12, 84–86, 111, 194

Hatch, Nathan 32, 55, 204
Hegeman, David 21–22, 27, 153, 190, 204
Heinlein, Robert 8, 62, 158, 203, 204, 207; *Stranger in a Strange Land* 7, 113–118, 204
Helms, Jesse 49, 62
Herbert, Frank 4, 7–8, 33, 106, 110, 112, 118, 127–128, 135, 141 158, 198ch5nn1,3,4, 204, 208; *Dune* series 4, 7–8, 33, 106, 118–126, 128, 135, 158, 198 ch5nn1,3,4
higher criticism 10, 40–41, 47, 51, 71, 75, 139, 194
Hitler, Adolf 1, 16–17, 48, 60–63, 66, 68, 73–74, 76–77, 81–83, 115, 175, 178, 189–191, 193, 208
Holiness Christians 9, 11–12, 38, 44, 66, 85, 93, 142, 162, 177, 194–195, 204
Holocaust/anti-Semitism 16–17, 44–45, 66–67, 74–75, 167–168
homosexuality 88, 143–144, 167–169

Index

iconoclasm 1–10, 19–20, 24, 35, 38, 44, 49–50, 71–72, 91–94, 97, 159, 172, 175–176, 178, 189
Ingersoll, Robert 60, 107, 190
Inherit the Wind see Lawrence, Jerome; Lee, Robert E.
Islam 7, 126, 165, 172, 188–189, 198*ch5n*3

Jack Chick tracts 35, 49, 154, 186
Jacobs, Harriet 97, 157
jazz 66, 70, 89, 93
Jesus Camp 3–4, 24, 31, 133, 165, 210; *see also* Fischer, Becky
"Jesus Freaks, Freaking Jesus" 1
Joel's Army 31, 83, 154, 207

Kant, Immanuel 163; *see also* Kantian disinterestedness
Kantian disinterestedness 22–23, 34, 59–60, 152, 194
Keller, Tim 2, 26–27, 153, 205
Kennedy, D. James 86, 111–112
Kingsolver, Barbara 19, 34, 143–144, 182; *Poisonwood Bible* 27, 31, 141, 143, 144, 181
Kinkade, Thomas 18, 24, 35
Knippers, Edward 63, 190–191, 203
Koop, C. Everett 86, 112, 198*ch4n*1
Ku Klux Klan 80, 93; influence on Thomas Dixon, *Birth of a Nation* 93

LaHaye, Tim 8, 24, 27, 142, 184; *Left Behind* 24, 184, 203, 208
Lambda Conspiracy 143–144, 204
Law and Order 24, 31, 166
Lawhead, Stephen 35, 186
Lawrence, Jerome 3–4, 7, 37, 51–52, 55, 97–105, 106, 110, 112, 116, 128, 143, 157, 181, 197*ch5n*1, 204–205; *Dune* parallels 126, 128; *Inherit the Wind* 97–105; *Planet of the Apes* parallels 133–141
Lee, Robert E. 3–4, 7, 37, 51–52, 55, 97–105, 106, 110, 112, 116, 128, 143, 157, 181, 197*ch5n*1, 204–205; *Dune* parallels 126, 128; *Inherit the Wind* 97–105; *Planet of the Apes* parallels 133–141
Lewis, C.S. 22, 26–30, 49, 70, 82, 84, 198*ch3n*1, 202, 208; mythopoeic 26–30
Lewis, Sinclair 6, 18, 37–39, 51–64, 65, 72, 74–83, 91, 105–110, 116, 180, 190, 192, 205; *Elmer Gantry* (character) 4, 31, 49, 51–64, 75, 106–107, 109; *Elmer Gantry* (film) 7, 31, 102, 105–110, 181, 203, 205; *Elmer Gantry* (novel) 3, 6, 37–38, 50, 51–64, 65, 76, 91, 97, 110, 190, 203; *It Can't Happen Here* (influences on, works influenced) 74–75, 79–80; *It Can't Happen Here* (novel) 65–67, 74–83, 205
Lindsay, D. Michael 23, 24, 49, 165, 193, 205; *see also* cosmopolitan evangelicalism; populist evangelicalism
London, Jack 39, 48, 56, 76, 81, 207; *Martin Eden* 23, 131, 194, 205
Long, Huey 74, 80

mainline Protestantism 6–12, 32–33, 37–40, 43, 50, 53–55, 57–58, 61–62, 66, 75, 82, 84–85, 89, 98, 104, 106–110, 140, 142–144, 147, 163, 166, 169, 188, 197*Intro n*1, 203, 206; *see also* higher criticism
Manzoni, Piero 16, 190
Mapplethorpe, Robert 62, 72, 208
Marsden, George 5–6, 11, 32, 38, 66, 103, 112, 205; DDM model 5–6; historiography 32, 112
Marx, Karl 5, 17, 25, 72–73, 78, 93, 97, 150, 162, 166, 168, 193
McCarthy, Joseph 17, 97–105, 135, 147, 150; *Inherit the Wind* 97–105
McLaren, Brian 9, 11, 29–31, 41–42, 169, 206; Emergent theology and *Damnation of Theron Ware* 41–42
McPherson, Aimee Semple 52, 74; portrayal in *Elmer Gantry* (film) 105–110
media 3, 30–32, 75, 81, 97, 103–104, 107–109, 112, 126–129, 145, 160, 163, 165, 199*ch6n*2, 204, 209
Mencken, H.L. 37, 58–59; portrayal in *Inherit the Wind* 97, 102, 104, 107
messiah 4, 7, 71, 112–126, 157–162
Methodism 11, 38, 40, 41–43, 44, 49, 51–52, 53, 57, 60, 89, 162, 198*ch2n*1
modernism (art) 6, 10, 15–19, 22–23, 36, 41, 47–48, 56, 63, 68–70, 72, 83, 92–93, 116–117, 188–191, 197*ch1n*1
monoform 127, 209
Morrison, Toni 87, 157; *Paradise* 93, 126
Mulder, Karen 2, 206
mythopoeic 9, 27–30, 69, 102, 113, 119–126, 155, 186, 194, 198*ch3n*1; *see also* Catholicism

Nazism 1, 16–17, 48, 62–63, 66–67, 69, 73–75, 77–83, 100, 167–168, 175; *see also* fascism
neo-evangelicalism 7, 11–12, 32, 54, 84–86, 142, 194, 196; *see also* evangelicalism, definition
Nietzsche, Friedrich 48–49, 95–96, 98, 99, 100, 104, 128, 131, 148, 157–158, 163, 173, 194, 196, 205; *see also* genius, cult of; Romanticism
Nixon, Richard 85, 111
Noll, Mark 112, 193
Nunez, Sigrid 167, 178–185, 201, 206; *Salvation City* 178–183

Peale, Norman Vincent 110–111
Pelley, William Dudley 79–81
Pentecostalism/Charismatic movement 9, 11–12, 25, 31, 33–34, 38, 44, 50–51, 54, 85, 88–89, 93, 108–109, 142, 162–163, 177, 191, 194–196, 198*ch4n2*, 202, 206
Peretti, Frank 27, 35, 133, 186
Perotta, Tom 173; *The Abstinence Teacher* 24, 53, 55, 166, 207
pietists 2, 8, 9, 11, 19–20, 22, 38, 54
Planet of the Apes series 4, 7, 31, 33, 106, 110, 112, 133–141, 197*Intro n1*, 198*ch5nn6,7,8*, 199*ch5n9*, 202–203, 209–210
populist evangelicalism 5, 18, 24–25, 27, 30, 34–36, 55, 77–78, 165, 186, 195–196; *see also* cosmopolitan evangelicalism; Lindsay, D. Michael
Postmillennialism 8, 195
Pragmatism 40–41, 47
Premillenialism 48, 100, 111, 145, 167–168, 195
Presbyterians 8, 11–12, 26, 37, 54, 57, 65, 137, 152, 186, 191; Orthodox Presbyterian Church 11, 26, 65
Privilege 7–8, 102, 106, 110, 112, 126–133, 180, 201, 203, 209–210; *see also* Watkins, Peter
prosperity gospel 9, 195–196; *see also* Seeker sensitive/church growth movement
Puritanism (in Margaret Atwood) 53–54, 145, 148

racism 33–34, 74–75, 85–97, 100, 135, 137, 139, 156–164

Rand, Ayn 7, 48, 62, 114, 118, 168, 194, 197, 202
The Rapture (film) 31, 50, 126, 179, 195
Rapture of the Arts 5–10, 188, 195
Reagan, Ronald 142, 145, 201
Reconstructionism 53–54, 83, 111–112; *see also* theocracy
Reformed Movement 1–2, 8, 10–12, 19–27, 43, 47, 50–51, 54, 62–63, 65, 69–70, 73, 82–84, 86, 89, 92–93, 111–112, 116–117, 142, 151–156, 165–166, 187–191, 193, 195, 197*Intro n3*, 204, 206
Robertson, Pat 86; ties to Reconstructionism 86, 111–112
Romanticism 6, 26–27, 72, 98, 163, 173, 191, 194, 196
Rookmaaker, Hans (H.R.) 8, 21, 25, 47, 50, 69, 72, 82, 92, 191, 197*ch1n3*, 203, 207
Rosemary's Baby 110, 113
Roszak, Theodore 9, 19, 53–54, 167–173, 190, 201, 207; *Devil and Daniel Silverman* 6, 9, 37, 53, 167–173, 207
Rushdoony, Rousas 111

Saved! 24, 31, 33, 166–167
Schaeffer, Francis 1, 6, 8, 11, 17, 20–22, 24–26, 47, 49, 50–51, 54, 62–63, 69–70, 72–73, 82–86, 92, 111–112, 117, 142, 144, 151–156, 166, 178, 187, 191, 193, 196, 197*ch1n3*, 204, 207
Schaeffer, Franky 21, 25–26, 93, 144, 151–156, 164, 170, 173, 179, 181, 190, 207; *see also* Eastern Orthodoxy
science 41–45, 47, 70, 95, 97–105, 116, 133–141, 205
science fiction 7, 67, 74–75, 111–141 (passim), 156–164, 178–183, 197*Intro n1*, 197*ch1n3*, 198*ch5n2*, 202–203
Scopes Trial 39, 65, 205; *Inherit the Wind* 97–105; *Planet of the Apes* 135, 139
Seeker-sensitive/church growth movement 7–11, 133, 193, 196
September 11, 2001 16–17, 165
Serling, Rod 134, 198
Serrano, Andres 62, 72–73, 191
sexuality 41, 45, 53, 115–116, 143–151, 167–168, 174
Shiner, Larry 2, 19, 26, 198*ch4n3*, 208
Siedell, Daniel 2, 49, 72, 82, 191, 197*ch1n3*, 199*ch8n1*, 208

Index

Smith, Gerald L.K. 65, 75, 80
spiritual capitalism/spiritual bourgeois 5, 9–10, 33–36, 38, 56–57, 85, 104, 104, 107, 109–110, 118, 137, 143, 150, 159, 162, 168, 196
spiritual proleteriat 2, 5, 9, 19, 34, 47, 54, 59, 101, 109, 146, 149, 181, 188, 196
spiritual warfare novel 35, 50, 133, 154, 186; *see also* Peretti, Frank
Star Trek: Deep Space Nine (DS9) 140; *The Original Series (TOS)* 113
Star Wars 113, 135
Sunday, Billy 38, 52, 190

Taylor, Roger 26, 35
theocracy 21, 53–54, 145–148, 159, 168, 207
Thompson, Craig 85, 93, 167, 173–178, 199*ch7n*1, 206, 208; *Blankets* 3, 9, 68, 167, 173–179, 184, 208
Tolkien, J.R.R. 9, 22, 26–30, 70, 102, 120–124, 202, 208; *Lord of the Rings* 120–123, 208
Tzara, Tristan 19, 47, 208

ubermensch 26, 99–100, 131, 158, 163, 193
Unitarianism 40, 44; relationship to Sinclair Lewis's works 52, 75, 78

Van Til, Cornelius 69, 154
Veith, Gene 1, 17, 21, 23–26, 208

The War Game 127, 206
Warhol, Andy 19, 48, 71
Watkins, Peter 106, 126–133, 141, 180, 201, 203, 206, 209–210; *see also Privilege*
Wells, H.G. 39, 56, 58, 62, 209
West, Nathanael 6, 67–74, 83, 201, 204–205, 209; *Miss Lonelyhearts* 67–74, 102
The Wicker Man 8, 106, 110, 113, 127, 203
Wilson, Michael: *Planet of the Apes* 134–139, 141, 198*ch5n*6
Winrod, Gerald 65, 67, 75–77, 80, 81
Winterson, Jeanette 85, 93, 141, 174
Wittgenstein, Ludwig 28–29, 192, 202, 209
Wolterstorff, Nicholas 8, 197, 209
women 41, 53–54, 143–151, 156–164
worldview theory 5, 9, 17, 20–27, 29, 35, 50, 62–63, 69, 73–74, 82–83, 92, 112, 116, 144, 151, 156, 171, 187–192, 196, 197*ch1n*3
Wright, Richard 83, 88, 93, 97, 157, 163

Year of the Sex Olympics 126, 210